EXPERTS AND POLITICIANS

PRINCETON STUDIES IN AMERICAN POLITICS:
HISTORICAL, INTERNATIONAL, AND
COMPARATIVE PERSPECTIVES

SERIES EDITORS

IRA KATZNELSON, MARTIN SHEFTER, THEDA SKOCPOL

*Labor Visions and State Power: The Origins of
Business Unionism in the United States*
by Victoria C. Hattam

The Lincoln Persuasion: Remaking American Liberalism
by J. David Greenstone

Politics and Industrialization: Early Railroads in the United States and Prussia
by Colleen A. Dunlavy

Political Parties and the State: The American Historical Experience
by Martin Shefter

*Experts and Politicians: Reform Challenges to Machine Politics
in New York, Cleveland, and Chicago*
by Kenneth Finegold

EXPERTS AND POLITICIANS

REFORM CHALLENGES TO
MACHINE POLITICS IN NEW YORK,
CLEVELAND, AND CHICAGO

Kenneth Finegold

PRINCETON UNIVERSITY PRESS   PRINCETON, NEW JERSEY

Library of Congress Cataloging-in-Publication Data

Finegold, Kenneth, 1957–
Experts and politicians : reform challenges to machine politics in
New York, Cleveland, and Chicago / Kenneth Finegold.
p.   cm. — (Princeton studies in American politics)
Includes bibliographical references and index.
ISBN 0-691-03734-5 (CL : acid-free paper)
1. Elections—New York (N.Y.)   2. New York (N.Y.)—Politics and
government—1898–1951.   3. Elections—Illinois—Chicago.
4. Chicago—Cleveland.   6. Cleveland (Ohio)—Politics and
government.   7. Populism—United States.   8. Progressivism
(United States politics)   I. Title.   II. Series.
JS1238.3.F56   1995
324.6'3'0973—dc20   94-22109   CIP

This book has been composed in Caledonia

Contents

Acknowledgments

H. Douglas Price, Amy Bridges, and Sidney Verba were insightful and encouraging dissertation advisors who continued their insights and encouragement long after I had received my Ph.D. Amy Bridges deserves special thanks for convincing me that revising my dissertation into a book was worth doing and for showing me how I could do it. Larry Bennett, Donald Davis, David Hammack, Paul Kleppner, Richard L. McCormick, R. Douglas Rivers, Martin Shefter, Theda Skocpol, and Stephen Skowronek made penetrating comments. I also benefited from the opportunities to present my work at annual meetings of the American Political Science Association and the Social Science History Association, at a seminar of the Joint Center for Urban Studies, and at seminars with political science departments at the University of Chicago, Cornell, Holy Cross, Michigan, Princeton, UCLA, Vanderbilt, and Yale. Jeffrey Colen and Neil Marantz bailed me out when I needed to do something in one place and found myself in another. Tim Bartlett, Alessandra Bocco, Malcolm DeBevoise, and Eric Schramm did fine editorial work for Princeton University Press.

Research travel was made possible by National Science Foundation Doctoral Dissertation Grant No. SES-83-09537 and a Newberry Library Resident Fellowship. A V.O. Key, Jr. Fellowship of the Joint Center for Urban Studies of MIT and Harvard University and a Richard D. Irwin Fellowship allowed me to concentrate on writing for a year. Harvard's Delancey K. Jay Prize for the best dissertation on constitutional government was also very nice. My original computations were funded by the Government Department Data Center at Harvard. Jim Lee and Brian Watts later helped me rework the data. I received enormous assistance from librarians and staff members at Harvard, Vanderbilt, Dartmouth, Rutgers, the New York Public Library, the New York County Board of Elections, the Cleveland Public Library, Case Western Reserve, the Western Reserve Historical Society, the Cleveland Citizens League, the Cuyahoga County Archives, the Cleveland Municipal Library, the Newberry Library, the University of Chicago, the Chicago Historical Society, and the Chicago Municipal Reference Library. Paul F. Gehl of the Newberry Library was particularly helpful. I especially thank the Newberry Library, for permission to quote and cite material from the Carter Henry Harrison Papers; the Oral History Research Office of Columbia University, for permission to quote and cite material from the memoirs of William H. Allen and Henry Bruère; the Western Reserve Historical Society, for permission to quote and cite material from the papers of Newton D. Baker, Henry E. Bourne, and Peter Witt; and the University of Chicago Archives, for permission to quote and cite material from the Charles E. Merriam Papers.

Elaine K. Swift, a loving wife and a dedicated scholar, helped me write this in many different ways. I am especially grateful for her comments on my drafts, her errands on my behalf, and her willingness to reschedule our respective cooking duties during the summer of 1993. My mother, Lillian Finegold, and my sister, Hope Alper, gave me love and encouragement throughout my work on this topic. So did my father, Robert Finegold, until his death. I miss him, and this book is dedicated to his memory.

Part I

RETHINKING REFORM

The practical politician, if asked why one area has strong
[municipal ownership] interest and another not, will inevitably
answer that in one case the "boys got out and worked" and in the
other they didn't. The theorist will inevitably give his explanation
in terms of the progress of ideas, and the change in public opinion
or the social will. The facts are not comforting for either answer.
Arthur F. Bentley, "Municipal Ownership Interest Groups
in Chicago: A Study of Referendum Votes, 1902–1907"

CHAPTER 1.

Machine Politics and Reform Politics

THE EARLY YEARS of the twentieth century are generally known as the "Progressive Era." During this period, new patterns of politics and policy emerged at the local, state, and national levels of American government. Party or class organizations that had controlled cities were displaced by coalitions declaring their antipathy to established sources of political power. New forms of urban government, such as the commission system and the city manager, replaced the partisan mayor and the ward-based city council. Innovative public policies widened the role of city government, encroaching on functions already shared by markets, charities, and party organizations. Experts with professional training and orientations became key urban actors. At the state and national levels, partisan cleavages and governmental structures were less drastically changed, but, as in cities, new policy functions emerged and expertise became more central to the operations of government. This period, then, was one of the recurring waves of reform traced by scholars such as Samuel P. Huntington, Martin Shefter, and Ronald G. Walters.[1]

What, exactly, is meant by "reform"? The label has often been claimed by any politician who challenges an incumbent or by proponents of any policy change. The concept becomes more meaningful if a more restrictive definition is adopted: reform is the attempt to change what is systematic about government, rather than, or in addition to, what is transitory. Thus those who seek the reform of politics do not merely wish to change the people who are in office, but the processes by which they were placed there and the institutions within which they operate. In early twentieth-century American cities, this meant above all opposition to machine politics, the manipulation of material incentives by party organizations.[2]

Who, it might be asked, were *not* reformers? Some business owners opposed reform of any sort, either because they profited from the developmental activities of machine regimes or because they were afraid change would scare away investment.[3] Also outside the ranks of reform were members of the party organizations, including leaders like Charles Francis Murphy of New York and Roger Sullivan of Chicago, as well as the regulars who followed them. Blue-blooded politicians who sought office in tenuous alliance with the party organizations, such as George B. McClellan (New York) and Carter Harrison II (Chicago), were not reformers either, though their strategic decisions had important consequences for the outcome of reform in their cities.

During the Progressive Era, the ideas and techniques of reformers in separate localities were shared through the recently constructed mechanisms of professional associations; civic organizations such as the National Municipal League; and a national, "muckraking" periodical press. Thus diffusion occurred both vertically, among the levels of government, and horizontally, among cities or states. Even in cities that were alike in size, region, and economic base, however, reform movements led to dissimilar political outcomes. The puzzle is to explain these different reform outcomes.

The different outcomes of reform across cities cannot be explained by existing studies, most of which either provide details about a single city or draw examples from many cities to paint a picture of the reform phenomenon as a whole. Some scholars have tried to understand reform through aggregate methods using large numbers of cities as cases.[4] But the aggregate approach may be more appropriate for explaining single outcomes like council-manager government or total expenditures than for explaining general patterns of politics and policy. A comparative case study seems more likely to capture the complex dynamics of reform within each city, and thus offers a better chance that reform outcomes can be understood. An aggregate approach, moreover, is not well-suited for studying large cities, which provide only a small set of cases.[5] Yet it is important that reform outcomes in large cities be considered as a distinct theoretical subject, for the politics of reform in these cities was different than in cities of small or medium size.[6]

I chose to compare New York, Cleveland, and Chicago because these three large cities provide examples of different outcomes for reform. In social science terms, selecting these cities as cases maximizes the variance of the dependent variable, defined quite broadly as the city's subsequent patterns of politics and policy. The short-run outcomes can most easily be measured by the number of elections won by reform mayoral candidates during the Progressive Era: one in Chicago, two in New York, and six in Cleveland. By long-run outcomes, I mean the extent to which reform candidates continued to challenge machine politics after the Progressive Era. Each critical period builds upon the achievements (or failures) of the last: the long-term outcomes of reform politics during the Progressive Era shaped each city's response to the internal and external challenges of the 1930s, and the outcomes of the Progressive Era and the New Deal shaped each city's response to the challenges of the 1960s.

In New York, a broad-based reform coalition came together and then split apart. John Purroy Mitchel was elected mayor of New York in 1913 by a coalition linking elites who had elected Seth Low in 1901 with working-class voters who had supported William Randolph Hearst in 1905 and 1909. But by 1917, Mitchel's coalition had come undone. The immediate consequences of the reform collapse were to strengthen the 1 many Democratic machine and the Socialist opposition. The contin subordination of Jews, Italians, and Germans to Irish leaders within the Democratic machine, however, left these groups available for mobilization by Fiorello La Guardia in the 1930s and 1940s.

Cleveland reformers were more radical than those who gained power in any other major city, with the possible exception of the Milwaukee Socialists. They were also among the reformers with the most sustained electoral success. Tom Johnson was elected to four two-year terms, holding office from 1901 to 1909. After an anti-reform Republican defeated Johnson and served one term, Newton Baker restored reform control with a more inclusive coalition than Johnson had constructed. The same coalition reelected Baker in 1913. In 1915, however, Peter Witt, Baker's designated political heir, was defeated in a multicandidate election. The survival of a radical tradition, linking Johnson and Witt with Dennis Kucinich, has distinguished Cleveland politics since the Progressive Era.

Reformers in Chicago won some victories at the ward level, but their citywide success was limited due to the absence of a broad-based alliance like those achieved under Mitchel or Baker. John Peter Altgeld, running for mayor on a municipal ownership ticket after serving as governor of Illinois, finished third in 1899. Edward Dunne served one term as mayor but, like Tom Johnson, was defeated over the street railway issue. Charles Merriam's defeat in 1911 showed that elite reformers could win support from the upper class but not from workers. After the failure of progressivism in Chicago, the Democratic organization was transformed from a collection of personal factions into the city's legendary, centralized machine.

To explain these different outcomes, this book proposes a rethinking of urban reform opposition to party organizations. Support for reform candidates in New York, Cleveland, and Chicago during the Progressive Era followed three distinct patterns. Traditional reform candidates were supported by native-stock elites. Municipal populist candidates were supported by foreign-stock ethnic groups and by segments of the working class. Progressive candidates were supported by coalitions combining traditional reform and municipal populist voters. Whether traditional reform and municipal populist voters could be united into a progressive coalition depended on the way in which experts were incorporated into city politics.

This analysis challenges the emphasis of many historians on the ethnic or class bases of machine and reform support. According to the ethnic interpretation, seen in the work of Richard Hofstadter, the party organizations embodied the culture of, did favors for, and won support from foreign-stock nationality groups. Reformers are depicted as native-stock Americans seeking to regain control of the cities.[7] A variant of the ethnic interpretation, put forward by Samuel P. Hays, reframes it in terms of class: reform campaigns then appear as elite efforts directed against party organizations based in the working class.[8] These approaches suggest that the electoral alignments of early twentieth-century cities were relatively stable, subject to change only as underlying demographic variables changed. I argue, in contrast, that some reform candidates won support from foreign-stock, working-class voters instead of, or in addition to, native-stock elites, and that electoral politics was relatively fluid, with the possibility of reform alliances across class or ethnic lines. Without discarding what we have learned about the social origins of some reformers from Hofstadter, Hays, and the historians and political scientists who have followed their leads, we should pay more attention to reform as politics.

Central to the reform politics of the Progressive Era were experts, politicians, and the relationships that linked them. Understanding the different relationships of experts and politicians helps us to understand why reform efforts produced different outcomes in New York, Cleveland, and Chicago. The relationship of experts and politicians in the Progressive Era also helps us to understand the patterns of politics and policy that have characterized each of these cities since this period. More generally, this study demonstrates the significance of expertise as a potential source of change in American politics and policy, and the importance of each city's electoral and administrative organizations as mediating institutions within a national system of urban political economies.

SIMILARITIES AND DIFFERENCES

The complex of socioeconomic changes that Hays calls "industrialism" created new urban problems that, as viewed by reformers, were exacerbated by the practices of machine politics. Yet the improvement of transportation and communication also made it possible for reformers to share methods that promised to simultaneously solve social problems and overturn party-based regimes. Reform ideas and techniques were spread by new professional and municipal associations and by a diverse periodical press, as well as by individual reformers. City governments throughout the nation, then, faced similar challenges. In every city the resolution of these challenges served to structure future political possibilities, but city-specific factors led to different outcomes and thus to different patterns of politics in the post-reform period.

As Hays has noted, the rapid expansion of the railroads in the late nineteenth century linked every important city in the nation, with a particularly "dense and complex network" in the industrial Northeast. The telegraph, the telephone, and the modern printing press together produced a comparable national communication system.[9] The most obvious effect of these changes was to create national markets, spurring industrialization. But the improvement of transportation and communication also created a national polity. Hugh Heclo has stressed the importance of political learning, a collective, "relatively enduring alteration in behavior that results from experience," as a force reshaping answers to the fundamental question of "what to do."[10] During the Progressive Era, perhaps for the first time, political learning could take place on a national scale, as reformers in one city learned about the successes and failures of their counterparts elsewhere and altered their own strategies and tactics.[11] Communication among reformers from different cities was facilitated when the federal Bureau of the Census developed standardized comparative statistics of municipal expenditures and services, organized according to function.[12]

Professional associations provided a vehicle for the exchange of experience among specialists in particular policy areas. During the Progressive Era, social workers and social scientists formed new organizations, while older organizations of teachers, doctors, lawyers, and engineers were reoriented toward more aggressive strategies of professionalization.[13] Within cities, experts learned to cooperate across professional boundaries. "In Chicago, for instance," Robert H. Wiebe points out, "the architect Allen B. Pond designed uniquely functional settlements for Jane Addams, who aided Margaret Haley in achieving professional status for teachers, who joined with John Fitzpatrick, progressive president of the Chicago Federation of Labor, in championing the rights of wage earners."[14] Such exchanges were facilitated by citywide groups such as the City Club of New York and the Municipal League of Philadelphia.[15] In 1893, these two groups took the lead in the formation of the National Municipal League, which provided regular communication about governmental organization in different cities, as well as studies of foreign approaches. The National Municipal League's efforts were supplemented by the work of more specialized groups, such as the National Civil Service League and the National Short Ballot Organization.[16]

Journalists provided another means of communication among urban reform movements.[17] The journalism of the Progressive Era is most famous for "muckraking" articles like Lincoln Steffens's series, "The Shame of the Cities," published in *McClure's*. Such exposés created an awareness of urban political corruption as a shared phenomenon. In magazines like *The Outlook*, *World's Work*, *The Public*, and *The Independent*, other writers went beyond exposure, analyzing the results of key elections, evaluating the records of reform administrations, and debating issues such as municipal ownership.[18]

Many of the leading urban reformers were themselves active in more than one city. In 1905 and 1909, William Randolph Hearst ran for mayor of New York on a platform of municipal ownership. His newspapers supported like-minded candidates in Chicago and other cities.[19] Tom Johnson, mayor of Cleveland from 1901 to 1909, first became active in politics by participating in Henry George's campaigns for mayor of New York, managing George's final campaign in 1897.[20] One of the most peripatetic reformers was Edward Webster Bemis, who was dismissed from the University of Chicago in what became a major academic freedom controversy; served as waterworks superintendent and tax expert for Johnson in Cleveland; and was appointed Deputy Commissioner of Water Works by New York mayor William Jay Gaynor, only to be fired for opposing the purchase of meters from a company in which Tammany politicians held shares.[21] Louis F. Post, editor of the Single Tax journal, *The Public*, was also active in all three of the cities studied here.[22]

The networks of professional and municipal organizations, the periodical press, and the mobility of individual reformers all contributed to the rapid diffusion of innovative forms of governmental structure. Commission government, in which elected commissioners serve collectively as a legislative body and individually as heads of departments, was first adopted by Galveston in 1901. The plan received more attention when it was put into effect in Des Moines in 1908. An investigation by President Charles Eliot of Harvard, favorable coverage by the *Literary Digest* and other journals, and campaigns by the League of American Municipalities helped to win adoption of the new scheme in 423 cities by 1915.[23] As complaints about the shortcomings of the commission system spread through similar channels, the council-manager plan supplanted it as the object of reformers' enthusiasm. This plan, which vested executive power in a professional city manager chosen by appointment, was first adopted by Sumter, South Carolina, in 1912. The National Short Ballot Organization, and later the National Municipal League, actively promoted the "Sumter plan." By 1921, 212 cities, including Cleveland, had council-manager charters.[24]

The diffusion of new techniques of extragovernmental influence was equally rapid. The New York Bureau of Municipal Research, established in 1907, was the first independent organization for the study of urban government. Afterwards, research bodies were created in Philadelphia, Detroit, Chicago, and other cities. These organizations were often staffed by veterans of the New York Bureau or graduates of its Training School.[25] The New York Bureau received much publicity from its budget exhibit, which illustrated the types of work done by the city and showed examples of avoidable waste. Mayor Henry T. Hunt of Cincinnati, a reformer, imported a member of the New York Bureau to set up a similar exhibit explaining what his city did and why it needed a tax increase.[26]

New policy approaches spread from city to city as well. The general zoning ordinance was invented in New York City in 1916; as of 1921, "over 10 million urbanites were in zoned cities."[27] Junior high schools (Columbus, Georgia) and junior colleges (Fresno, California) were among the modern education programs developed in one city during the Progressive Era and imitated by others.[28] The Lexow Committee's 1894 investigation of the New York police provided a model for probes into other police departments. Ways of reforming the police were communicated through professional associations and research bureaus.[29] Sanitation was another service reshaped by reformers during the Progressive Era. In New York, Colonel George E. Waring achieved unprecedented results through reorganization of the sanitation force, symbolized by the workers' white uniforms. Supporters of Cleveland's Mayor Johnson boasted that he had copied this "White Wing" system during his first term in office.[30]

As a result of the rapid diffusion of governmental structures, extragovernmental techniques, and policy proposals, the content of reform initiatives in different cities was often alike. The outcome of reform attempts, however, varied greatly, from ineffective protest against the current regime in some cities to sustained control of others. In New York, the Bureau of Municipal Research helped expand the traditional reform constituency that elected Seth Low mayor in 1901 into a progressive coalition for John Purroy Mitchel in 1913. In Cleveland, the Civic League helped expand the municipal populist constituency that elected Tom Johnson mayor in 1901, 1903, 1905, and 1907 into a progressive coalition for Newton Baker in 1911 and 1913. In Chicago, Edward Dunne received municipal populist support and Charles Merriam received traditional reform support, but despite the formation of the Bureau of Public Efficiency no progressive coalition could be constructed.

These cases pose a double problem for theoretical interpretations of reform. Any explanation must make sense of the similarities among reform movements. This is the issue to which existing explanations of reform have most frequently been addressed. But these explanations must also tell us why the outcomes of reform in New York, Cleveland, and Chicago were so different.

MACHINE AND REFORM IN URBAN POLITICAL ECONOMY

Explanation of the origins and outcomes of municipal reform is a crucial problem in the emerging literature of urban political economy. Among the authors who have made important contributions to this body of work are Amy Bridges, Stephen Elkin, Stephen Erie, Ester Fuchs, Dennis Judd, Paul Kantor, Ira Katznelson, John Mollenkopf, Martin Shefter,

Clarence Stone, and Todd Swanstrom.[31] Although they disagree on many points, these authors share a conception of cities as "semisovereign" entities that operate with some degree of independence, yet are also part of larger economic and political structures at the state, national, and even international levels. They share also a research strategy of examining the interaction of politics and economics in cities through analysis that is comparative and historical. And, with all who study political economy in any context, they share a focus on the intersection of the economic processes of production and consumption, organized by markets, with the political processes of self-government, organized by representative institutions. One of the important findings of the urban political economy literature is that American cities have more autonomy to pursue a range of public policies than in the influential model of Paul Peterson, in which municipal governments' unavoidable need for revenue forces them to adopt policies that facilitate economic development and prohibits policies of economic redistribution.[32] Another is that cities of the South and West, such as Houston and Los Angeles, followed significantly different patterns of political development than northeastern cities like New York and Chicago, with whose histories most scholars are more familiar.[33]

Central to much of the new urban political economy is the concept of regime, which was applied to city politics by Aristotle and is widely used in comparative politics and international relations. A pattern of governance that endures beyond individual leaders or electoral coalitions, a regime can be constituted through the formal institutions of a city charter or through informal arrangements of public-private cooperation. It provides a set of rules for determining, in Harold Lasswell's classic formulation, "who gets what, when, how." At the same time, it provides a moral order that defines what is good, and thus who *should* get what, and why.[34]

Several of the scholars associated with the study of urban political economy have joined with urban historians to advance a new interpretation of the American political machine as the basis for one kind of urban regime. This rethinking represents a second wave of revisionism about machine politics. The earliest students of the machine were themselves reformers; for James Bryce, Moisei Ostrogorski, Lincoln Steffens, and Gustavus Myers, to analyze the machine was to demonstrate its corruption and its violation of a universal public interest.[35] Robert K. Merton's functionalist analysis of the machine replaced the reform view as the standard approach within American political science.[36] Merton used the example of the machine to illustrate his fundamental distinction between manifest functions, intended and recognized by participants, and latent functions that were neither intended nor recognized. The patronage, graft, and electoral operations noted by reform-minded observers were the manifest functions of the machine. The latent functions of the machine, which explained its survival, were to centralize power despite the fragmentation of formal city government, and to provide personalized services (and opportunities for individual mobility) to the needy. If support for machine politics was based on the provision of services, then assumption of those services by the national government, with its superior resources, made the machines superfluous. Mertonian functionalism thus fit well with what became known as the "Last Hurrah" thesis, after the novel that conveyed it more vividly than any social scientist: the argument that the New Deal led to the death of the machine.[37]

Mertonian functionalism also fit well with Hays's revisionist analysis of reform. If the machine addressed the needs of the immigrant working-class masses, who could have opposed it except native-stock elites seeking to regain power in the cities?[38] In support of this interpretation, one could cite the nativistic and antidemocratic statements of reformers such as Andrew Dickson White and Woodrow Wilson as well as specific reforms, such as at-large elections and the city-manager system, that favored elite control over city governments.[39] Melvin Holli only partially modified this analysis with his distinction between the sort of reformers described by Hays, whom he labeled "structural reformers," and "social reformers" like Detroit's Hazen Pingree and Cleveland's Tom Johnson, who sought to improve conditions for the urban masses.[40]

Recent scholarship has challenged Merton's analysis of the machine on each of its major points. First, party organizations in most cities at most times were not centralized "machines" at all, but loose aggregations of ward leaders or sets of antagonistic factions.[41] Because centralized organizational control was the exception rather than the rule, most party organizations were incapable of performing the coordinating functions that Merton attributed to them. If party machines were functional substitutes for centralized government, as Merton suggests, then centralizing reforms should have had a negative effect on machine formation. Alan DiGaetano has shown, to the contrary, that formal centralization made machine formation *more* likely, by giving party leaders the resources they needed to subordinate ward bosses.[42]

A second problem with Merton's functional view of the machine is that the party organizations did not do very much to help their immigrant and working-class constituents. The "new" immigrants from Eastern and Southern Europe, including Jews, Italians, and Poles, and the black immigrants from the American South, were excluded from the party organizations or placed in subordinate positions, and thus received few of the alleged benefits of machine politics.[43] Even for the Irish, the ethnic group that often (but not always) provided leadership for the Democratic party organizations, machine politics was of dubious value and may have actually retarded economic mobility.[44] The real beneficiaries of organizational politics were the organizations' leaders, who exchanged franchises, contracts, and regulatory decisions for personal wealth under the arrangements that reformers denounced as graft. Both Richard Croker of New York's Tammany Hall and "Bathhouse" John Coughlin of Chicago's First Ward, for example, owned stables of racehorses. The organization leaders were thus "predatory," in the specifically political sense in which Margaret Levi uses the term to refer to rulers who "as much as they can, design property rights and policies meant to maximize their own personal power and wealth."[45]

A third problem with Merton's model is that the "Last Hurrah" thesis is wrong: the New Deal did not kill the machine. Because so many New Deal policies of social provision combined federal funding with local direction, these policies did not displace the bosses but gave them added resources. In many cities, including Chicago, Pittsburgh, and Kansas City, organizational leaders allied with the Roosevelt administration and used federal money and patronage to build centralized machines that had previously proven impossible to construct.[46] Reports of the machine's death are, in fact, greatly exaggerated.[47] The case of New York, which for many is the paradigmatic reform city,[48] justifies such skepticism. New York party organizations were buffeted by the reform victories of the Progressive Era, by the later reform administrations of Fiorello La Guardia (1934–45) and John Lindsay (1966–73), and then by the fiscal crisis of the 1970s, which essentially placed city government under external receivership. These assaults did in fact demolish the Manhattan Democratic organization that had once been Tammany Hall. Yet the party organizations of the other four boroughs (Brooklyn, Queens, the Bronx, and Staten Island) survived to play major roles in the coalition constructed by Edward Koch, the erstwhile reform Democrat who won three mayoral elections and governed the city from 1978 to 1989.[49]

This rethinking of machine politics has been incorporated into the literature of urban political economy.[50] There has not been a comparable rethinking of reform. Instead, Hays's interpretation has been accepted as the standard analysis, with exceptions sometimes made for Holli's social reformers.[51] Yet it is necessary to challenge the earlier revisionism about reform as well as about machine politics if the study of urban political economy is to achieve its goals. Without a rethinking of reform, it is not possible to explain political outcomes, in either the short or the long run, because we cannot understand why and to what extent machine politicians lost unless we understand why and to what extent their reform opponents won. Without a rethinking of reform, urban political economy is also incomplete as a normative endeavor. If the content of urban political reform and the sources of support for reform candidates are misunderstood, any evaluation of the reform regime will be misleading. So too will any evaluation of the machine, for a regime can only be evaluated in comparison with its alternatives. The early evaluation of reform as good and machine as bad was reversed with the incorporation of Merton and Hays into the study of urban politics. The most recent research has made it more difficult to idealize the machine. It should be equally difficult to demonize reform. The new interpretation of reform politics presented in this book, taken together with the anti-Mertonian, revisionist interpretation of machine politics, makes it possible to evaluate particular regimes in particular cities, both by understanding who really got what, and by understanding what these regimes defined as good through their conceptions of citizenship, education, and the meaning of political conflict.

THREE PATTERNS OF REFORM POLITICS

Interpretations of reform in the Progressive Era have always been linked to judgments about it. Reformers' heroic self-images were accepted by one generation of scholars but rejected by the next. The difficulties of maintaining the boundary that separates analyses of reform support from evaluations of key actors or central ideas, and of defining such elusive concepts as "progressivism," "machine," and "reform," have led some historians to reject these concepts entirely.[52]

This book argues that it *is* possible to make sense of urban reform, by distinguishing among three patterns of reform politics. One pattern, which I describe as traditional reform, fits the Hays model of reform support as disproportionately native-stock and elite. A second pattern of support for reform, which I describe as municipal populist, came from very different sources: foreign-stock groups (particularly the "new" immigrants) and parts of the working class. This pattern of reform has received less notice from urban historians. A third pattern, which has also been overlooked, was for traditional reform and municipal populist voters to be brought together to form what I describe as a progressive coalition. The economic and ethnic composition of New York, Cleveland, and Chicago gave rise to continual revolts against machine politics by both traditional reformers and municipal populists. Formation of a progressive coalition was less frequent, and more contingent. A necessary condition for such a coalition was the prior incorporation of experts into the municipal polity by political entrepreneurs pursuing their own electoral goals.

As my case studies of New York, Cleveland, and Chicago show, reform success and machine failure (or reform failure and machine success) were intertwined. The most basic distinction in the study of party organizations, David Mayhew points out, is between places that have them and places that don't. New York, Cleveland, and Chicago each had patronage-based party organizations during the Progressive Era, and to some extent each of the three cities still does.[53] Whether each city's party organizations were aggregated at the level of ward leaders, citywide factions, or genuine, centralized machines was important to the course of reform, and whether experts and politicians could bring together traditional reform and municipal populist voters to form a progressive coalition was similarly important to the course of organizational politics.

This analysis does not yield easy explanations of reform outcomes. Instead, it demands comparative case studies with attention to the consequences of short-term strategic decisions. Like the progressive coalition I have described, this approach to the problem of urban reform combines what is usually distinct. The study of electoral politics has been separate from the study of organizational development, and the study of ideas has been tangential to both. But each part is weaker by itself. The study of elections can become sociocultural determinism, the study of institutions can lapse into abstract evolutionism, and the study of ideas can lose track of the contexts that determine whether ideas will have practical influence. Taking these approaches together to explore the incorporation of expertise, it becomes possible to explain why electoral coalitions do or do not form, when institutions develop, and how ideologies are created and disseminated.

Part I of the book introduces this argument. In this chapter, I have situated the argument within the study of urban political economy. In Chapter 2, I explain why similarities and differences in reform outcomes are best understood in terms of the three coalitional patterns summarized above and the political incorporation of expertise. In the course of doing so I critically examine the interpretations of reform by historians who have emphasized its social, ideological, or bureaucratic aspects. The next three sections of the book present my case studies of progressivism, electoral change, and public policy. Part II (Chapters 3–5) examines New York; Part III (Chapters 6–8), Cleveland; Part IV (Chapters 9–11), Chicago. An introduction to each part provides an overview of my arguments about that city. Part V (Chapter 12) reviews the relationships of experts and politicians and summarizes my findings about ethnicity, suburbanization, expertise, and policy for incorporation into the literature of urban political economy. The Appendix explains the quantitative methods (generalized least squares regression and linear programming) used to estimate patterns of voting behavior throughout the book.

CHAPTER 2.

Incorporating Experts

THE ARGUMENT of this book is that the incorporation of experts into city politics made possible what I call "progressivism": an electoral coalition between elite "traditional reformers" and "municipal populists" supported by portions of the working class. This interpretation treats urban politics as autonomous; that is, as not strictly determined by such social categories as class, ethnicity, or race.

The most common historical approach to the study of reform, in contrast, has been to identify reform with a particular social group.[1] Because reform attitudes have been seen as manifestations of deeper economic and cultural characteristics, group interpretations have not been sensitive to the dynamics of electoral politics within each city. The estimates of electoral behavior presented in Chapters 3 through 11 indicate that class and ethnic variables were consistently important, but in more complicated ways than a simple identification of reform with any one group. Thus, we should view social groups as building blocks for urban reform movements, with city-specific patterns of elite strategy and expert organization determining which groups were included in the construction of reform coalitions and how they fit together.

TRADITIONAL REFORM

The traditional reform constituency was comprised of native-stock, upper- and middle-class voters. These voters supported reform candidates because, in their view, government by the party organizations was too costly, or too closely identified with the Irish or other immigrant groups. Traditional reform candidates achieved success in citywide elections as early as 1857, when New York's elites mobilized in opposition to the inchoate machine of Mayor Fernando Wood.[2] Later in the nineteenth century, similar campaigns were aroused by revelations about Tammany rule under Bosses William M. Tweed and Richard Croker.[3] During the Progressive Era, Seth Low, William Ivins, and Otto Bannard in New York, Harvey Goulder and Theodore Burton in Cleveland, and John Maynard Harlan and Charles Merriam in Chicago were all supported by traditional reform voters.

A variety of historians and social scientists have interpreted all reform as traditional reform and attributed the characteristics of these voters to all opponents of machine politics. James Weinstein and Samuel P. Hays, for example, depict urban reform as business's alternative to the rule of ward-based machines. At the local level, Weinstein argues, even small firms were capable of class-conscious action, mobilizing to replace expensive mayoral systems with more businesslike government by commission or city manager.[4] The nonpartisan ballot, a feature of most commission or manager plans, made it difficult for working-class opponents of business candidates to win elections, thus reducing the threat of Socialist or labor control.[5] Hays too traces the business origins of the commission and manager plans. He places more emphasis, however, on the change from election by ward to citywide elections in the selection of city councils and school boards.[6] This shift not only replaced popular decision making with technological rationalization, but altered the composition of governing bodies from lower- and middle-class groups to "upper class, advanced professional, and large business groups."[7] Hays also interprets the municipal research bureau as "a springboard for influence" by business.[8]

Richard Hofstadter's emphasis on the conflict between the Anglo-Saxon heritage of individual political action and immigrant support for the machine suggests that he too has traditional reformers in mind.[9] Edward C. Banfield and James Q. Wilson expand upon this conflict. The battle of machine and reform, they say, is one aspect of the tension between a public-regarding Anglo-Saxon ethos that stresses service to the community and a private-regarding immigrant ethos that emphasizes group recognition and material benefits. To a greater extent than other authors, Banfield and Wilson distinguish the effects of class from the effects of ethnicity, arguing that as members of different ethnic groups ascended into the middle class, they took on the Protestant ethos. Banfield and Wilson speculate that Jews, who often allied with Protestants in support of reform, most rapidly achieved this transformation.[10]

Neo-Marxist interpretations of reform as the political ideology of a new middle class similarly fit traditional reform better than they do other patterns of reform support. Magali Sarfatti Larson develops this theme (which can also be traced back to Hofstadter) in her analysis of the "professional project," the conquest and assertion of social status by collectively self-defined experts.[11] Although the professions were connected to the central bureaucratic institutions of the corporation, the state, and the modern university, they derived their identity from their apparent independence, and so embodied the general concealment of class in American society. For Barbara Ehrenreich and John Ehrenreich, the early twentieth century marked the emergence of a distinct "Professional-Managerial Class," which does not own the means of production but is separated from the working class because its function is the control of the workers. Ehrenreich and Ehrenreich find the ideology of this new class in Thorstein Veblen's technological anticapitalism, in the platform of Eugene Debs's Socialist party, and in the thought of the early New Left as well as in the ideas of municipal reformers during the Progressive Era.[12]

Evidence for these group-based interpretations of reform most frequently comes from studies of the social origins of leading reformers.[13] Hofstadter based his conclusions upon early profiles of Progressive party activists, nationally and in California, which identified their subjects as overwhelmingly middle class and well educated.[14] Hofstadter's work, in turn, led to a flurry of studies testing his hypothesis by examining the social origins of other groups of reformers. Hays, for example, rejects Hofstadter's interpretation on the basis of his own finding that members of the two principal Pittsburgh reform organizations had upper-class backgrounds.[15]

The origins of followers, however, may be more important for reform politics than the origins of leaders, which exhibit little variance. Several studies compared reformers to a control group and found that there were no significant differences in their social origins.[16] Even the Socialist party, which explicitly appealed to proletarian unity, drew its leaders from the middle class.[17] Since activity in either the reform or the Socialist causes offered little promise of personal economic reward, it is not surprising that members of the lower classes could not devote themselves to leadership roles. Yet the Socialists, and some of the reformers, received considerable working-class support.

To reason from the social origins of leaders alone, then, is to ignore the patterns of collective choice between leaders and followers and the possibilities that these patterns differed between cities or changed over time, even if the class and ethnic pool from which the leaders were selected was uniform and constant. To trace these patterns, electoral evidence is necessary. Election results do not tell us how candidates were selected or excluded. But they do tell us who won and who lost and, with some additional work, with whose support. The electoral evidence presented for New York, Cleveland, and Chicago in Chapters 3 through 11 suggests that the upper or middle classes that most often provided the leaders of reform (as well as its opponents) only sometimes provided the bulk of reform supporters. Traditional reform was thus but one pattern of reform, and group-based approaches that depict it as the only pattern of reform support should be rejected.

Scholars who have emphasized the relationship between reform and suburbanization also end up identifying reform with the native-stock middle class. The development of mass transportation, Richard Wade has argued, made possible the expansion of the city. New residential areas were created at the urban periphery. Though these were suburbs, annexation kept them within the limits of the political city. The residents of these communities needed coordinated services. They expressed this need, according to Wade, by supporting reform movements. The party machine, in contrast, was rooted in the neighborhood life of the center city.[18] Zane L. Miller has applied this perspective to Cincinnati, while Michael P. McCarthy has used it to understand the sources of reform in Cleveland and Chicago.[19]

The method most commonly used to confirm Wade's argument is map drawing. "Voting results," Wade suggests, "could be plotted on a map; reform majorities dwindled, then disappeared, as they crossed over the lines demarcating the oldest parts of town."[20] Such maps show how the inhabitants of peripheral wards voted, but they do not prove that location explains their preference for reform candidates: the apparent relationship between pro-reform voting and suburban location might be an artifact of the method. The estimates of Chapters 3 through 11, based on ecological regression and linear programming, suggest that suburbanization only mattered in elections when an issue with a specifically locational dimension, usually streetcar policy, was especially salient.[21]

MUNICIPAL POPULISM

Business, middle-class, and suburban interpretations agree on one point: reform was not supported by, and was in some sense directed against, the predominantly immigrant-stock, inner-city working class. Yet municipal populist reform constituencies, composed of segments of the ethnic working class, date to before the Civil War. One such workerist reformer of the antebellum period was Mike Walsh of New York.[22] In 1886, Henry George, inventor of the Single Tax, mobilized municipal populist support in his candidacy for mayor of New York. Like Walsh, George expressed a widely felt resentment at the practices and policies of the factions that competed for control of the Democratic party.[23] During the early twentieth century, municipal populist voters supported William Randolph Hearst in New York, Tom Johnson in Cleveland, and John P. Altgeld and Edward Dunne in Chicago.

Support for municipal populism came most frequently from the upper strata of the working class. Because this group was better educated than unskilled workers, it was more easily roused by policy appeals. Because it was economically more secure, at least in good times, the material incentives party politicians could most easily offer, such as emergency aid or jobs as laborers, were of less value to it. Municipal populist candidates also tended to draw electoral support from members of ethnic groups who were denied full recognition by the major parties. In New York, for example, the domination of the Republican party by Anglo-Saxon Protestants, and the domination of the Democratic party by Irish Catholics, left Jews, Germans, and Italians available for mobilization by antiparty reformers.

Municipal populist candidates were not Socialists: they called for public ownership of utilities but accepted private ownership of the rest of the means of production. Though more likely to look to Henry George than to Karl Marx, they carried out policies similar to those of Socialist administrations in other cities. Because of the Socialists' evolutionary ideology; their emphasis on winning elections by attracting non-Socialist votes; and the limits placed on them by hostile governors, state legislators, and judges (all of which also constrained non-Socialist reform administrations), the Socialist city administrations of the early twentieth century never closed the gap between the introduction of central purchasing and collective ownership of the means of production. Socialist city governments eliminated graft, improved administrative methods, and built better parks and sewers. Milwaukee Socialists even established a Bureau of Economy and Efficiency, headed by John R. Commons. The longest surviving Socialist city governments, in Milwaukee and Bridgeport, ended up as pro-business economy administrations by another name. Walter Lippmann, then a Socialist, noted the equivalence of municipal socialism and reform:

> The first comment I read in the *Call* [a Socialist daily newspaper, published in New York City] on John Purroy Mitchel's administration announced that he was a pinhead. Now on the subject of municipal government Mitchel is undoubtedly not a pinhead. One could draw up a tremendous indictment against Mitchel, but on the question of his competence, administrative skill, and integrity no Socialist I know has the right to open his mouth. We become positive hypocrites, for if Mitchel were in Schenectady or Milwaukee, he would be doing just about what he has been doing and we should be hailing him as an example of the extraordinary capacity which the Socialist movement produces.[24]

Voters also seemed to understand that Socialists and some kinds of reformers were close in practice, if not in theory. When municipal populist or progressive candidates were competitive, the Socialists did poorly, as their putative supporters voted for reform. When a progressive coalition could not be formed (as in Chicago), or collapsed (as in the New York election of 1917), political space was opened up for the Socialist alternative, and the party's candidates proved stronger at the polls.

If Socialists and reformers in power did much the same things, the advantage of the reformers was that it was easier for them to gain and hold power, for they could not be so readily repressed. Sometimes opposition to socialism took the form of collaboration of the major parties against successful Socialist candidates, as in the Schenectady elections of 1913 or the New York state elections of 1918. Elsewhere, forceful tactics of repression were used, particularly after the United States entered World War I and the national Socialist party declared its opposition to intervention, conscription, and the sale of war bonds. Anti-Socialist tactics included imprisonment, deportation, refusal to seat legally elected officials, and mob violence.[25] Municipal populists who abjured socialism, even those as radical as Tom Johnson, were treated much more gently by their conservative opponents.

Working-class, foreign-stock support for reform, though overlooked by scholars who connect reform with native-stock elites, has been recognized in studies of electoral behavior at the state level; in work by J. Joseph Huthmacher and John Buenker on what they call "urban liberalism"; and in Melvin Holli's distinction between structural and social reform. Sophisticated quantitative studies of state-level voting during the Progressive Era have demonstrated that some reform candidates received working-class support and that patterns of electoral support were more volatile than if they had been rigidly determined by class or ethnicity. Roger Wyman's examination of voting patterns in Wisconsin uses correlation, regression, and examination of wards with particular class and ethnic characteristics to show that upper- and middle-class Anglo-Saxon voters were *less* likely to support the reform governor and senator, Robert La Follette, than ethnic, working-class voters.[26] Michael Rogin and John L. Shover's study of support for Hiram Johnson, California governor and senator, finds a similar pattern. Rogin and Shover also explore change over time: using ecological correlations and examination of assembly districts categorized by class, they suggest Johnson's base of support shifted between 1910, when he was opposed by working-class voters, and 1914, when they were his greatest strength.[27] Martin Shefter has used ecological regression methods to corroborate Rogin and Shover's analysis of support for reform in California, but he concludes that the pattern of voting for Charles Evans Hughes in New York did not undergo a comparable transformation.[28]

Workers, Huthmacher argues, "provided an active, numerically strong, and politically necessary force for reform."[29] In so doing, they helped to build an urban liberalism that was consolidated during the New Deal. Looking primarily at the state level, John D. Buenker has extensively documented Huthmacher's thesis, showing how urban legislators representing, and often themselves part of, the new-stock working class supported welfare measures and governmental reforms. Buenker's list of urban liberals combines reformers such as Tom Johnson (Cleveland), Hazen Pingree (Detroit), and Edward Dunne (Chicago), whom I would categorize as municipal populists, with machine (or would-be machine) politicians like Charles F. Murphy of New York's Tammany Hall and Boston's James Michael Curley and Martin Lomasney.[30] Though neither Huthmacher nor Buenker argues that reform was an exclusively ethnic, working-class phenomenon, each suggests the role of the new-stock workers cannot be dismissed as easily as it has been by those who identify reform with the upper or middle class.

My categories of traditional reformer and municipal populist, finally, build on Holli's conceptions of structural and social reformers.[31] As described by Holli, structural reformers supported by elites, including Seth Low and John Purroy Mitchel (New York) and James D. Phelan (San Francisco), distrusted democracy, wanted rule by the "best men," and were primarily interested in reducing expenditures. In contrast, social reformers backed by the working class, like Hazen Pingree (Detroit), Tom Johnson (Cleveland), and Brand Whitlock (Toledo), sought to make utilities cheaper and safer and to provide amenities to the masses. The structural approach dominated the theory and practice of reform, but in Holli's view the social reform program represented a more constructive response to the needs of urban society.

Holli's characterizations of reformers are often overstated. On the one hand, some of Holli's structural reformers also worked to improve social conditions. Seth Low's biographer, for example, points out that important advances in education, public health, and tenement regulation took place under his administration.[32] Professionally trained reformers interested in the conditions of the working class played a larger role under Mitchel than under previous mayors of New York, reform or Tammany. On the other hand, there were limits to the concerns of even the best known and most ardent of Holli's social reformers. Tom Johnson, for example, was sensitive to the lifestyles of lower-class, foreign-stock whites, but he showed little interest in the problems of Cleveland's black population.[33]

A second criticism is that the same reformers were often interested in social and structural change. Johnson attacked the efforts of the Republican state legislature to alter Cleveland's "federal plan" of government. Under Mitchel, Henry Bruère of the Bureau of Municipal Research proposed both appointment of a city manager (structural) and establishment of unemployment exchanges (social). New York comptroller Bird S. Coler, active as a fiscal reformer, called for "a movement with a broad and liberal policy for building up, not a mere negative force to stop progress in order to show a smaller expense account."[34] And for Benjamin De Witt, a contemporary adherent and historian of reform, "municipal home rule," "the charter movement," "the efficiency movement," and "the social movement" were complementary.[35]

These problems suggest that Holli's scheme forces reformers into excessively tight conceptual boxes. Holli's approach to electoral patterns, similarly, makes coalitions that brought together social and structural reform voters inconceivable. Yet a coalition of the traditional reform voters who had supported Seth Low and the municipal populist voters who had supported Hearst elected John Purroy Mitchel mayor of New York in 1913, and Newton Baker received similarly broad-based support in the Cleveland mayoral election of 1913. The overwhelming majorities indicate that in these elections Mitchel and Baker were able to cross the class and ethnic boundaries that had earlier divided reformers in their cities.

What bound these coalitions together? Why was Charles Merriam of Chicago unable to put together a similar winning coalition? If Holli's dichotomy cannot provide answers to these questions, neither can group approaches, for the emphasis of group approaches on ethnocultural conflicts prevents them from explaining how these conflicts could be overcome in particular elections. In fact, the emphasis of group-based analyses on slowly changing demographic variables means they can say little about any short-term changes. In all three cities, however, such changes were often quite sharp: the actions of politicians seeking to organize electoral majorities with policy appeals made the urban politics of the Progressive Era much more fluid than group approaches would allow it to have been.[36]

PROGRESSIVISM AND THE INCORPORATION OF EXPERTISE

What made progressive electoral coalitions possible in New York and Cleveland, but not in Chicago, was the role of experts. Some kinds of experts, such as engineers, have always been important in city *government*. The role of experts in city *politics*, however, was new in the Progressive Era. People such as William H. Allen and Frederic C. Howe, educated as social scientists according to the research model recently imported from Germany, were potentially well-suited to develop rhetoric and proposals that could simultaneously appeal to the very different constituencies of traditional reform and municipal populist voters. Professionally trained experts emerged in all three cities, but political and economic elites, acting upon their own strategic calculations, established different relationships with the new experts. To understand who experts were, what they believed, and what relationships they formed with politicians in New York, Cleveland, and Chicago is to understand reform outcomes in these cities.

During the Progressive Era and today, in cities and more generally, experts can be incorporated into politics in a variety of ways. Every organizational context has its own distinctive features, but Figure 2-1 suggests

Are Experts

Autonomous from Business?

Are Experts Linked with Politicians?	Yes	No
Yes	Political Experts	Policy Planning Networks
No	Gadflies	Servants of Power

FIGURE 2-1 Alternative Roles of Experts in Relation to Business and Politics

four basic roles. Experts who are neither autonomous from business nor directly connected with political authority can be described by the phrase that Loren Baritz uses for industrial social scientists: "servants of [economic] power."[37] Experts under business control who are linked to politicians as well serve as nodes in the corporate "policy planning networks" described by G. William Domhoff.[38] Domhoff himself uses the concept much too broadly when he applies it to describe experts who do have significant autonomy from business.[39] Yet there are some organizations for which the concept is a good fit: at the Committee for Economic Development (CED), for example, the business-based trustees have final say over policy recommendations.[40] Autonomous experts who lack regularized connections to political authority are gadflies, a role made familiar in our time by Ralph Nader and his progeny.[41] Peter Witt played this role in Cleveland politics before he joined Tom Johnson's administration and after his defeat in the mayoral election of 1915. William H. Allen played it in New York after he left the Bureau of Municipal Research and devoted himself to attacks on the Rockefeller interests that had curtailed the Bureau's original program of political activism.

Only experts who are organized to be both linked with politicians and autonomous from business can truly be considered political experts. To put it another way, only then are they themselves both experts and politicians. The Bureau of Municipal Research played this role before its Rockefeller-inspired restructuring, and Mayo Fesler of the Civic League played it for Newton Baker in Cleveland. At the national level, the Keynesian economists of the Brookings Institution played this role during the Kennedy and Johnson administrations. Brookings has always operated with a significant degree of autonomy, protected by by-laws limiting the influence of the business-oriented trustees. Brookings was usually in opposition to the policies of the Roosevelt and Truman administrations, but a change in leadership and personnel allowed it to establish ties with the Democrats during the Kennedy-Johnson years.[42] The agricultural economists who worked to make production control the basis for New Deal agricultural policy provide other examples of the type.[43] As Richard Kirkendall says, "These social scientists refused to be mere 'servants of power.'"[44]

The municipal experts of the Progressive Era were the first products of the new doctoral programs in American universities. Henry Bruère and William H. Allen (New York) studied under Simon Patten at the University of Pennsylvania; Frederic Howe (Cleveland), under Richard Ely, Albert Shaw, and Woodrow Wilson at Johns Hopkins; Charles Merriam (Chicago), who went on to train many experts himself, under William A. Dunning and John W. Burgess at Columbia. This training was a powerful experience: Howe went so far as to open his autobiography by explaining, "I am not nearly so old as the records of births in Meadville, Pennsylvania make me seem. My life really began in the early nineties instead of the late sixties. It began at Johns Hopkins University. Under the influence of Richard T. Ely, Woodrow Wilson, Albert Shaw, James Bryce, I came alive."[45]

Despite their stress on practical knowledge, many of these teachers espoused fanciful racial theories emphasizing the democratic traditions of the Anglo-Saxon peoples and disparaging immigrants.[46] Howe and his contemporaries abandoned the racial theories and took the notion of practical knowledge more seriously. E. L. Godkin expressed the older generation's attitudes when he blamed corruption on the influence of immigrants, particularly the Irish, under universal suffrage.[47] Howe rejected such explanations. In his view, the problems of the modern city were not "personal" but economic and institutional.[48]

The new experts acted in accord with Theodore Roosevelt's advice to the 1894 Conference for Good City Government: "There are two gospels I always want to preach to reformers, whether they are working for civil service reform, for municipal reform, or for any other reform. The first is the gospel of morality; the next is the gospel of efficiency. . . . I don't have to tell you to be upright, but I do think I have to tell you to be practical and efficient."[49] In the course of their careers in philanthropy, journalism, or academics, the younger experts developed a common worldview that saw efficiency and social welfare as not only compatible, but inseparable: lack of efficiency prevented municipal programs from accomplishing goals such as eliminating disease, improving education, and alleviating poverty.[50] Bruère, for example, criticized commission governments for ignoring social needs and described living conditions and employment as essential aspects of progress.[51] Lower municipal spending in the name of "economy," to Delos F. Wilcox, was "likely to prove to be penny wisdom and pound foolishness."[52]

The experts' conception of municipal research emphasized its educational aspects. The public, particularly the poor, was to understand the operations of the municipal government and so demand an end to waste.[53] One method for accomplishing this education was extensive publicity, including photographs, cartoons, and other techniques, borrowed from business advertising, to make data accessible. The result, in William H. Allen's words, was to be "Unescapable Information, Not Merely Obtainable Information!"[54] Another method of civic education was to establish community centers as intermediaries between the government and the public. The Wingate Community Center in the Gramercy area of New York, for example, provided a range of services, including a program of study courses on labor problems and other topics, cosponsored by Local 25 of the Ladies' Waist and Dress Makers' Union and offered in Yiddish and English.[55]

Through such methods, the government could inform the citizenry— and the citizenry could control the government. As Allen noted, "Where the public is not currently helped to understand, not only will and must the public misunderstand and mistrust even government by experts, but those very experts themselves almost inevitably acquire contempt for the public's ability and right to understand expert government."[56] Charles A. Beard saw the first hope of "reconciling democracy and expert service" in "the rising intelligence of laymen which enables them to exercise independent and critical judgment about the achievements of the expert. The steady refusal of the public to accept the final verdict of educational experts is a cheering sign."[57] James A. Morone identifies as one paradox of progressive reform that "government would be simultaneously returned to the people and placed beyond them, in the hands of the experts."[58] Civic education, through which the people would themselves become experts, was supposed to resolve this contradiction.

The municipal experts of the Progressive Era, along with other reformers, shared a political vision of a society where "all classes of citizens, whether rich or poor, find that their interests and their honor lie together." One would then see, Howe wrote, "the identification of all classes with the state, rather than against it."[59] This ideal of a classless polity mirrored the progressive coalition that could be assembled with the mediation of experts. Because they simultaneously stressed economy, which appealed to traditional reform voters, and social welfare, which appealed to municipal populists, the policy proposals developed by experts could provide the basis for unity between what would otherwise be two distinct reform constituencies.

Looking at it another way, cooperation with experts allowed reform politicians to exercise a kind of leadership between what James MacGregor Burns calls "transactional leadership," which takes existing incentive structures as given, and Burns's "transformational" leadership, which alters the preferences of followers.[60] Leaders like Tom Johnson did not necessarily change the public's goals, among which material security and ethnic recognition remained the most important. But they did transform the politics that followed from those goals by constructing hitherto impossible coalitions. That they did so in conjunction with the municipal experts who developed their appeals suggests the need to identify the institutional conditions for this intermediate type of leadership.

IDEOLOGY AND ORGANIZATION

This view of the municipal experts of the Progressive Era draws on, but is distinct from, ideological and organizational approaches to the study of reform. Hays warns "that ideological evidence is no safe guide to practice, that what people thought and said about their society is not necessarily an accurate representation of what they did."[61] Authors presenting ideological interpretations, in contrast, see these ideas themselves as fundamental in understanding reform.

What brought the adherents of reform together, these authors argue, was not class or ethnicity, but shared beliefs about the current conditions and future improvement of government and society. Ernest S. Griffith, author of a multivolume history of American city government sponsored by the National Municipal League, rejects the revisionism of Hays or Hofstadter and their disciples; their findings, he suggests, apply at best only to particular localities. "Social consciousness and a sense of public duty, not wealth or the lack of it," he concludes, "seem much more nearly to have been the common denominator" among reformers. For Griffith, reform in the Progressive Era can be summarized as "pragmatism with a conscience."[62] Maureen A. Flanagan's case study of the charter reform movement in Chicago argues for the primacy of "ideas about cities as places to live" in explaining divisions over the reconstitution of city government. Analysis of urban reform, she says, "necessitates both trying to understand what participants intended as a result of their stance on reform issues and recognizing that ideas are not the passive products of a person's (or group's) place in society defined by interest-group or class needs."[63] "The basic riddle in progressivism," for David P. Thelen, "is not what drove groups apart, but what made them seek common cause." What brought them together, he argues, was the depression of 1893–97, which "generated broadly based new issues which all classes could unite behind," including tax reform and "corporate arrogance." "Perhaps," he says, "there are, after all, times and places where issues cut across class lines."[64] Richard L. McCormick dates the turning point later than Thelen does, but he offers a similar interpretation of reform as a response to widely held perceptions. The discovery that business was responsible for corruption, McCormick argues, led to a nationwide regulatory revolution in 1905 and 1906. To understand reform, McCormick advises, one must partially adopt the perspective of the "typical textbook" written before the group approach became influential and take seriously reformers' expressions of outrage at the relationship of economic and political elites.[65]

In making these arguments, scholars such as Griffith, Flanagan, Thelen, and McCormick echo the reformers' own conception of what they were doing. Writing in 1915, De Witt traced reform to the recognition that under a Constitution that placed strict limits on public authority, "the government was being *used*—not in the interests of the many, but in the interests of the few." "Slowly," he said, "Americans realized that they were not free."[66] He defined the "Progressive movement" by three tendencies, each representing a common belief:

> The first of these tendencies is found in the insistence by the best men in all political parties that special, minority, and corrupt influence in government —national, state, and city—be removed; the second tendency is found in the demand that the structure or machinery of government, which has hitherto been admirably adapted to control by the few, be so changed and modified that it will be more difficult for the few, and easier for the many, to control; and, finally, the third tendency is found in the rapidly growing conviction that the functions of government at present are too restricted and that they must be increased and extended to relieve social and economic distress.[67]

As the ideological interpretation of reform suggests, new beliefs were associated with shifts in reform politics from a relatively narrow to a relatively broad pattern of electoral support. But the ideological interpretation of reform cannot explain why these shifts took place, or why no such shift occurred in Chicago. The organizational approach, pioneered by Robert Wiebe, provides insights into the ideologies that glued together progressive coalitions. Like Larson or Ehrenreich and Ehrenreich, Wiebe emphasizes the role of professionals and managers in reform. "The heart of progressivism," he says, "was the ambition of the new middle class to fulfill its destiny through bureaucratic means." But if this group was at the center, business executives, farmers, and workers also took part in the "revolution in values." What they shared was not, as Flanagan, Thelen, or McCormick might argue, specific ideas, but a general form of consciousness, the orientation toward organization as the way to solve the problems of urban-industrial life. And for Wiebe, reform was not a response to discrete periods of economic crisis or political revelation, but an aspect of the continuing adjustment to the end of the isolated local community.[68]

Augustus Cerillo, Jr., has applied Wiebe's ideas to the study of reform in New York City, describing the development inside and outside government of a professionally trained policy elite. The formation of this elite marked the shift from the old, moralistic style of urban reform to an organizationally oriented approach epitomized by the Bureau of Municipal Research. Cerillo sees the new policy elite as responsible for a range of administrative reforms that provided the basis for a continuing governmental role in social welfare.[69]

Cerillo traces the rise of the policy elite during both reform and Tammany-supported administrations. He also shows the influence of the Bureau of Municipal Research on electoral politics. What is missing from his sketch is an explanation of why successive mayors cooperated with municipal experts, and how this interaction shaped the incorporation of expertise. For Wiebe's concept of a national shift toward organizational action to be useful in understanding the outcomes of urban reform, some attention must be paid to the distinctive, dynamic patterns that characterized the development of expertise in each city. What seems necessary, in short, is to introduce politics into Wiebe's abstract conception of the "search for order."[70]

POLITICIANS, EXPERTS, AND POLITICAL SCIENTISTS

To develop ties to experts required that politicians overcome their own frequently expressed preference for experience over academic learning and subjected them to attacks along the same lines from others. Whether these costs were worth incurring depended on the structure of local party organization. The citywide machine of legend was in fact the exception rather than the rule. More common patterns of organizational party politics were the division of control among competing factions or independent ward bosses.[71]

The electoral strategies of organization and anti-organization reflected the extent to which party politics was consolidated. Carter Harrison of Chicago, for example, had much in common with George McClellan of New York. Both had the same names as their famous fathers.[72] Both had achieved the mayoralty through uneasy accommodation with organizational politicians, and both had aspirations for higher office. But Harrison, unlike McClellan, took no steps to bring experts into his administration. This was because Harrison faced different political circumstances. In the context of a Democratic party dominated by Tammany, alliance with the Bureau of Municipal Research made sense for McClellan as a way to separate from the machine. In the context of the more fragmented Chicago Democratic party, Harrison could stay in power by winning over whatever factions had deserted him in the last election, rather than by allying with experts.

The structure of local party organization, in turn, reflected the structure of local government. Governmental consolidation encouraged party consolidation, and governmental fragmentation encouraged party fragmentation. Independent bases of patronage and authority, such as Chicago's park districts or New York's boroughs, allowed rival politicians to maintain their organizations even when they were out of power at the top.[73] Of the three cities examined in this book, Chicago, a jumble of boards and districts, had the most fragmented city government.[74] Cleveland, under the Federal Plan of 1891 or the Home Rule Charter of 1913, was the most centralized; although the usual city-county division of authority remained in place, municipal officials were responsible to the mayor.[75] New York, with its five boroughs, can be considered somewhere in between. As Wallace Sayre and Herbert Kaufman point out, each of the five boroughs, which are also counties, essentially developed its own party system. New York politics thus became organized by jurisdictions that were smaller than the city, yet larger than the ward.[76]

In all three cities studied here, experts entered municipal politics as traditional reformers: they enthusiastically joined the campaigns of Low in New York and Harlan in Chicago and worked to defeat would-be boss Robert McKisson in Cleveland. But whether experts continued to act as traditional reformers, allied with municipal populists, or helped to form progressive coalitions depended on the interaction of governmental and party organizations, politicians' strategic calculations, and the experts' own political learning.

The limitations of Low's tenure as mayor—his emphasis on "goodness" over administrative effectiveness, his alienation of ethnic voters by enforcement of Sunday laws, and, above all, his failure to win reelection—

led experts to reevaluate their relationship to traditional reform.[77] The Bureau of Municipal Research, organizational home to Allen and Bruère, was formed within the traditional reform Citizens' Union, but soon broke off to pursue its own agenda with funding from John D. Rockefeller, J. P. Morgan, and other titans of big business. The Bureau developed ties to Mayor McClellan, who sought to distance himself from Tammany after winning election with machine support in 1903 and 1905. Among the products of McClellan's alliance with the Bureau was the development of the first municipal budget in the United States. McClellan's alliance with the Bureau also led to the removal of two borough presidents for inefficiency; this was the first time any American city officials had been removed for inefficiency, as opposed to corruption. The ties between City Hall and the Bureau of Municipal Research were continued under McClellan's successor, William J. Gaynor, who had a similarly tenuous relationship with Tammany.

The Bureau's ties to McClellan and Gaynor helped give its members the skills to develop a program that included both ways to make government cheaper and ways to make it a more effective tool for social policy. This program could appeal to traditional reform and municipal populist constituencies at the same time. As Cerillo has shown, the efficiency rhetoric of the 1913 Mitchel campaigns conveyed different messages to New York's upper and lower classes. The very positions that made Mitchel attractive to the lower classes, moreover, aroused the fears of upper-class reformers and newspapers that he had radical tendencies.[78] The value of the rhetoric of efficiency was that it could contain appeals to both constituencies. The concept of efficiency replaced Seth Low's emphasis on "good men," by which he meant Anglo-Saxon Protestants listed in the Social Register, and which could not attract municipal populist support.[79]

Running on it, in close association with members of the Bureau, Mitchel was elected mayor in 1913. Once Mitchel was in office, however, governmental experts came into conflict with business over the adoption of reforms. New policies and structures might eventually have served business interests. In the short run, however, new social programs meant higher taxes, and governmental changes threatened to create instability that might scare away investment. Business's view won out, as Mitchel gave in to demands to curtail reforms, or implemented them in ways aimed only at reduced expenditures. The Bureau of Municipal Research was itself reshaped in the interests of business, as it gave up its watchdog role in New York government in return for increased funding from the Rockefeller family. Business's victory was only temporary: Mitchel's rejection of policies that might have allowed him to maintain the municipal populist portion of his coalition contributed to his defeat by a Tammany candidate in 1917.

Cleveland experts were initially attached to the Municipal Association, an organization comparable to New York's Citizens' Union. But the Municipal Association's unwillingness to challenge business leadership and its manipulation by Mark Hanna in the election of 1899 left Frederic Howe, for one, available to Tom Johnson.[80] Experts sympathetic to Johnson were loosely organized within his administration, rather than in a business-funded research body. Implementing these experts' proposals without concern for business opinion, the Johnson administration adopted many policies that were farsighted and others that were far-fetched.

Cleveland's Baker was identified with an ideology expressed in the word "civitism," which Baker coined as a municipal analogue to patriotism.[81] As an all-inclusive, consensual ideology, civitism corresponded to Baker's broad coalition and fit his political needs much better than Henry George's Single Tax doctrine, which Tom Johnson had championed and which Baker had endorsed as a member of Johnson's cabinet. Civitism was encouraged by policies such as establishment of a municipal orchestra. As Baker's civitism replaced Johnson's emphasis on the Single Tax, the Municipal Association, renamed the Civic League, took on a research orientation under the leadership of Mayo Fesler, who had done graduate and undergraduate work in political science and history at the University of Chicago. After Baker left office, municipal populists and traditional reformers split once again, resuming a series of conflicts that include Dennis Kucinich's battles during the 1970s.

In Chicago, experts remained within the narrow roles of traditional reformers. The Chicago Bureau of Public Efficiency was organized on the model of the New York Bureau of Municipal Research but never developed the New York Bureau's interest in social policy. Charles Merriam became the candidate of the Bureau of Public Efficiency, just as Mitchel became the candidate of the Bureau of Municipal Research. Yet Merriam, running on a narrower platform, could not attract enough ethnic working-class voters to build a progressive coalition and become mayor. These voters became instead the foundation of the machine that was to make Chicago politics famous.

Successful or not, politicians' strategic choices had lasting consequences for the politics of their cities. These political choices also had lasting consequences for American political science. Political science, like the other academic disciplines, was defined and organized during this period of professionalization. Alternative models for the relationship between the study and practice of politics and government were connected with the electoral alternatives of the Progressive Era. In association with traditional reform, research showed how to achieve greater economy. In association with municipal populism, research investigated social conditions. In association with progressivism, research explored both governmental efficiency and social change and provided the basis for the reorganization of political conflict.

The eventual defeat of progressivism in all three of the cities studied here contributed to the national separation between political science and practical politics. After its withdrawal from New York politics, the Bureau of Municipal Research helped to create the abstract discipline of "public administration." And after his losses in the Chicago mayoral elections of 1911 and 1919, Charles Merriam helped to reorient and reorganize the study of politics, thus creating what we know as political science. The traditional reform model survives in latter-day municipal research bodies like the Cleveland Citizens League, but it has little to do with academic political science. The municipal populist model, carried on by unrecalcitrant experts like William H. Allen of New York and Peter Witt of Cleveland, has been institutionalized in public interest research groups and similar organizations, but they are even further outside disciplinary boundaries. There are contemporary counterparts to the New York Bureau of Municipal Research or the Chicago Bureau of Public Efficiency, but their reports are not discussed at academic conferences or published in academic journals as they were during the Progressive Era. Professional programs like Harvard's Kennedy School of Government and policy institutes like the Brookings Institution or the Heritage Foundation are closer to academic political science, but they function as vehicles for elite training and interaction, without the emphasis on popular education seen as central in the Progressive Era.

Political scientists have begun to devote more attention to our own history as a discipline.[82] The relationship of progressivism and political science suggests that we should be careful not to do so in a purely idealist fashion that locates the conflicts of approaches in the world of pure thought, above the political conflicts to be studied. Instead, we should be alert to the connections between the study of politics and patterns of electoral division.[83] New ways of thinking about politics create new ways of organizing political conflict. But the outcomes of political conflict make some ways of thinking about politics dominant and define other ways as marginal. Like New York, Cleveland, and Chicago, political science has been shaped by the reform outcomes of the Progressive Era. As political scientists, we too are experts. To understand why we study what we study, and why we are situated where we are situated in relation to the politicians of our time, we need to look at the urban experts and politicians of the Progressive Era.

Part II

NEW YORK: FROM TRADITIONAL REFORM
TO PROGRESSIVISM

> It was a period of disillusionment for me, for I worked for a time
> with the Mitchel administration, and the Bureau of Municipal
> Research. I know of nothing actually accomplished by the sterile
> Mitchel administration excepting Edward M. Bassett's launching of
> the zoning system. The zoning boat was loaded down with all kinds
> of junk; it had reciprocating engines instead of turbines; it made
> little speed, but it floated and went places. Almost all the rest of
> the Mitchel proposals were pipe dreams. It was an honest outfit
> committed to saving rubber bands, using both ends of the pencil
> and similar efficiency devices, and to the impossible promise of
> making vast physical improvements without spending more money.
> *Robert Moses,* Working for the People: Promise
> and Performance in Public Service

NEW YORK CITY provides a good test of competing interpretations of reform, for three distinct patterns of electoral support for reform candidates
can be identified between 1901 and 1917. Seth Low won the mayoralty in
1901 and lost it in 1903. Each time, he received traditional reform support, as did two unsuccessful mayoral candidates, William Ivins in 1905
and Otto Bannard in 1909. In 1905 and 1909, William Randolph Hearst's
independent campaigns received municipal populist support. Hearst was
backed most strongly by ethnic voters, particularly those from the lower
middle and skilled working classes. In 1913, John Purroy Mitchel was able
to combine traditional reform and municipal populist support to win an
overwhelming victory as a Fusion candidate. Mitchel's ability to unite the
supporters of Hearst and Low suggests the limitations of any theory identifying progressivism as a movement by one class or nationality, directed
against a traditional "negative reference group." In 1917, however, Mitchel's attempt to win reelection failed by a large margin, as Tammany Hall
returned to full political power.

The incorporation of administrative expertise into city government
helps explain these electoral patterns. But the incorporation of administrative expertise can only be understood in relation to electoral change.

The most important links between administrative reformers and city government were established under the Tammany-elected administrations of George B. McClellan, Jr., and William Jay Gaynor, in response to Hearst's mobilization of an antimachine constituency. Under McClellan and Gaynor, a new organization of experts, the Bureau of Municipal Research, developed close ties to city government. The administrative reformers of the Bureau provided the electoral appeals that made possible Mitchel's construction of a coalition between native middle-class and ethnic working-class reform voters in 1913. Under Mitchel, professionally trained reformers, interested in the conditions of the working class, played a larger role in policy development than ever before. The dependence of the Bureau on business funding, however, meant that business was able to defeat reforms that threatened to upset the urban economic order. The reshaping of the most comprehensive reform proposals to meet the constraints imposed by big business helped to bring about Mitchel's 1917 defeat.

The next three chapters explore the sequence of outcomes that constituted reform in New York. Chapter 3 reviews the origins of machine politics, traditional reform, and municipal populism in the context of the city's economic and ethnic structure. I then turn to the election, administration, and defeat of Seth Low. Chapter 4 examines Hearst's challenge and its impact upon municipal government. Chapter 5 discusses the election, administration, and defeat of John Purroy Mitchel. I conclude this part of the book by suggesting how the outcomes of the Progressive Era shaped New York's responses to the New Deal, the War on Poverty, and the fiscal crisis of the 1970s. Table II-1 summarizes the elections covered in these chapters.

TABLE II-1
New York Mayoral Elections, 1901–1917

Year	Traditional Reform	Municipal Populist	Progressive Coalition	Organization Candidates	Socialist Party
1901	**Low**			Shepard	Hanford
1903	Low			**McClellan**	Furman
1905	Ivins	Hearst		**McClellan**	Lee
1909	Bannard	Hearst		**Gaynor**	Cassidy
1913			**Mitchel**	McCall	Russell
1917	Mitchel Bennett			**Hylan**	Hillquit

Note: Winning candidate in **bold**.

CHAPTER 3.

Seth Low and Traditional Reform

EARLY TWENTIETH-CENTURY politics in New York, to a greater extent than in Cleveland or Chicago, was dominated by a single party organization. But as the 1901 election of Republican Seth Low as mayor demonstrated, Tammany Hall's position within the city's Democratic party could not always be translated into electoral victory. With Low's election, the native-stock, elite reform coalition that had often been mobilized against Tammany achieved success. This success, however, proved to be as temporary as previous reform administrations. Although Low made efforts to reach out to the foreign-stock, working-class voters who represented a second source of opposition to Tammany, he was defeated for reelection in 1903.

From the mid-nineteenth century through the end of the Progressive Era, New York politics was an arena in which ethnicity, class, and electoral organization were closely related, and several alternative winning coalitions were possible. David Hammack describes the ethnic class hierarchy: "In sum, the native Americans and British were heavily overrepresented at the top; Germans were solidly ensconced in the middle; Irish were well represented in the clerical, skilled, and semiskilled ranks and had almost double their share of laborers; eastern Europeans [mostly Jews] were overrepresented in the entrepreneurial ranks and dominated the garment trades; and Italians were well represented only among petty entrepreneurs and garment workers and had three times their share of laborers."[1] Wealthy Germans and Jews, excluded from native-stock society, formed their own clubs and charitable organizations. Middle-class mutual benefit associations were organized by nationality or religion. Ethnic labor unions created a common class identification for recent immigrants who had been oriented toward their home-country villages, but they also divided workers of different nationalities from each other. In 1900, the Central Labor Union, founded after rallies in support of tenant farmers in Ireland, merged with the German Central Labor Federation to form the Central Federated Union. The Jewish labor movement had its first great success with the International Ladies Garment Workers strike of 1909. Italian workers, more likely than members of other groups to plan to return home once they had earned enough money, resisted unionization.[2]

Tammany Hall achieved dominance within the Manhattan Democratic party by defeating such rival organizations as Irving Hall and the County Democracy, curbing the ambitions of maverick political entrepreneurs like Fernando Wood, and controlling the "rapacious individualism" personified by "Boss" William M. Tweed.[3] Dominance within the Manhattan Democratic party, however, did not guarantee success in citywide elections. One set of limits could be traced to the consolidation of Manhattan, Brooklyn, and outlying towns into the five boroughs of Greater New York. Both the original metropolitan charter of 1897 and the more enduring one of 1901 left borough-level organizations with substantial patronage resources. Thus, for example, Tammany was unable to gain effective control of Brooklyn Democrats until 1910, after the death of the Brooklyn Democratic leader Patrick McCarren, who had said, "I would rather be a serf in Russia than a satrap of Tammany."[4]

TRADITIONAL REFORM AND MUNICIPAL POPULISM

In addition to challenges within the Democratic party, Tammany faced continual extraparty reform movements, backed by either native-stock elites or foreign-stock workers. The Irish had long provided Tammany's core support, yet as Henry George's 1886 mayoral campaign demonstrated, even Irish voters could be mobilized by the right kind of anti-Tammany candidate.[5] By the Progressive Era, moreover, the Irish made up a relatively small and decreasing proportion of the electorate. According to the 1910 federal census, 11.7 percent of the city's population were first- and second-generation Irish. This figure, to be sure, understates the Irish population, since the Irish had been in the United States long enough to produce a third generation that would not be counted. However, Germans would be undercounted in the same way, and their first- and second-generation population was 12.7 percent of the city. Recent waves of Eastern European immigrants had made Jews the largest ethnic group in New York. The 1910 census, which did not directly report the number of Jews, found that first- and second-generation immigrants from Austria, Hungary, and Russia represented 23.5 percent of the population; surveys showed that in New York, each of these nationality groups was predominantly Jewish. Though this figure is inflated by the inclusion of non-Jewish members of these nationality groups, it excludes German Jews, who were earlier arrivals to the U.S. A contemporary study based on mortality rates estimated that 22.0 percent of New York was Jewish. The 1910 census showed 22.4 percent of New York was native-stock, including native-born with native parents and first- and second-generation English and Scottish. First- and second-generation Italians were 11.1 percent of the population; the black population was 1.9 percent.[6] All these groups except the Irish were either excluded or subordinated by the Tammany regime and thus could potentially be mobilized against it.[7]

Low's unsuccessful mayoral campaign of 1897, and his successful one in 1901, continued a series of traditional reform campaigns in which native-stock elites sought to contain party leaders whose greed and/or social expenditures created a fiscal burden. Reformers defeated Fernando Wood in 1857, after he had proposed an extensive public works program to aid the unemployed. The elite Committee of Seventy put Tweed in jail and elected its own mayoral candidate, William Havemeyer, in 1872. William R. Grace was elected over Tammany's Hugh Grant in 1884, and William L. Strong was elected by another Committee of Seventy in 1894. Strong's campaign drew upon the Lexow Committee's revelations of police corruption under Tammany rule and upon the anti-vice crusade of Reverend Charles H. Parkhurst and other moral reformers. Morgan and Vanderbilt were among Strong's financial backers. Strong himself said, "No one who has had experience in the administration of city affairs will contend that it is other than a business proposition. That is all there is to it." During Strong's administration, the Citizens' Union was organized to replace elite reformers' temporary committees with an ongoing, independent local party.[8]

The elite that supported these traditional reformers was capable of cohesive political action despite economic shifts and social divisions. New York's port, the basis for the city's mercantile wealth and for its rapid growth during the early nineteenth century, lost some of its trade to Chicago and other railroad cities after 1870. Gradually, the merchants were displaced by manufacturers. Unlike their counterparts in Cleveland or Chicago, who produced iron, steel, and meat in huge plants, New York manufacturers gained their wealth from clothing, publishing, and specialty goods, all produced in small factories. New York was also a site for banks, insurance companies, law firms, and corporate headquarters. Though sharp status distinctions were made between the old "Knickerbocker" mercantile families and the new industrial millionaires of the "Four Hundred," with each group looking down upon the other, economic conflict between them was muted by diversified ownership and by the training of members of mercantile families for positions in industrial firms.[9]

A very different pattern of reform was a municipal populist campaign backed by the organized working class. During the Jacksonian era, Tammany was challenged by the Workingmen's party. Later, Michael Walsh, who called the working classes "the only honest, virtuous part of the Democratic party," forced Tammany to accept him and his Spartan Association on Walsh's own terms. John Morrissey had a similar political career during the 1870s. Henry George's Independent Labor party of 1886 brought Socialists, Samuel Gompers's trade unionists, and Irish nationalists together with supporters of George's own Single Tax doctrines. Though Abram Hewitt, supported by Tammany and "Swallowtail" elite Democrats, won the election, George received 31 percent of the vote and finished ahead of the Republican candidate, Theodore Roosevelt. George did particularly well among Germans, Jews, and second-generation Irish voters.[10]

Tammany's response to these external threats, ironically, improved its ability to dominate its intraparty rivals. After the fall of Tweed and the election of Havemeyer, John Kelly built a centralized and fiscally responsible party organization, which allied with segments of the business community and regained the mayoralty. George's independent labor candidacy led Tammany to organize political clubs that gave it a more secure base among upwardly mobile Irish voters.[11] By the end of the nineteenth century, then, New York had a party machine. But that machine faced opposition from elites when it spent too much or became too identified with immigrant ways, and from workers when it allied too closely with elites or excluded particular ethnic groups. The Republican party organization, though unable to defeat the Democrats by itself, was available for alliance with reformers.

THE ELECTION OF 1901

Such an alliance, with support from a traditional reform coalition of upper- and middle-class native-stock voters, elected Seth Low mayor of New York. The Low coalition was assembled in 1901, and disassembled in 1903, by a politics of coalition-building among organized political elites. Low's candidacies neither drew upon nor produced mass electoral change. But the Low administration's policy appeals to working-class, foreign-stock voters did have some electoral impact. And the traditional reform constituency to which Low appealed remained available for the broader movements that followed.

In 1897, Low, then president of Columbia University and formerly Republican mayor of pre-consolidation Brooklyn, ran for mayor of New York on the reform Citizens' Union ticket. Low finished behind the Tammany candidate, Robert A. Van Wyck, but ahead of the Republican, Benjamin F. Tracy. The combined votes of Low and Tracy would have defeated Van Wyck. Henry George ran another independent campaign but died two days before the election. Though huge crowds attended George's funeral, his son, Henry George, Jr., received only 4 percent of the vote as a stand-in candidate.[12]

In 1901, the prospect of defeating Tammany, considered vulnerable after the state legislature's Mazet Committee investigation into corruption, encouraged the Republican party of Boss Thomas C. Platt to unite with the anti-Platt Citizens' Union behind a Fusion ticket headed by Low.[13] The Fusion coalition also included the Greater New York Democracy, a dissident faction led by John C. Sheehan. Sheehan had been leader of Tammany for three years while its boss, Richard Croker, raced horses in England, but was deposed upon Croker's return. The Sheehan group had at first sought an independent Democrat as candidate, but accepted Low. During Low's administration, the Greater New York Democracy received a share of patronage that, according to Republicans and Citizens' Union members, exceeded its contribution to the vote.[14]

Low defeated Edward M. Shepard, the Democratic candidate, 296,813 votes to 265,177. Who supported Low? From what demographic groups were his supporters drawn? Did his candidacy follow or cut across existing party lines? We do not have data such as that provided by modern surveys, showing the voting behavior and other characteristics of individuals. We do have aggregate data on voting in this and other elections, and on demographic characteristics, grouped by Assembly District (AD). The effect of these variables on voting behavior can thus be explored by combining generalized least squares (GLS) regressions with linear programming. (See Appendix for methodological details.) Unfortunately, the demographic categories for which the 1900 census provides data at the Assembly District level are rather crude. White voters are categorized as foreign-born, native-born with foreign parents, and native-born with native parents. This categorization makes it difficult to separate the effects of generation from those of nativity, since different ethnic groups arrived in the United States at different times. Estimates for the small number of nonwhites could not be computed separately without collinearity problems, so this group was included with the native-born, with native parents as "other." The ratio of the number of families to the number of dwellings was used as an indicator of suburbanization. The 1900 AD data do not provide any good measure of class that is independent of spatial location. Another problem is that the 1900 census provides data by ADs only for Manhattan and the Bronx, then both part of New York County, limiting the sample to 36 of 61 districts.

Estimates of ethnic group support for each candidate, calculated as the expected vote from a district composed entirely of that group, with suburbanization set at the mean value, are given in Table 3-1.[15] Low did best among native-stock (including black) voters. However, he received some support from native-born voters with foreign parents. Low also did better than Shepard among the foreign-born, most of whom presumably did not vote. A large number of the foreign-stock Low voters were probably Jews. Even in his unsuccessful Citizens' Union campaign of 1897, Low had done

TABLE 3-1
Voting Behavior by Ethnic Group, 1901

	Low (Fusion) %	Shepard (Dem.) %
2nd Generation White	19–34	66
Foreign White	4–33	0
Other	50–86	7–50

Note: Suburbanization set at mean value.
N = 36 (Manhattan/Bronx only).

well on the Jewish Lower East Side, and a contemporary observed that in 1901,

> It is almost incredible, but is nonetheless a fact, that the entire machinery of the fusion campaign was largely directed to that portion of the city mostly inhabited by the Russian Jewish citizens. It was there that the successful candidates for mayor and district attorney made their strongest appeals and received the most encouraging response. . . . To the Russian Jew, with a mind quick to grasp simple business propositions, this problem of municipal reform was a very simple matter.[16]

Regression estimates suggest that the suburbanization variable did not have a significant effect on either candidate's vote. Contrary to the hypothesis of Richard Wade and other scholars, its coefficient in the equation for Low was slightly less than its coefficient in the equation for Shepard.[17]

Estimates for the partisan sources of support for the two major candidates in 1901 suggest, predictably, that Low did best among Republicans (between 50 and 94 percent) and Shepard among Democrats (84 percent). But Low did win the support of a small number of Democrats (estimated between 8 and 44 percent), while the percentage of Republicans supporting Shepard is estimated at zero.

LOW AS MAYOR

Melvin Holli has characterized Low as a structural reformer who "never seemed to realize that his municipal reform had nothing to offer the voters but sterile mechanical changes and that fundamental social and economic conditions which pressed upon the vast urban masses of immigrants and poor could not be changed by rewriting charters or enforcing laws." Similarly, Augustus Cerillo has identified Low with the nineteenth-century emphasis on government by good men, which he contrasts with the progressive emphasis on improved administration.[18] These generalizations do not completely capture the policy record of his administration. Low's franchise and tax policies were aimed primarily at improving the collection of revenues and thus allowing the reduction of the overall property tax rate, though it is not obvious who ultimately benefited from this reduction. In two years as mayor, however, Low spent twice as much on new school construction as had been spent in four years under his Tammany predecessor, Van Wyck; the same was true for municipal parks and buildings.[19] The Health Department's efforts to control disease and promote preventive medicine improved fundamental conditions at city expense. And establishment of the Tenement House Department to enforce the state tenement house code represented an administrative reform that, in the housing reformers' view, addressed not only the problem of housing itself, but poverty, crime, vice, and other social ills believed to originate in inadequate shelter. The housing reformers can be faulted for ignoring the extent to which the cost of improvements would be passed on to renters, but code enforcement did entail city expenditures designed to improve the living conditions of the poor. Low also embraced the movement to build free public baths. The public bath movement was based on paternalism as well as on beliefs in the healing power of water that now seem quaint. Yet Low's construction of ten baths in Brooklyn and Manhattan received working-class support, and the Tammany administrations that followed Low continued the program.[20]

The Low administration policy most closely associated with native-stock Protestant morality was the intermittent crackdown on Sunday drinking. Low tried to avoid the issue by following his earlier practice as mayor of Brooklyn, enforcing the state excise law only against the least respectable and most flagrantly violative saloons. During Low's first year, the policy was occasionally more stringently enforced, but this reflected his inability to control the police or District Attorney William Travers Jerome, rather than explicit mayoral policy. Many more arrests were made in 1903, after Francis V. Greene had been appointed Police Commissioner, but even then Sunday drinking remained widespread.[21] In all, the Sunday drinking policy seems to have been a concession to defenders of Protestant morality such as Reverend Charles Parkhurst, who had been part of Low's electoral coalition, rather than a manifestation of deep-rooted anti-immigrant attitudes.

Far more popular among foreign-stock voters than the attack on drinking was the reform campaign against prostitution, a vice with which Tammany politicians had many connections. Because he opposed prostitution, Jerome was popular among the Jews of the Lower East Side despite his crackdown on saloons. He set up a special office in the neighborhood and asked residents, "Is the honor of Jewish women sold for brass checks nothing to you?"[22]

Though Low's policy record was mixed, the individuals he chose to implement these policies followed a clear pattern. Theodore Lowi's study of cabinet-level appointments shows that Low tended to select gentlemen from the Social Register and the City Club, active in social organizations but without professional training. The proportion of the mayoral cabinet with job-oriented skills, for example, was lower under Low than under Van Wyck or under any of Low's successors, reform or machine.[23] Low's rejection of housing reformer Lawrence Veiller, who did have a professional background, as Tenement House Commissioner is cited by Holli as an example of Low's conservatism, but Veiller ended up deputy commissioner anyway. More revealing is the process by which Low selected Robert Weeks deForest as Veiller's superior. Low consulted the vice president of the elite Charity Organization Society, who recommended deForest, president of the Society. DeForest, in turn, was convinced to accept the position by Josephine Shaw Lowell, described by Low's biographer as the "grand dame of the social reformers."[24]

THE ELECTION OF 1903

In 1903, George B. McClellan, Jr., a "clean" Tammany candidate, defeated Low by 314,782 votes to 252,086. Contemporary observers such as Lincoln Steffens and Theodore Roosevelt (who commented that "the dog has returned to its vomit") interpreted Low's defeat as a rejection of reform. However, many ethnic, partisan, and personalistic explanations were advanced as well.[25] The estimates of ethnic group support presented in Table 3-2 help to sort out these competing explanations. In 1903, as in 1901, Low voters were disproportionately native-born, and Democratic voters disproportionately second-generation foreign-stock. Again, first generation foreign-stock voters gave more support to Fusion than to Tam-

TABLE 3-2
Voting Behavior by Ethnic Group, 1903

	Low (Fusion) %	McClellan (Dem.) %
2nd Generation White	8–10	79
Foreign White	5–26	0
Other	50–77	0–9

Note: Suburbanization set at mean value.

$N = 36$ (Manhattan/Bronx only).

many. Such Low policies as disease control and tenement regulation, then, may have had some positive electoral impact among the group most directly affected by them. Suburbanization did not have a significant effect on the vote for either candidate, and actually had a greater positive effect on the Democratic vote than on the vote for Fusion.

But why did support for Low drop among the native and second-generation voters? Estimates that Low received nearly 100 percent of Republican support, while McClellan received all the Democratic support, suggest that the answer had more to do with partisanship than with policy.[26] Before the 1903 campaign, many Republicans and Citizens' Union members expressed bitterness toward Low, who, they claimed, had given a disproportionate share of patronage to Democrats. After an attempt to displace Low as Fusion candidate failed, Republicans apparently voted for him once again. However, in this election, unlike that of 1901, only Republicans voted for Low. Low lost his original Democratic support for several reasons. First, with Croker's retirement, Charles F. Murphy became leader of Tammany Hall in 1902. The next year, Murphy was able to bring the anti-Croker Greater New York Democracy, which had played an important role in the 1901 result, back into Tammany. Second, Murphy offered Democratic nominations to Edward M. Grout, comptroller, and Charles V. Fornes, president of the Board of Aldermen. The two independent Democrats had been elected as Fusion candidates in 1901. After they accepted the Democratic endorsements, they were dropped from the 1903 Fusion ticket, weakening Fusion's appeal to anti-Tammany Democrats. Third, Democrats charged that Low had violated his pledge of nonpartisanship by campaigning for Governor Benjamin Odell, a Republican, in 1902. Finally, Tammany argued widely that a victory in the mayoral election was necessary if the party was to carry New York State in the 1904 presidential contest. Roosevelt's graphic judgment to the contrary, then, the election of 1903 seems less a repudiation of reform, which would have been expressed by Republicans as well as Democrats, than a return to customary patterns of partisan behavior.

In some ways, Seth Low fit the model of the traditional, "structural" reformer. He appointed the well-bred to office and was predominantly supported by native-stock Republicans. However, his 1901 coalition also included some Democrats and foreign-stock voters. Had it not, he could not have been elected mayor in a city where Democrats were a majority and 80 percent of the population was first- or second-generation foreign-born. Low's defeat in 1903 did not represent a rejection of reform, but the reincorporation into the Democratic majority of national Democrats who had left the party after the Mazet Committee exposures and the factional disputes of Croker's last years. Low's policies included both enforcement of the old ethnocultural prohibitions and comprehensive health and housing reforms. The latter elicited a small but significant electoral response by first-generation voters, showing that they could be mobilized by policy appeals as well as by the material incentives of the machine. Two of Low's reform successors, Hearst and Mitchel, demonstrated more clearly the possibility of mobilizing ethnic, working-class voters against machine politics.

CHAPTER 4.

Hearst, McClellan, and Gaynor:
Municipal Populism and the Tammany Response

IN 1905 AND 1909, William Randolph Hearst ran independent campaigns for mayor on a platform of municipal populism. Hearst's electoral coalition overlapped Low's to some extent, but drew much more heavily on lower-middle-class and skilled-working-class votes, as well as on the support of immigrant-stock groups. Though Hearst never became mayor, his electoral threat helped to shape the administrations of Mayors George B. McClellan, Jr., and William Jay Gaynor, indirectly contributing to the rationalization of city government.

THE ELECTION OF 1905

Hearst entered politics under Tammany auspices and broke with the machine only when it frustrated his ambitions.[1] He was elected to Congress as a Tammany candidate in 1902 and 1904. In 1904, he sought the Democratic nomination for president and received considerable Western support, but he was rejected by Tammany leader Charles Francis Murphy and other conservatives as a radical who, like William Jennings Bryan, would lead the party to defeat. In 1905, Hearst was unable to secure the Tammany nomination for mayor. An attempted fusion with the Republicans also collapsed, though Hearst and the Republicans did work out an arrangement for joint assembly and aldermanic nominations. McClellan was renominated despite Tammany suspicions; Hearst ran as candidate of the Municipal Ownership League; and the Republican party nominated William Ivins after Charles Evans Hughes declined to run. McClellan charged that Ivins was in the race to help Hearst, while Hearst said Ivins's candidacy was designed to help the Democrats. Hearst was not only endorsed by his own newspapers, the *Journal* and the *American*, but by Joseph Pulitzer's *World* and by the *Tribune*, whose publisher, Whitelaw Reid, had been the Republican vice-presidential candidate in 1892.

Judge Samuel Seabury's participation in the Hearst campaign further indicated the extent to which Hearst cut across previous political cleavages. Seabury was descended from a distinguished native-stock family. Like many of his contemporaries, he was converted to reform by reading

Henry George's *Progress and Poverty*. Seabury worked in George's 1897 mayoral campaign, which ended with George's death shortly before the election. In 1901, Seabury won his position as justice of the city court by running on the Fusion ticket with Seth Low and William Travers Jerome. In 1905, Seabury declined Hearst's efforts to nominate him as the Municipal Ownership mayoral candidate, running instead as the Municipal Ownership candidate for supreme court judge. Seabury later became famous when he served as counsel to the state investigation that brought down Tammany mayor Jimmy Walker. He then played a key role in the selection of Fiorello La Guardia as Fusion mayoral candidate.[2]

In his speeches and in his newspapers, Hearst urged municipal ownership of major utilities, including gas companies and transit lines. Emphasizing the links between the utilities and Tammany Hall, Hearst argued that municipal ownership would reduce corruption as well as lower rates and improve safety. Hearst also defended unions and strikes, which helped win him the support of many labor leaders. These positions were not very different from those of the Socialists, who were generally reformist and especially so in their municipal campaigns. Opponents' charges to the contrary, however, Hearst explicitly rejected socialism, which he claimed would be unnecessary if the privileges enjoyed by the utilities and the trusts were abolished.[3] He called himself an "urban Jeffersonian."[4]

The results of the election were controversial: Hearst partisans charged that Democratic frauds included repeaters, imported voters, and the ejection of ballot boxes from pro-Hearst districts into the East River. The final recount gave Hearst 800 additional votes, mostly by allowing ballots originally declared void (one alleged Tammany tactic was to mark up a ballot while counting it, using a piece of lead hidden in the fingernail). This gave McClellan a 2,791 vote victory over Hearst, with Ivins over 90,000 votes behind.[5] Though the strong probability of even greater fraud than recognized by the courts renders the vote count suspect, analysis of the 1905 returns provides some insights into the sources of Hearst's support.

Table 4-1 presents estimates of transition probabilities from 1903 to 1905.[6] (See Appendix.) These estimates suggest that Hearst mobilized an anti-Tammany coalition that overlapped only partly with the coalition mobilized earlier by Low. An estimated 24 to 45 percent of 1903 Low voters backed Hearst in 1905. But a comparable proportion of 1903 McClellan voters, estimated at 33 to 36 percent, defected to Hearst in 1905. Though the estimate that Hearst captured 100 percent of the earlier Social Democratic (Socialist) vote is certainly impossible, it does suggest that in 1905 Socialists gave Hearst stronger support than they gave their own party's candidate.[7] The Socialist effort to maintain their support by emphasizing the limits of Hearst's radicalism and pointing out his hypocrisy in de-

TABLE 4-1
Transition Rates, 1903–1905

1903	1905			
	Ivins (Rep.) %	McClellan (Dem.) %	Hearst (Mun. Own.) %	Lee (Soc.) %
Low (Fusion)	54	10–46	24–45	0
McClellan (Dem.)	0	37–64	33–36	0–2
Furman (Soc. Dem.)	0	0	100	36–48

N = 61 (all boroughs).

nouncing Tammany after serving as its congressman thus seems to have failed.[8] Another pattern of partisan switching suggested by Table 4-1 was for normally Republican voters to vote Democratic. Contemporary commentators attributed McClellan's victory not only to fraud but to the votes of upper-class Republicans who accepted the Tammany candidate to keep the radical Hearst from becoming mayor. Two historians who have examined the vote of normally Republican districts in Manhattan have also emphasized this phenomenon.[9]

THE ELECTION OF 1909

Hearst ran for mayor again, with less success, in 1909. In between these mayoral elections he won the 1906 Democratic gubernatorial nomination, with Murphy's support, but "knifing" by Tammany and the Brooklyn Democratic organization apparently cost Hearst the election, won by Republican Charles Evans Hughes. Hearst then set up the Independence League, which ran Hearst-controlled candidates for president and governor in 1908. In 1909, Hearst tried to run Judge William Jay Gaynor as the League's candidate for mayor but was outmaneuvered when Murphy gave Gaynor the Democratic nomination.[10] Hearst ended up running for mayor himself on the Civil Alliance ticket, against Gaynor and Otto Bannard, nominated as a Republican-Fusion candidate. Two of the key figures of the 1905 campaign could be found on different sides: Seabury supported Gaynor, while Ivins, who had supported Hearst's attempts to convince the courts to invalidate the 1905 results, endorsed Hearst in 1909. By 1909, Hearst's organizational base had deteriorated to the point where it was unable to prevent Tammany subversion. Hearst also did not receive labor leaders' endorsements as he had in 1905. Though his newspapers remained politically effective, Hearst received only 153,843 votes to

250,678 for Gaynor and 177,682 for Bannard. Fusion candidates endorsed by Hearst won the other two citywide offices and the presidencies of four of the five boroughs, thus gaining a majority on the Board of Estimate.[11]

The 1909 vote provides more evidence about the sources of Hearst's core support than the 1905 results. In contrast to 1905, no major charges of fraud were advanced after the 1909 election. The Assembly Districts (ADs) by which voters were grouped were reapportioned in 1906; the new districts were used for both the 1909 election and the 1910 census. Hence it is possible to analyze the 1909 election results by use of the ethnic data of the 1910 census, which gives population by country of origin as well as by generation for ADs in all boroughs. In using this data to analyze voting in 1909 and later elections, percentages were computed for the largest ethnic groups in the city: German (first and second generation), Irish (first and second generation), Italian (first and second generation), Jewish (first- and second-generation Austrian, Russian, and Hungarian), and native (native-born with native parents, plus first- and second-generation English and Scottish). These groups represented 80 percent of the city's population, with the remainder including nonwhites, whites from smaller ethnic groups, and whites of mixed ethnic background. As with the 1900 data, dwellings per family was used as a measure of suburbanization. Dummy variables for class were derived from data on the illiterate proportion of the population ten years and older.[12] Votes for each candidate were calculated as percentages of potential voters, that is, of the total number of males of voting age.

Table 4-2 shows the expected voting behavior by each major ethnic group, with suburbanization and class variables set at mean values. These estimates suggest that Hearst's strength was with Germans, Italians, and Jews, rather than with Irish or native-stock voters.[13] The first three groups were available for mobilization by a third party, since none of them had been fully accepted into either the Irish-dominated Democratic party or the native-dominated GOP. Germans and Jews also had European so-

TABLE 4-2
Voting Behavior by Ethnic Group, 1909

	Bannard (Fusion) %	Gaynor (Dem.) %	Hearst (Mun. Own.) %
German	0	30–50	32–43
Irish	0	50	0
Italian	0	14–50	6–49
Jewish	1–26	9–37	11–23
Native	55	9–39	0

Note: Suburban and class variables set at mean values.
N = 63 (all boroughs).

TABLE 4-3
Voting Behavior by Social Class, 1909

	Bannard (Fusion) %	Gaynor (Dem.) %	Hearst (Mun. Own.) %
Upper	14–15	17	12–17
Middle	12–15	17–18	12–17
Lower	12–15	17–19	8–17

Note: Ethnic and suburban variables set at mean values.
$N = 63$ (all boroughs).

cialist traditions, which Hearst was apparently able to draw upon more effectively than the Socialist candidate. The impact of suburbanization was the same in 1909 as in earlier elections: it did not have a significant effect on the vote for any candidate, and its estimated effect on the vote for the Democratic candidate was greater than its effect on the vote for either of the two reformers, Hearst or Bannard.

The relationship between class and support for Hearst was curvilinear. McClellan later observed that Hearst's "strength was chiefly among what has since become known as the white-collar proletariat, the clerks, small employers, and small shopkeepers."[14] But Hearst also received the support of skilled, unionized workers. In 1905 he was endorsed by many labor leaders, and a *New York Herald* survey found that 72 percent of workingmen, compared to only 11 percent of businessmen, supported him.[15] Given the biases of prescientific polling, these workers were probably drawn from the labor aristocracy rather than from the poorer members of the urban proletariat. In 1909, Hearst received less support from labor leaders, but he remained strongest among the intermediate economic strata. Table 4-3 shows estimates for voting by class, as measured by dummy variables for AD illiteracy levels. Differences among these crude categories are slight, but they do give some support to the hypothesis that Bannard's strongest support came from the upper class, Gaynor's from the lower class, and Hearst's from either the upper class or the intermediate groups, the lower middle class and the skilled workers.

THE BUREAU OF MUNICIPAL RESEARCH

Hearst never became mayor of New York, but his campaigns stimulated the incorporation of expertise into city government and thus had important effects on subsequent politics and policy. The selection of McClellan and Gaynor as Democratic candidates gave the party organization an elegant veneer at the cost of loss of control. McClellan's conflicts with Tammany during his first term led Murphy to seek to replace him in 1905, but the Hearst threat and the influence of the Brooklyn organization forced Murphy to consent to McClellan's renomination. During the campaign, McClellan asserted that he was independent from the machine. He proved his independence after winning reelection, replacing Tammany appointees with his own men. As Theodore J. Lowi's data show, McClellan's appointees (over both terms) more frequently had job-oriented professional or bureaucratic backgrounds than the appointees named by his reform predecessor, Seth Low.[16] McClellan's administration, particularly his second term, can thus be considered the "take-off period" for the bureaucratization of New York City government.

Even more importantly, McClellan's second term saw the establishment of the Bureau of Municipal Research and the development of close ties between the bureau and City Hall. The Bureau of Municipal Research began in 1906 as the Bureau of City Betterment, part of the Citizens' Union.[17] In May 1907, the Bureau of Municipal Research was founded as an independent organization with funding from Andrew Carnegie, John D. Rockefeller, and R. Fulton Cutting. William H. Allen, Henry Bruère, and Frederick Cleveland served as directors. Mayor McClellan cooperated with the new, extragovernmental organization as it scrutinized the activities of city officials. McClellan defended the Bureau of City Betterment's study of the Health Department, which introduced the concept of the budget into municipal finance: the study, he said, was "not so different from what we did on the Ways and Means Committee of the House of Representatives."[18] When the Bureau expanded its budgetary analysis to survey all departments, McClellan convened a budget conference of three representatives from City Hall and three from the Bureau.

The Bureau's most famous activity during the McClellan administration was its participation in the investigation of the borough presidents of Manhattan and the Bronx. Utilizing information gathered by the Bureau, John Purroy Mitchel, who had been appointed special counsel and later commissioner of accounts by McClellan, showed that the two Tammany officials were incompetent. Both were then removed by Governor Hughes. During the investigation of the Bronx borough president, McClellan asked Bruère to complain about holding the hearing in the official's home borough. This allowed the mayor to claim he was forced to move the hearing to Manhattan, where it was more difficult for Bronx Democrats to disrupt the investigation.

As mentioned above, Gaynor was nominated by the Democrats to prevent his nomination by Hearst. Like McClellan, Gaynor asserted his independence from Tammany during his campaign and demonstrated it after his election. Lowi's data show that Gaynor's appointments continued the trend toward selection of individuals with bureaucratic or professional backgrounds.[19] During the 1909 campaign, Tammany politicians denounced the "Bureau of Municipal Besmirch." According to Tammany pamphlets and displays, the Bureau slandered city officials in order to lower bond prices, so that its wealthy contributors could buy the bonds at discount prices. But Gaynor, Tammany's candidate, established his own ties to the Bureau despite his personal dislike for its leaders. The Bureau's development of a general ledger account, begun under McClellan, was completed under Gaynor. On one occasion, Gaynor asked the Bureau to help him save a Park Commissioner who had proved unable to handle his job. The Bureau of Municipal Research was even more closely connected with Mitchel, elected president of the Board of Aldermen in 1909, and with the other members of the Fusion majority on the Board of Estimate. Proposals introduced by the Fusion members were generally drafted and typed by the Bureau. Under Comptroller William A. Prendergast and Manhattan borough president George McAneny, Bruère recalled, the Bureau became "a rather unofficial adjunct of the city government."[20]

The studies and proposals of the Bureau of Municipal Research in cooperation with McClellan, Gaynor, and the Fusion Board of Estimate aimed to achieve both economy and social welfare goals. Generalizing from the New York experience, Henry Bruère stated the five standards of the efficiency movement as "efficiency of service program," "efficiency of organization," "efficiency of method," "efficiency of personnel," and "efficient citizenship."[21] Of the five, efficiency of method, the use of procedures adopted from current business practice, was closest to Melvin G. Holli's image of structural reform.[22] The budgeting, accounting, and purchasing methods introduced by the Bureau all addressed this goal. Efficiency of organization was also compatible with business government and structural reform, though Bruère rejected the structural reform of commission government as an inadequate substitute for administrative research. The Bureau studied the city administration for the state Ivins Commission as a prelude to charter reform and helped the Fusion borough president of Manhattan reorganize his Department of Public Works. For Bruère, efficiency of personnel did not mean just adoption of civil service, but new techniques of investigation and training. To train public officials, the Bureau established its own Training School with funds donated by Mary Harriman. Students were taught by Bureau staff members, using laboratory methods. Robert Moses was a Training School graduate.

The Bureau goals of efficient service and citizenship went beyond business demands for economy or traditional reformers' desire for good government. "It frequently happens," Bruère wrote, "that the most costly inefficiency is not extravagance or waste in executing work performed, but failure to so plan work that it will adequately meet community requirements. If departmental activities are misdirected, it is poor consolation to the taxpayer and to the public to know that taxes are comparatively low, that supplies are purchased at reasonable prices and that employees give full day's service."[23] The efficient service program was illustrated by the work of the Division of Child Hygiene, established on the recommendation of the Bureau. By visiting sick babies, following up on defects reported in school, and creating safe municipal milk depots, the Division reduced child mortality. The Bureau also developed new ways of mapping tuberculosis cases and studied tenement conditions. Each of these activities resulted in increased city expenditures.

Efficient citizenship meant providing the average person with usable information without "making every public spirited inhabitant of a city a fact depository regarding city business," for the working citizen could only devote a limited time to government activity.[24] The budget exhibit of 1908, attended by 50,000 and publicized and copied throughout the country, drew on the methods of advertising and of recent World's Fairs to reach the average citizen and provide a model for the reporting of public affairs by newspapers and civic agencies. One display showed six-cent hat hooks for which the city had paid sixty-five cents. After 1908, the city itself sponsored the annual budget exhibit.

As Irwin Yellowitz has observed, "Hearst's success proved how fallacious it was to regard the working-class vote as stolidly machine-bound."[25] Hearst's appeal was strongest among the upper strata of the working class. Because this group was better educated than unskilled workers, it was more easily mobilized by the policy appeals of Hearst and his press. Because it was economically more secure, the material incentives traditionally offered by the Democratic machine, such as emergency aid and jobs as laborers, were of less value to it. Hearst's appeal was also greatest among ethnic groups denied full recognition by the existing parties.

In 1905 and again in 1909, Tammany sought to counter Hearst's electoral threat by nominating McClellan and Gaynor as mayoral candidates. Unlike the previous Tammany mayor, Robert A. Van Wyck, who was socially respectable but subject to obvious control, McClellan and Gaynor could campaign and govern with relative independence. McClellan and Gaynor each saw his best strategy for reelection and possible higher office, including the presidency, as the cultivation of his own constituency through a reformed and more effective administration. Neither mayor's strategy, it must be noted, was successful. McClellan's political career ended with the death of Brooklyn boss Patrick McCarren, his primary patron, in 1909. And when Gaynor died in 1913, he was running for reelection without party designation.[26]

Nonetheless, McClellan and Gaynor's political strategies had important consequences for the administration of public policy. These strategies, as well as the retention of McClellan and the advancement of Gaynor by the Democratic party, were shaped by the competition of the Hearst movement. By mobilizing a new constituency for reform that threatened to detach foreign-stock workers from the Democratic party, Hearst's candidacy forced the reluctant reorientation of Tammany and the institutionalization of reform under the auspices of the mayors the machine had elected. Even so, Hearst supporters remained available for mobilization against Tammany and coalition with the more traditional reform elite that had supported Seth Low. In 1909, such a coalition was able to elect a majority of the Board of Estimate. Led by John Purroy Mitchel, the president of the Board of Aldermen, the Fusion Board of Estimate relied heavily upon the Bureau of Municipal Research to develop policy proposals. Four years later, the pattern of alliance in support of a program developed by the Bureau was repeated with the election of Mitchel as mayor.

CHAPTER 5.

John Purroy Mitchel and the
Politics of Municipal Research

JOHN PURROY MITCHEL was elected president of the Board of Aldermen in 1909 as one of the Fusion candidates nominated by both the Republicans and William Randolph Hearst's Civil Alliance. In 1913, again with Hearst's endorsement, the thirty-four-year-old Mitchel, an Irish Catholic and an independent Democrat, was elected mayor on the Republican-Fusion ticket. Mitchel received support from the immigrant-stock voters of intermediate social class who had backed Hearst in 1909 *and* from the native-stock, upper-class voters who had backed Otto Bannard in 1909 and had earlier backed Seth Low. The pattern of support for Mitchel in 1913 thus provides an example of a progressive coalition cutting across the class and ethnic boundaries that normally shaped New York politics. However, Mitchel could not sustain this coalition. Mitchel's administration continued the trend toward expertise in government, but the policies developed by the new professionals were consistently implemented in ways that served the most narrowly conceived, immediate interests of business. Carried out in this fashion, these policies helped to detach the Hearst bloc from the Mitchel coalition, contributing to Mitchel's defeat in 1917.

THE ELECTION OF 1913

Hearst support helped Mitchel to win the 1913 Fusion nomination over New York County District Attorney Charles Whitman and Manhattan Borough President George McAneny.[1] Mitchel gained the support of Hearst and his followers by opposing the terms of the Brooklyn Rapid Transit and Interborough Rapid Transit contracts concluded under Mayor William Jay Gaynor, and by advocating eventual public ownership of the subways. Mitchel also shared Hearst's views on the need for public milk stations. These positions aroused the fears of upper-class reformers and newspapers that Mitchel had radical tendencies, but his record as an opponent of corruption and inefficiency who had participated in the removal of the Manhattan and Bronx borough presidents attracted the traditional Fusion elements. During the campaign, the arrest of Police Lieutenant

Charles Becker, the head of the vice squad, for the murder of Herman Rosenthal, allegedly his partner in an illegal gambling house, and the impeachment of Governor William Sulzer for disobedience to Tammany leader Charles Francis Murphy were invoked against the Democratic candidate, Edward McCall.[2] Gaynor, dumped by Tammany for his independence, declared that he would seek reelection on his own ticket. The strong possibility that Gaynor would split the reform vote with Mitchel ended in September, when the mayor died during a vacation at sea.[3]

Mitchel's campaign platform was developed by the Bureau. Mitchel, Henry Bruère recalled,

> asked me to prepare a general program based upon the work that had been done by the Fusion Administration and the contacts of the Bureau of Municipal Research. We were to include our own individual views, his own views, a combination of the points of view regarding what might be brought about by way of improving the character and scope of the services of the city government, the use of public funds, and the questions of how many should be raised. In short, if we had full control of the city government, we were to state what we would do with it. That was done.[4]

As Augustus Cerillo, Jr., has suggested, Mitchel's campaign employed the old reform slogans, but interpreted them in the Bureau's terms. Thus, Fusion rhetoric could appeal both to voters who wanted honest (and cheaper) government and to those who wanted to make government more effective.[5]

Much of Mitchel's speech accepting the mayoral nomination, for example, was devoted to the case of the workman on the Equitable Building being constructed across from where Mitchel was speaking. This man, Mitchel said, made a contract with the mayor. Each year, he paid twenty-five to thirty dollars in taxes, collected in the form of higher rent. In return, he expected to receive good schools, parks and playgrounds, pure food and water, public health, freedom from vice, honest weight at the market, clean streets, and a well-run hospital. Mitchel said he himself could be trusted to keep this contract, but Tammany could not.[6] This argument attacked Tammany corruption while appealing to ethnic, working-class voters. The nativist overtones of earlier reform rhetoric had been replaced by the notion of efficiency, as it was introduced into reform politics by the Bureau of Municipal Research.

Tammany's response to the new reform rhetoric was to accuse Mitchel and the other Fusion officials of burdening the taxpayer by spending money on experts from Cleveland, Chicago, and other cities. "There is not one taxpayer of our city," the Democrats said, "who can countenance for one moment Mr. Mitchel's 'efficiency' plans, because the record in each case is that the city pays heavy bills for experts and gets nothing in

TABLE 5-1
Transition Rates, 1909–1913

| | 1913 | | |
1909	Mitchel (Fusion) %	McCall (Dem.) %	Russell (Soc.) %
Bannard (Fusion)	100	0	0
Gaynor (Dem.)	0	88–93	0
Hearst (Civ. All.)	100	37–50	10–12
Cassidy (Soc.)	26–50	0	100

$N = 63$ (all boroughs).

return." Tammany claimed a record of economy and asked the voters to "compare these achievements by public-spirited Democratic business administrations having the welfare and good name of New York at heart, with the grotesque waste of the public funds by the faddists and theorists on the Fusion ticket, who for four years have been bleeding property owners by boosting assessments to the confiscation point with an audacity that would stagger the most daring suburban real estate boomers." The Democrats also depicted Mitchel as a stooge of Hearst.[7] The Socialist candidate, Charles Edward Russell, said that both Mitchel and McCall were controlled by the "Invisible Government" of big business. The only difference between the Democratic and Fusion slates was between "the side of the house that is called Ryan and Belmont," and "the side of the house that is called Kuhn, Loeb and Co."[8]

Mitchel received 358,161 votes, McCall 233,919, and Russell 32,057. Mitchel won his majority by combining the Hearst and Fusion blocs of 1909. Table 5-1 shows estimates of transition rates from 1909 to 1913.[9] The estimates for the 1909 Bannard and Hearst votes, while numerically impossible, strongly suggest that Mitchel was able to combine the bulk of the Bannard vote with at least a major portion of the Hearst supporters, while McCall was able to hold on to the normal Democratic vote.

Estimates of the vote by major ethnic groups, presented in Table 5-2, similarly suggest the transfer of support from Hearst to Mitchel. Mitchel did much better than Bannard had done (Table 4-2) among Jews and Germans. Voters in both groups had given substantial support to Hearst. Comparison of the estimates in Tables 4-2 and 5-2 also suggests that Mitchel may have done less well among native-stock voters than Bannard. Perhaps some of them were unwilling to vote for an Irish Catholic, even on a Fusion ticket. Though Mitchel was the grandson and namesake of a well-known Irish patriot, his estimated support among Irish voters is zero. As in earlier New York elections, the estimates do not support the

TABLE 5-2
Voting Behavior by Ethnic Group, 1913

	Mitchel (Fusion) %	McCall (Dem.) %	Russell (Soc.) %
German	35–50	29–50	9–12
Irish	0	41–50	0
Italian	6–50	14–50	0
Jewish	14–50	7–35	3–5
Native	50–82	1–36	5

Note: Suburban and class variables set at mean values.
N = 63 (all boroughs).

suburbanization hypothesis: the effect of suburbanization on the vote for the machine candidate, McCall, is greater than its effect on the vote for Mitchel.

MITCHEL AS MAYOR

Mitchel's appointments continued the trend toward reliance on individuals with professional or bureaucratic backgrounds.[10] And, as he had done in his earlier positions, Mitchel relied heavily on the Bureau of Municipal Research for policy proposals. According to Bruère, Mitchel, "more or less, adopted" the campaign platform drafted by the Bureau "as the policy basis for his administration. A man proposes and others disposed, but to a large extent we set forth after his election to carry it out."[11] Bruère was made City Chamberlain, a position that had been without significant responsibilities, but one he used to maintain contact with all departments and develop a comprehensive plan for administrative reorganization.[12] Mitchel also established ties to the Public Education Association, another professional and research body outside city government.[13]

Under Mitchel, the Bureau of Municipal Research, the Public Education Association, and other extragovernmental, expert organizations helped to develop policies for increased employment during the 1914–15 depression; for comprehensive educational reform; for the improvement of charitable organizations, prisons, and public health; for zoning; and for removal of dangerous railroad tracks. Yet these policies were consistently implemented so as to achieve short-term economies rather than long-range social reorganization. Conflict between business and experts led to the resignation of one of the Bureau's founders, William H. Allen, who established a rival organization, and to the reorientation of the Bureau away from the problems of New York City. Ironically, capitalists were the long-term losers. Not only did each policy fail in itself, but all contributed to Mitchel's defeat. The political activities of big businessmen thus helped to bring about the return of Tammany and the expansion of the Socialist movement.

In response to the economic crisis of 1914–15, which left 18 percent of New York's wage earners out of work, Mitchel established the Mayor's Committee on Unemployment and Relief. The selection of the committee chair symbolized the subordination of socially oriented reformers to businessmen interested in cheap city government: Mitchel picked Judge Elbert Gary of United States Steel. The idea of the committee had been developed by Henry Bruère, whose proposals included immediate emergency public works and an emergency loan fund. Comptroller William A. Prendergast, however, refused to release money for public works, and employers were reluctant to contribute to the emergency fund. The Gary Committee then established workshops. These reduced their wages twice in two months and finished with a surplus. Conflict over the committee's published conclusions also ended with the victory of cost-conscious business executives over socially conscious reformers. Bruère and other reformers wanted the report to advocate a national system of employment bureaus and compulsory unemployment insurance. Business objections softened the stand to a proposal for "careful consideration" of this plan, and the Mitchel administration did not give the question any further attention. [14]

The implementation of the Gary school plan provides another example of a comprehensive reform pared down by the Mitchel administration to a means of reducing expenditures. [15] The plan, developed by William Wirt, a disciple of John Dewey, in Gary, Indiana, provided for one part of the students to receive conventional classroom instruction while the other part received more practical training in workshops, playgrounds, and other special facilities. At midday, the two "platoons" would switch. In theory, the plan not only solved the problem of overcrowding, but offered an expanded concept of education appropriate to an industrial society and a model of a democratic, self-sustaining community in which students' work met the needs of the school. For these reasons, the Gary experiment won the approval of Dewey, Randolph Bourne, and a delegation from New York's Public Education Association.

Under Mitchel, however, the Gary Plan was introduced as a way of intensifying the use of existing school buildings and improving teacher productivity. Tristam Walker Metcalfe, the education columnist of the *New York Globe*, wrote that the plan was becoming "more and more, as each day passes, a device for reducing school costs and less and less a plan for enriching the educational opportunities for the children." [16] Morris Hillquit, the Socialist candidate for mayor in 1917, took a similar view, praising the plan itself but not the way it had been made into "a pure scheme for effecting economies in the education of the children by saving the cost of building schools and keeping down the salary list of teachers."[17] Twelve Bronx schools were converted and the aim of converting the entire school system was announced before the experience of the first two experimental schools could be evaluated, necessary facilities added, or teachers retrained. As a result, the plan aroused the opposition of teachers, whose workday was extended an hour; of parents, who feared their children were being tracked into narrowly industrial schooling; and of students, whose strikes against the plan turned into riots. The Gary Plan was particularly unpopular among Jews. Tammany made extensive use of the issue in the 1917 campaign, pointing to Mitchel's appointment of two educators from the Rockefeller Foundation and the Rockefeller-funded General Education Association to the Board of Education. Ignoring the fact that one of these appointees took a more comprehensive and critical view of the plan than either Mitchel or Prendergast, Democratic politicians used the Rockefeller connection as evidence that the Gary Plan was designed as a tool of the rich.

The charities investigation also represented reform turned askew. This investigation into the conditions of children at private institutions receiving city aid was carried out under a commissioner and deputy commissioner with professional backgrounds. Bruère later expressed his regret that it proved impossible to consider the question objectively; the city, he said, could have provided payments and technical advice to institutions that fell short of standards. Instead, the investigation was widely viewed as an attack on Catholic institutions. The wiretapping of a Brooklyn priest actively opposed to the inquiry, and Mitchel's court testimony alleging a Catholic conspiracy, did not make him more popular with his own religious group.[18]

With the recommendation of John D. Rockefeller, Jr., who had sponsored her work with the Bureau of Social Hygiene, Katharine Bement Davis, superintendent of the Bedford Hills Reformatory for Women, became Mitchel's corrections commissioner. She was the first woman in city history to receive a cabinet-level appointment. Davis drew on her own research and that of other "social hygiene" experts in introducing innovative measures such as outdoor work for prisoners and the abolition of striped clothing. Budgetary concerns, however, blocked her plans for a new women's prison and a drug treatment center.[19]

Mitchel's first appointee as health commissioner was Dr. Sigismund S. Goldwater, the superintendent of Mount Sinai Hospital. When Goldwater returned to Mount Sinai in March 1915, he was replaced by his deputy, Dr. Haven Emerson. Goldwater and Emerson's accomplishments included reorganization of their department, creation of health education districts on the Lower East Side and in Queens, and the rewriting of the Sanitary Code. For the most part, these activities were carried out by transferring funds and personnel from other activities, and thus required little additional expense from the economy-conscious Mitchel administration. In 1915, budget cuts forced the department to close its nose-and-throat clinics for schools. The Health Department's budget request for that year complained about "the lack of a sufficiently liberal social program generously supported by the Board of Estimate" and said that "public health is purchasable; within natural limitations a city can determine its own death rate. Health insurance is as reliable and profitable an investment for the municipality as it is for the individual."[20]

In 1916, New York adopted the nation's first comprehensive zoning law. Groundwork for regulating the height, area, and use of buildings was done by the First Zoning Commission, appointed during the Gaynor administration and led by George McAneny, the Fusion borough president of Manhattan. After the state legislature approved the necessary amendments to the City Charter, Mayor Mitchel appointed the Second Zoning Commission, which drafted the ordinance. McAneny, by then president of the Board of Aldermen, was again a key figure; Mitchel endorsed the Commission's report. The immediate impetus for the innovation of zoning was the desire of Fifth Avenue merchants to protect themselves from loft-based garment manufacturing; the merchants feared the presence of the garment workers would drive customers from their stores. Broader business support came from real estate interests that sought to buttress falling rates by restricting new development. Both these groups were more satisfied with the zoning ordinance and the pluralistic bargaining that characterized its implementation than the architects and engineers of the Board of Estimate's City Planning Committee. These experts had hoped to make zoning the basis for systematic land-use planning, but fears about economic and legal consequences prevented this from happening during the Mitchel years.[21]

Mitchel aroused additional popular resentment with the West Side Plan, which provided for the city and the New York Central Railroad to remove the dangerous tracks along the Hudson River. Opponents charged that the railroad would come out ahead in the proposed land swap and perpetual franchise grant. The Hearst press, reflecting its publisher's continued interest in transportation issues, was especially vocal in its criticism. Overriding Mitchel's mayoral veto, the state legislature and the Republican governor approved a bill limiting franchises to fifty years and requiring that the State Public Service Commission participate in any plan.[22]

Throughout Mitchel's administration, then, potentially broad-ranging progressive reforms were implemented in narrowly cost-conscious ways.

This pattern has been attributed to Mitchel's personal conservatism or to his lack of political sensitivity.[23] But it also reflects the relative resources of business and the new professionals within the policy elite. Mitchel depended on big business to finance his two mayoral campaigns and the city government itself. During the 1917 campaign, contributions from big business, including Rockefeller, Morgan, and Carnegie interests, allowed Mitchel to spend an unprecedented eight dollars and seventy cents per vote received. Morgan helped the city out of the fiscal crisis of 1914–15, brought on by the national depression, by organizing a syndicate of banks to market $80 million in bonds in order to meet the city's obligations. The terms of this loan symbolized the impact of business influence on the Mitchel administration: the banks imposed a "pay-as-you-go" policy by which improvements that were not self-sustaining had to be financed from current revenues rather than bond issues. The pay-as-you-go policy limited costs, but it also limited action to meet pressing needs such as construction or expansion of schools.[24]

Against the financial resources of business, experts could offer only ideas. Even use of this resource could be blocked, for their institutional bases depended on business funding. In 1914, responding to criticism of the Mitchel administration by the Bureau of Municipal Research, the Rockefeller Foundation offered to provide ten thousand dollars a year to the Bureau if it would separate itself from its training school and end its out-of-town surveys, its published bulletins, and its role in educational policy. The offer, which effectively stripped the Bureau of its watchdog role, was accepted by the Bureau board. William H. Allen, who opposed the deal, resigned from the Bureau. He later set up the Institute of Public Service, which spent much of its time criticizing Rockefeller activities.[25]

Thus the Bureau, which had established ties to City Hall during a period of ostensible Tammany rule, was forced to play a more restricted role during a reform administration for which it had provided much of the program. In opposition, businessmen and experts could agree on the need for research, since it promised both lower taxes and more effective government. In power, however, the two groups came into conflict, for the implementation of reform proposals as the reformers themselves had envisioned them threatened to make government cost more, not less. In New York, the connections between business, government, and experts gave businessmen the power to ensure that their interpretation of reform won out. The social planning of the Bureau and other outposts of the new professionals may have represented the long-term interests of capital, but these interests could not be enforced against the constraints imposed by capitalists. The same conflict was illustrated during the depression of 1914–15: as Judge Gary's committee was seeking to reduce unemployment, his corporation, U.S. Steel, laid off 50,000 workers.[26]

The dominance of the economic elite was further demonstrated when Mitchel adopted its favorite cause, military preparedness. In 1915 and 1916, the mayor participated in highly publicized upper-class military camps held in Plattsburg. After the United States entered the First World War, Mitchel questioned the patriotism of many of his political opponents, including State Senator Robert Wagner. This intolerance and Mitchel's pro-war stance alienated many German, Irish, and Jewish voters.[27]

THE ELECTION OF 1917

The Gary Plan, the unemployment committee, the charities investigation, the West Side Plan, and Mitchel's aggressive militarism all became issues in the 1917 campaign.[28] The Democrats nominated John F. Hylan, a little-known Brooklyn judge. Hearst had broken with Mitchel early in his administration, apparently over appointments. Initially mentioned as a candidate himself, he gave Hylan his full support. The Socialist candidate was Morris Hillquit, who ran on his party's antiwar platform and his own record as a labor lawyer. The recent enactment of the direct primary by the state legislature made it possible for Mitchel to be denied renomination as a Republican. Mitchel was originally declared the winner, but a recount gave the victory to his opponent, William S. Bennett. Bennett, who received no organizational support, attacked Mitchel for his alleged extravagance and Democratic affiliation. Though Bennett was from Manhattan, he seems to have appealed most strongly to Republicans in Brooklyn and Queens: he was endorsed by the *Brooklyn Standard Union* and won primary majorities in those two boroughs. His nomination shows the effects of the direct primary. In 1913, Republicans had preferred Charles Whitman, a member of their own party, to Mitchel, but went along with Mitchel's nomination to preserve Fusion unity. By requiring that an independent Democrat like Mitchel win a majority among Republicans, as well as among representatives of the broader Fusion movement, the primary made such cross-party nominations more difficult.

Even with all the votes that Bennett received in the general election, Mitchel would have been defeated. Hylan received 298,149 votes, Mitchel 149,260, Hillquit 141,739, and Bennett 53,163. A 1917 reapportionment makes it impossible to directly compare voting data from the 1913 and 1917 elections. To allow such comparisons, the 1917 data for all boroughs were recalculated onto the 1913 Assembly District (AD) boundaries.[29] The transition rates estimated using this data are presented in Table 5-3. The relatively low estimate for the transition rate from Mitchel$_{1913}$ to Mitchel$_{1917}$, and the correspondingly high estimates for transitions from Mitchel$_{1913}$ to Bennett$_{1917}$, Hylan$_{1917}$, and Hillquit$_{1917}$, suggest

TABLE 5-3
Transition Rates, 1913–1917

1913	1917			
	Mitchel (Fusion) %	Bennett (Rep.) %	Hylan (Dem.) %	Hillquit (Soc.) %
Mitchel (Fusion)	42	15	27–42	9–20
McCall (Dem.)	0	4–11	100	0
Russell (Soc.)	0	0	100	100
Abstain[a]	50–62	1–50	0	4–50

Note: 1917 data recalculated onto 1913 ADs.
[a]Includes abstaining and voting for minor candidates.
N = 63 (all boroughs).

the breakup of the progressive coalition that had elected Mitchel. Estimates for the behavior of 1913 McCall and Russell voters, which should be interpreted cautiously because they sum to more than 100 percent, suggest that the Democrats and Socialists were able to hold onto their respective electoral bases while gaining former Mitchel voters responding to the war and other issues.

Mitchel's losses came among the more radical parts of his 1913 coalition, the voters he had absorbed from the Hearst movement. Table 5-4 shows estimated transition rates from the 1909 election to the election of 1917. In the latter election, Mitchel held on to the bulk of the traditional reform vote that had gone for Otto Bannard in 1909, while doing less well among the 1909 Hearst voters than either Hylan or Hillquit. This pattern contrasts with the 1909 to 1913 transition rates shown in Table 5-1 above, which suggest that in his first election, Mitchel captured far more of the 1909 Hearst vote than his Democratic or Socialist opponents.

TABLE 5-4
Transition Rates, 1909–1917

1909	1917			
	Mitchel (Fusion) %	Bennett (Rep.) %	Hylan (Dem.) %	Hillquit (Soc.) %
Bannard (Fusion)	84	15–19	10–50	0
Gaynor (Dem.)	0	11	50–89	0
Hearst (Civ. All.)	48–59	13–17	100	91
Cassidy (Soc.)	0	14–50	0	100

Note: 1917 data recalculated onto 1913 ADs.
N = 63 (all boroughs).

TABLE 5-5
Voting Behavior by Ethnic Group, 1917

	Mitchel (Fusion) %	Bennett (Rep.) %	Hylan (Dem.) %	Hillquit (Soc.) %
German	0	5–15	50–64	39–42
Irish	0	0	16–50	0
Italian	2–47	0	12–50	2–44
Jewish	1–22	1–8	10–44	19–21
Native	46	8–11	12–46	0–22

Notes: 1917 data recalculated onto 1913 ADs. Suburban and class variables set at mean values.

$N = 63$ (all boroughs).

Analysis of ethnic support also suggests that Mitchel's losses came from the defection of Hearst supporters. Table 5-5 shows estimated support by ethnic groups. The recalculated 1917 electoral data was used to allow use of 1910 census data and comparison with Table 5-2, which showed voting behavior by ethnic group in 1913. This comparison suggests that support for Mitchel dropped most among Germans and Jews; Hearst had done well among both groups. To a greater extent than in 1913, Mitchel's 1917 vote came from native-stock voters. Hillquit won support not only among Jews, with whom the Socialists were often identified by opponents, but among Germans, Italians, and even native-stock voters.[30] Holding all other variables equal, coefficients for the suburbanization variable suggest that in 1917, Mitchel received less support from suburban voters than any of his three opponents.

The influx of new professionals into City Hall and the development of ties to the Bureau of Municipal Research, an extragovernmental research organization, stemmed from the responses of Democratic politicians to the electoral competition of Hearst's municipal populism. In 1913, Bureau proposals provided the basis for Mitchel's election by a multi-ethnic, multi-class coalition between the previously distinct reform constituencies of Low and Hearst. But the ultimate dependence of both Mitchel and the Bureau on big business made it impossible for these proposals to be enacted in ways that might maintain the coalition. By 1917, Mitchel had lost the support of that part of his coalition earlier mobilized by Hearst. Mitchel's election shows that experts could be incorporated into political life in ways that reshaped electoral cleavages. But the policy proposals that allowed them to do so went beyond business demands for economy. Because both the experts and the politicians with whom they were allied depended on business for support, the experts' policy agenda could not be implemented or even maintained during an administration they had helped elect.

THE NEW MACHINE

The defining characteristic of politics in twentieth-century New York City has been its bureaucratization. Generalizing from New York, Theodore Lowi described the "modern city" as "well run but ungoverned because it now comprises islands of functional power before which the modern mayor stands impoverished. No mayor of a modern city has predictable means of determining whether the bosses of the New Machines—the bureau chiefs and the career commissioners—will be loyal to anything but their agency, its work, and related professional norms."[31] There was no evidence of this displacement of the "Old" party machines by municipal bureaucracy under Mayor Hylan or his successor, James J. Walker, who was even closer to Tammany.[32] Yet the bureaucratization of New York politics that occurred under Fiorello La Guardia can be traced back to the earlier period of reform success that ended with Hylan's defeat of Mitchel in 1917. With Hylan and then Walker as mayor, Tammany returned to full citywide power. But because the progressive coalition had collapsed, Tammany regained power by default. When Tammany was weakened by scandal, La Guardia was able to put the old progressive coalition back together, and then to draw upon the experts of the Progressive Era and their proposals to do what neither Low nor Mitchel had been able to do: win reelection.

"We have had all the reform that we want in this city for some time to come," Mayor Hylan wrote the Civil Service Reform Association at the beginning of his administration.[33] Hylan's Board of Estimate abolished the City Planning Committee and fired its staff.[34] The mayor also announced that he would not allow experts to study his administration and officially barred the staff of the Bureau of Municipal Research from city offices. The Bureau responded by withdrawing further from participation in New York City government. Three years later, in 1921, the Bureau and the Training School were merged into the new National Institute of Public Administration. The Institute played a key role in the development of "public administration" as a general set of rules, divorced from political conflict. As Jane Dahlberg notes, "Research became individual, conducted by students as outside observers rather than as participants." Welfare and economy concerns were still combined, but the Institute no longer paid specific attention to New York affairs.[35]

Despite Tammany's ascendancy and the Bureau's retreat, the factors that had encouraged traditional reform and municipal populist opposition to Tammany—its corruption, its exploitation of the working class, and its subordination of non-Irish ethnic groups—had not changed. Tammany thus remained vulnerable to reform efforts. In 1933, following the Seabury corruption investigations and Walker's resignation, La Guardia was elected mayor as an anti-Tammany Fusion candidate. Mitchel, William Leuchtenburg wrote, was "humorless and self-righteous . . . a colorless leader who resembled not at all that latter-day fusionist, Fiorello La Guardia."[36] Despite their contrasting personalities, there were important political similarities between the two. Each came to office combining business and working-class support. Neither quite fit into his ethnic group: Mitchel was an Irish Catholic who developed close ties to the native-stock social elite, La Guardia an Italian Protestant. And each made policy under severe constraints imposed by banks in return for bailing the city out of fiscal crisis.

Unlike Mitchel, however, La Guardia was able to stay in office for twelve years, winning reelection in 1937 and 1941. A key difference was that under La Guardia, professionals oriented to social reform were better able to dictate the course of policy because they enjoyed access to federal funds. As Martin Shefter has shown, the New Deal in Washington made possible the "Little New Deal" in New York. The comprehensive, if wrong-headed, restructuring of New York's transportation system by Robert Moses, a graduate of the Bureau of Municipal Research Training School, contrasts with Mitchel's need to bribe the New York Central to improve the dangerous conditions on the Upper West Side. The La Guardia administration's provision of public relief during the Great Depression was very different from the policy of low-paying workshops initiated by the Gary Committee. Planning was institutionalized under the City Planning Commission, established by the 1938 City Charter. In each case, experts under the Mitchel administration had offered proposals as wide-ranging as those adopted under La Guardia. The expert most successful at bringing federal funds into New York was Moses; during 1936, for example, his skills brought one-seventh of all Works Progress Administration funds into the city. Throughout his career, Moses worked with men and women he met while investigating city government as a student of the Bureau Training School. If Moses's ideas and contacts were shaped by his training with the Bureau of Municipal Research, his extreme pragmatism grew out of his disillusionment with the failure of the Bureau during the Mitchel administration.[37]

New York's "Little New Deal," in turn, shaped the city's response to the War on Poverty and the fiscal crisis of the 1970s. La Guardia's administrations gave New York politics its modern bureaucratic form, and bureaucratization shaped the implementation of the War on Poverty in New York: community action groups gained control of their own agencies, but the civil servants threatened by this autonomy were bought off with salary and benefit increases. John Lindsay, with the help of the RAND Corporation, the Ford Foundation, and university experts, was able to construct a new version of the progressive coalition, linking white elites with the black and Puerto Rican poor to win reelection in 1969.[38] The city's inability to meet the claims of both municipal workers and the poor, however, led to the fiscal crisis of the 1970s. Unionized employees were better able than unorganized minority groups to curb their losses during the retrenchment that followed.[39] David Dinkins, New York's first black mayor, revived Lindsay's elite-minority coalition in 1989, but his subsequent efforts to consolidate an electoral majority were hampered by a lack of resources: hostile Republican administrations gave him little federal support, while an enduring recession exacerbated the effects of a long-term process of deindustrialization upon the municipal economy.[40]

New York politics after the Progressive Era suggests that what the experts of the Bureau of Municipal Research lacked was not vision or political skill, but the outside resources needed to win implementation of their ideas in their original form and spirit. During the New Deal and the Great Society, when the federal government supplied later generations of experts with more adequate resources, patterns of politics and policy in New York were reshaped. During the Progressive Era, the ideas of Allen and Bruère might have served capitalism better than the capitalists' own demands for retrenchment. The plans of these experts might have also made it possible for Mitchel, like La Guardia or Lindsay, to keep a multiethnic, multi-class coalition intact. Judging from the results of the 1917 election, it is hard to see how they could have made things worse.

Part III

CLEVELAND: FROM MUNICIPAL POPULISM
TO PROGRESSIVISM

As time went on our organization gathered to itself a group of
young fellows of a type rarely found in politics—college men with
no personal ambitions to serve, students of social problems
known to the whole community as disinterested, high-minded,
clean-living individuals. Over and over again the short-sighted
majority which cannot recognize a great moral movement when it
appears as a political movement, and which knows nothing of the
contagion of a great idea attributed the interest and activity of
these young fellows to some baneful influence on my part.
"Johnson has them hypnotized," was the usual explanation
of their devotion to our common cause.

Tom L. Johnson, My Story

AS IN NEW YORK, organizational party politics in Cleveland was opposed
by distinct traditional reform and municipal populist constituencies that
briefly came together to form a progressive coalition. Cleveland reformers, however, enjoyed more sustained electoral success than their
counterparts in New York. Tom Johnson, supported by a municipal populist coalition, was elected mayor in 1901 and reelected in 1903, 1905, and
1907. Newton Baker, who broadened Johnson's support by appealing to
traditional reform voters as well, was elected mayor in 1911 and reelected
in 1913. In New York, the immediate effects of the dissolution of the
progressive coalition were to strengthen Tammany Hall and the Socialist
party, but in Cleveland Peter Witt's defeat in 1915 was followed by structural instability and the revival of municipal populism as an independent
political force.

The outcome of reform in Cleveland was different from that in New
York because Johnson and Baker incorporated experts into city politics in
different ways than did New York's reform mayors, Seth Low and John
Purroy Mitchel. In New York, as explained in Part II, experts were part of
the Bureau of Municipal Research, an organization that was independent
of city government and relatively autonomous from business. Cleveland

experts entered city politics as part of a traditional reform group, the Municipal Association. They were then incorporated directly into city government as heads of departments within Johnson's municipal populist administration. During the Baker administration, city government developed ties to autonomous organizations like those between the Mitchel administration and the Bureau of Municipal Research. But under both reform administrations, Cleveland's experts were more successful at translating their preferences into policies than their counterparts in New York. The role of experts in politics, in turn, reflected the pattern of party organization confronting experts and politicians in each city at the beginning of the twentieth century. No party organization held a dominant position in Cleveland comparable to that of Tammany Hall in New York. Instead, factions that were loose amalgamations of ward leaders competed for local, state, and national positions within the two parties. Individuals with professional training and orientations responded to the maneuvers of these factional leaders.

Patterns of party organization, then, combined with leaders' policy commitments to shape the incorporation of expertise into Cleveland city politics, and the incorporation of expertise determined the outcomes of Cleveland reform. The next three chapters trace these relationships; Table III-1 summarizes the elections discussed. Chapter 6 begins with the

TABLE III-1
Cleveland Mayoral Elections, 1899–1915

Year	Traditional Reform	Municipal Populist	Progressive Coalition	Organization Candidates	Socialist Party
1899				McKisson Farley	Kirchner
1901		Johnson		Akers	Ballar
1903	Goulder	Johnson			Homas
1905		Johnson		Boyd	Clifford
1907	Burton	Johnson			Cheyney
1909		Johnson		Baehr	Wilert
1911			Baker	Hogen	Ruthenberg
1913			Baker	Davis	Robb
1915		Witt		Davis Norton Salen	Ruthenberg

Note: Winning candidate in bold.

distinctive economic and ethnic characteristics of early twentieth-century Cleveland. Economic and ethnic factors indirectly influenced the reform outcomes of the Progressive Era by shaping the context of organizational party politics. But these societal variables did not directly determine reform outcomes. To understand the course of reform, it is necessary instead to examine a political dynamic beginning with the conflict between the Republican factions of Mark Hanna and Robert McKisson, and the formation of the Municipal Association as a traditional reform body opposed to McKisson's effort to use the mayoralty to construct a citywide machine.

By attracting experts away from the Municipal Association and into his administration, Tom Johnson reshaped Cleveland politics. Chapter 7 discusses patterns of electoral support and public policy under Johnson's administration, which lasted from his election in 1901 to his defeat in 1909. In 1911, Newton Baker, a former member of the Johnson administration, was able to regain power for Cleveland reformers by assembling a progressive coalition that remained intact until 1915. Chapter 8 compares Baker's electoral coalition with Johnson's and evaluates the significance for public policy of the way each mayor drew upon the skills of municipal experts. It then explores the dissolution of the Baker coalition in 1915 and shows how the outcome of reform during the Progressive Era has continued to structure political conflict in Cleveland.

CHAPTER 6

McKissonism and the "Muny"

INDUSTRIALIZATION and immigration did not produce a dominant political organization in Cleveland politics. Several political entrepreneurs tried to construct party machines, but their creations did not endure. The most successful of the would-be machine builders, Robert McKisson, was able to elect himself mayor in 1895 and 1897. By 1899, however, McKisson was not even able to dominate his own Republican party. In the long run, the significance of McKissonism was the unintended invigoration of reform rather than the desired consolidation of organizational control.

Like other large northeastern cities, Cleveland became industrialized during the late nineteenth century. Compared with New York, its economy was more dependent on manufacturing, including the production of iron and steel, chemicals, boxes, bicycles, rubber goods, electrical supplies, and automobiles. Oil refining was also important until 1896, when John D. Rockefeller closed his local refinery. Linked to other cities and raw materials by Lake Erie and the railroads, Cleveland remained a commercial and financial center during the period of industrialization. Mercantile and industrial capitalists were united in the Cleveland Chamber of Commerce, created by the expansion of the mercantile Board of Trade in 1893. The Chamber was the first such organization in the nation to encompass all economic sectors and participate widely in municipal affairs. This unusual degree of cohesion between mercantile and industrial capital was, perhaps, a response to the city's history of violent labor conflict: lockouts, importation of strikebreakers from other states, and use of the militia were common employer practices.[1]

Cleveland's population was almost as heavily foreign-stock as that of New York. In 1910, only 27.7 percent of the population was native-stock, defined as native-born with native parents, English, or Scottish.[2] A New England tradition of political morality, dating from the settlement of northern Ohio as Connecticut's Western Reserve, survived among these voters.[3] Germans (17.9 percent) were the largest foreign-stock group. Slavs (including Poles, Czechs, Slovaks, Slovenes, Croats, and Serbs) were proportionally more significant than in New York. There were also sizable Irish, Jewish, Italian, and black communities, but each of these groups represented a smaller percentage of Cleveland than of New York.[4]

The dynamics of class and ethnic politics in nineteenth-century New

York led to the reorganization of Tammany Hall as an Irish working-class machine. No such machine emerged in Cleveland during the nineteenth century. A politics of material incentives did flourish among the Irish, as well as among Italians, Jews, blacks, and other minorities.[5] But none of the ethnic leaders was able to expand his power beyond his ward or group to create a citywide machine. In the absence of an Irish-dominated machine, the Cleveland Democratic party was not distinctively Irish, nor were the Cleveland Irish distinctively Democratic.[6]

Class conflict, elite cohesion, and the absence of an Irish machine all shaped the outcome of reform efforts. But none of these factors can directly explain what happened in Cleveland during the Progressive Era. Despite the city's history of violent antagonism between capital and labor, Newton Baker was able to construct a progressive coalition that cut across class lines. Cleveland businessmen were more unified than their counterparts in New York, but businessmen in New York were better able to control the course of reform. Finally, the absence of an Irish machine and the survival of a New England political tradition among native-stock voters notwithstanding, traditional reform candidates such as Harvey Goulder and Theodore Burton were unable to win mayoral elections.

To understand reform outcomes in Cleveland, then, it is necessary to look at governmental structures and patterns of party organization. The municipal charter of 1852, which remained in effect until 1891, gave the mayor of Cleveland little power. Most administrative authority rested with a jumble of elected or appointed boards.[7] Under this system, ward organizations and party factions existed among both Republicans and Democrats, but no dominant machine was created in either party. Among the Republican ward leaders were "Czar" Harry Bernstein, who was able to control the vote of the Russian Jewish Fifteenth Ward, and William Welfeld, whose base was the Polish Twelfth Ward. Democratic ward leaders included Charles P. Salen, an important ally of Tom Johnson in his early mayoral campaigns.[8]

John Farley, a Democrat, and Mark Hanna, a Republican, were each able to bind some of these ward organizations into factions, but neither was able to create a party machine. Farley, a professional politician and contractor, served as mayor from 1883 to 1885 and again from 1899 to 1901. He also served as director of public works under Robert Blee, mayor from 1893 to 1895. Though both positions gave him significant patronage resources, Farley lacked the ethnic base for a true political machine: as a Protestant of Northern Irish descent and strong Orange sympathies, he was repellent to Irish Catholics.[9] Though Hanna was, during the same period, able to mastermind the rise of William McKinley to the governorship and then to the presidency, his "control of Cleveland was never so absolute as legend asserts."[10]Hanna held the allegiance of some Republican ward leaders, but his mayoral candidate lost to McKisson in the 1895 Republican primary.[11]

Policy and administration during this period reflected the absence of a centralized machine. To win council approval for his street railway franchises, Hanna, like Tom Johnson and other utility magnates, had to buy individual councilmen; he could not rely on the backing of a disciplined party organization.[12] The "Axworthy defalcation" of 1888 shows further the consequences of the absence of machine-enforced discipline for city government. As James B. Whipple explains, Thomas Axworthy, the city treasurer,

> disappeared, leaving a shortage of over half a million dollars. Most of it represented city funds which he had loaned in his own name and which he could not produce on demand. Apparently becoming panic-stricken, he withdrew additional funds and departed for Canada. A few weeks later a letter to the mayor explained what he had done, and naively closed with, "Good bye and may God bless the City of Cleveland." Subsequent investigation did not probe too deeply, but it did disclose that all treasurers had been using municipal funds as their own with the tacit understanding that it was all right, and that bookkeeping methods had been careless and inaccurate to the point of juggling figures to make the balance correct. Ultimately the Forest City recovered its money from Axworthy or his bondsmen, and three years later Mayor Gardner believed the defalcator should be permitted to return, having been sufficiently punished by his exile. The suggestion was never carried out, but it was indicative of the rather lax standards of public servants who would welcome home a fugitive from justice, a robber of public funds which had been placed in his trust.[13]

Whipple's implication is that Axworthy's embezzlement reflected the low level of public morality. Yet without any underlying ethical shift, the construction of the Tammany machine transformed the politics of corruption in New York from a free-wheeling individualism that produced similar incidents to a more restrained acceptance of opportunities for "honest graft" brokered by the party organization.[14] Between 1895 and 1899, Robert McKisson tried to effect a parallel transformation in Cleveland.

MCKISSON AND MACHINE BUILDING

Adoption of the "Federal Plan," enlarging the authority of the mayor, allowed McKisson to attempt to construct a citywide machine. McKisson's machine-building strategy, like that of many other would-be bosses in American urban history, did not succeed, for he was unable to win over members of the Republican faction associated with Mark Hanna. Moreover, McKisson's efforts aroused opposition along both traditional reform and municipal populist lines. One new traditional reform group, the Municipal Association, soon defined its mission as opposition to McKisson. Like the Citizens' Union in New York, this traditional reform group provided an initial framework for the incorporation of expertise into city politics. Experts' political experience within the Municipal Association, however, made them available for direct incorporation into city government. When Cleveland experts left traditional reform, therefore, it was to serve in Tom Johnson's administration, rather than to participate in an autonomous research body like the Bureau of Municipal Research.

McKisson's attempt to consolidate political power was made possible by the "Federal Plan" charter, so called because it placed the mayor and council in a relationship analogous to that of the president and Congress. The charter, enacted by the state legislature in 1891 in response to demands from local elites, gave the mayor, formerly a figurehead, power to veto legislation. The mayor could also appoint, with council confirmation, the directors of the executive departments that replaced the old boards. One feature of the charter that was very different from the national constitution was that the mayor and his cabinet were given seats in the council: though they had no votes, they could participate in council debates.[15]

McKisson was elected mayor in 1895 as the candidate of the Republican faction of Representative Theodore Burton and Senator Joseph Foraker. He won the Republican nomination over a Hanna candidate, and then defeated the Democratic incumbent, Robert Blee.[16] McKisson sought political power, not personal financial gain.[17] During his four years as mayor, McKisson tried to use patronage to construct a citywide machine. Several historians have suggested that this shows the naivete of Clevelanders (or anyone else) who believed charter revision could prevent corruption.[18] Yet, while the Federal Plan certainly did not end the use of power for individual ends, it did have an impact on organizational party politics: McKisson relied on the powers granted to the mayor by the Federal Plan in his attempt to build a machine.

McKissonism was thus an unintended consequence of the structural reforms of 1891.[19] Under the new appointment powers, McKisson selected political allies as cabinet directors.[20] These officials replaced city employees who were Democrats or Hanna Republicans with members of their own faction. At the beginning of McKisson's administration, one-third of the waterworks employees were replaced every two weeks, arousing protests from the Chamber of Commerce that the civil service protections of the Federal Plan had been violated. Police officers were also purged. Services were allocated politically, with extra staff sent into swing districts at election time. When McKisson ran for a third term in 1899, city workers were assessed 5 to 7 percent of their earnings as a campaign contribution. This practice led to a minor rebellion among pumphouse employees, which suggests that it was an innovation in the city. Business contracts were also used as political rewards.

Ethnic appeals, by McKisson and by ward leaders allied with him, were another part of McKisson's machine-building strategy. During the 1899 campaign, "Czar" Bernstein reportedly told his Jewish constituents that McKisson, if reelected, would free Alfred Dreyfus, the French soldier (and Jew) the French government was then imprisoning unjustly for treason. McKisson, like his rivals, rushed his immigrant supporters through the citizenship process.[21]

McKisson's biographer has noted that many of the policies of his administration helped to modernize Cleveland. These included work on a new water supply tunnel, sewer system, and city hall; campaigns against impure ice and adulterated milk; and construction of five additional bridges.[22] Of course, each of these policies also generated patronage that could be used to political advantage. Moreover, some of McKisson's policies did not contribute to municipal progress and were especially harmful to its poorest residents. For example, he gave a sanitation contract to friends who failed to carry it out and allowed merchants supplying the city relief department to cheat recipients with short weights, denying further assistance to those who complained.[23]

In 1897, McKisson was renominated over two opponents. He then defeated the former mayor, John Farley, in the general election, though McKisson's majority was five thousand less than in 1895.[24] In 1899, Farley defeated McKisson to regain the mayoralty. Farley was able to do so because he was supported not only by his own faction of the Democratic party but by Hanna Republicans, municipal populists, and traditional reformers.

Hanna's political resources included wealth, close ties to President William McKinley, and, after his appointment to replace John Sherman in March 1897, a seat in the United States Senate. For Hanna, unlike McKisson, politics was a secondary activity; Johnson quoted him as saying, "When I can't combine business and politics, I will give up politics."[25] Hanna unsuccessfully opposed McKisson's nomination in 1895. In 1897, McKisson's opponents lacked financial support, which suggests that Hanna did not play an active role in the campaign. Conflict between Hanna and McKisson became more intense later in 1897, when McKisson tried to block Hanna's election as senator.[26] In 1898, a riot broke out at the county convention after McKisson used city police to seize control. Hanna supporters held a rump convention, which was recognized as legitimate by the state Republican party. In 1899, Hanna backed Judge Carlos N. Stone against McKisson in the Republican mayoral primary, then contributed twenty thousand dollars to Farley's campaign against McKisson in the general election.[27]

Municipal populists represented a second source of opposition to

McKisson. During the 1880s, Dr. L. B. Tuckerman ran independent mayoral campaigns that emphasized public health and municipal ownership of utilities. Municipal populism was organized in the Franklin Club, which held weekly meetings to discuss these and other radical ideas. Among the political leaders who emerged from this milieu was Peter Witt, a blacklisted iron molder who became active in campaigns for the Populist party in 1894 and for William Jennings Bryan in 1896, and who later served in the Johnson and Baker administrations.[28] During a strike, Witt commented that "every lickspittle of a politician, from Mayor McKisson down, can see the rights of property, but not the rights of man." Other members of the Franklin Club criticized McKisson for corruption and mismanagement.[29] In 1899, however, McKisson won some municipal populist support by portraying himself as the defender of the workers against the upper class, calling for municipal ownership of all public utilities, an eight-hour day and a minimum wage of one dollar and fifty cents on city contracts, and reduction of the water tax.[30] After McKisson's defeat in the spring mayoral election of 1899, municipal populist support went to the independent gubernatorial candidacy of Samuel "Golden Rule" Jones, the reform mayor of Toledo. Witt managed the Jones campaign in Cuyahoga County, carrying it for Jones even though the candidate finished third statewide.[31]

THE MUNICIPAL ASSOCIATION

Traditional reform opposition to organizational party politics also predated McKisson: as noted earlier, the initiatives of local elites had led to the charter revisions of 1891. Opposition to McKisson, however, was institutionalized in the Municipal Association, an organization that, as the Citizens League, remains active in Cleveland affairs today. The Municipal Association grew out of the anti-Bryan alliance between Republicans and conservative Democrats in 1896. Harry A. Garfield, a Cleveland lawyer and the son of the former president, sought to continue this bipartisan cooperation in local affairs.[32] On November 14, 1896, a meeting of twenty-six agreed to form a permanent civic organization.

A constitution for the new organization was approved at a larger meeting on December 5. According to the constitution, the purposes of the Municipal Association were "to induce citizens and taxpayers to take a more active and earnest part in municipal affairs," "to disseminate instructive information relative to the Government of the City of Cleveland," "to devise and advocate plans for its improvement," "to promote businesslike, honest and efficient conduct in municipal affairs," "to secure the choice of competent officials," and "to encourage the faithful performance of public duty, to secure the enactment and enforcement of the economic, intelligent and progressive management of the offices of the city government." Membership was open to any citizen or taxpayer who did not hold public office, was willing to sign a pledge of support for the organization's principles, and would pay annual dues of one dollar.[33]

At its inception, the "Muny," as it came to be known, drew most of its members from business. Of the 116 present at the December 5 meeting, ninety-nine listed a business address. Telephone exchanges, a sign of wealth, were listed for 110 of the members. Business figures in the Municipal Association included financiers such as Samuel Mather, of Pickands, Mather & Co., industrialists such as H. A. Sherwin of Sherwin-Williams Co., and corporate lawyers such as Harry Garfield.[34] The executive committee of the organization, Henry E. Bourne noted, included many representatives of big business who had contributed heavily to the McKinley campaign. Yet, as Bourne observed, the minds of these people were on their businesses. They had little notion of what the organization should undertake and knew little of the details of city and county administration.[35]

The Municipal Association hired experts to do what businessmen could not do: explore the details of local government and decide what the organization's tasks should be. Thus, it was within a traditional reform framework, as secretaries of the Municipal Association, that experts began to participate in Cleveland politics. Frederic C. Howe, chosen as temporary secretary at the founding of the Association, was a lawyer in Harry Garfield's firm. But he had studied at Johns Hopkins under Richard Ely and Woodrow Wilson and saw this contact with the German research method as the formative experience of his life. After serving as secretary, Howe wrote one of the Municipal Association's first bulletins, arguing that the proposed twenty-five year streetcar franchise should be rejected because the value of the franchise was rapidly increasing.[36] Howe's successors as secretary included Henry E. Bourne, who had a graduate degree from Yale and was professor of history at the College for Women of Western Reserve University, and Delos F. Wilcox, a Columbia Ph.D. whose dissertation had been a treatise on municipal government in Michigan and Ohio.[37] As secretary, Bourne developed methods for investigating the finances and performance of public officials, while Wilcox collected and published biographical data on local candidates.[38]

Tensions existed between these experts and the elite that led and financed the Municipal Association. When Bourne was named as secretary, one lawyer protested that such an academic type would be more familiar with abstract ideas than practical politics. Many members complained that Howe's streetcar pamphlet was too radical. And Wilcox was forced to resign when he criticized the anti-McKisson city council for its subservience to streetcar interests. Garfield, he said, was running the Association against McKisson, rather than for good government.[39]

THE ELECTION OF 1899

As Wilcox claimed, by 1899, the drive against McKisson had been defined as the major task of the Municipal Association. In 1897, the group provided information on the candidates but made no endorsements. Two years later, it took a more active stance against McKisson's attempt to construct a political machine.[40] "If the Municipal Association stands for anything," its bulletin proclaimed, "it is that such evils as these may be uprooted and forever eliminated from our city government. If it is ever to lift its voice in favor of municipal reform and against municipal viciousness, now is the time." Calling McKisson's candidacy "an insult to the manhood, a threat to the property, and a menace to the safety of the people of Cleveland," the Association endorsed his primary opponent, Judge Stone.[41] After McKisson defeated Stone, a committee headed by Garfield called upon Farley. When he pledged that he would not seek a second term or build a machine, the Municipal Association endorsed him in a bulletin that devoted one page to his merits and forty-seven to reiterating its charges against McKisson.[42]

With Hanna Republicans and the normally Republican traditional reform voters supporting Farley, and some of the normally Democratic municipal populist voters supporting McKisson, the election of 1899 did not follow the lines of national party politics. Estimates suggest that as many Republicans (1900 McKinley voters) supported Farley as backed McKisson (between 35 and 40 percent). Democrats gave more generous support to their party's candidate (from 42 to 67 percent, versus between 30 and 41 percent for McKisson).[43] What these estimates cannot measure are the relative contributions of Hanna and the Municipal Association to McKisson's defeat. A Farley associate, speaking to Howe the night of the election, suggested that traditional reform support did not explain the result: "'Of course we were glad,' he said, suspecting no indiscretion, 'to have the support of the Municipal Association, but you know that didn't elect us. We should have been beaten but for Mark Hanna's contribution of twenty thousand dollars to the campaign.'"[44]

The election of 1899 did not immediately transform Cleveland politics. McKisson remained the leader of a faction within the Republican party. His allies won Republican mayoral nominations in 1901 and 1905, and McKisson himself unsuccessfully sought the nomination in 1909.[45] Despite his promises to the Municipal Association, Farley resumed his earlier style of politics and pushed a streetcar franchise through the city council.[46] And when Tom Johnson was elected mayor in 1901, voting patterns were closer to those of the 1900 presidential election than to those of the 1899 mayoral contest.

Nonetheless, Cleveland politics did change after 1901, and the way it changed reflects the heritage of McKissonism. Under the Federal Plan, a politician who was willing to work with Hanna rather than oppose him for power at the state level might have succeeded in constructing a local Republican machine despite the protests of the Municipal Association.[47] But experts' political learning as part of the Municipal Association drive against McKisson was important in the long run, for it influenced patterns of electoral alignments and policy initiatives during Tom Johnson's administrations. Johnson was able to remain in power with the support of a municipal populist coalition held together by policies initiated and administered by experts. Had McKisson succeeded in building a citywide machine, Johnson would have found it more difficult to mobilize foreign-stock voters. Had experts been fully incorporated into the traditional reform drive against McKisson, they would not have been available to serve in Johnson's administration. Instead, experts within the Municipal Association experienced conflict with business and manipulation by politicians. After 1901, therefore, the Johnson administration could replace the Municipal Association as the vehicle for college graduates with specialized training who wanted to enter city politics.

CHAPTER 7

Tom Johnson: Municipal Populism in Power

THE ELECTION OF 1901, in which Tom Johnson became mayor of Cleveland, followed earlier patterns of municipal politics. During his first term, however, Johnson reshaped Cleveland politics by directly incorporating experts into his administration. Individuals with specialized training and orientations became heads of city departments or held other official positions. Unlike their counterparts in New York, they were able to use their positions within city government to make their ideas into public policies. Some of these policies proved to be farsighted, while others were simply far-fetched. But, taken together, the policies introduced by experts allowed Johnson to construct an enduring reform coalition while serving as, in Lincoln Steffens's words, "the best Mayor of the best-governed city in the United States."[1] Johnson's supporters claimed that he had made Cleveland "a city set upon a hill."[2]

THE ELECTION OF 1901

Johnson, a Democrat, was elected mayor without strong support from either the traditional reform or the municipal populist constituencies. Few reformers of either type took part in Johnson's initial mayoral campaign.[3] To traditional reformers, Johnson was a radical. He had served two terms as a congressman, during which he articulated the social philosophy of Henry George, advocating a Single Tax on land to capture the "unearned increment" that accrued to landowners from the growth of the surrounding community, and opposing the tariff as the foundation of monopoly.[4] On the local level, Johnson interpreted Georgeism to include municipal ownership of street railways and other utilities, which would lower fares, improve service, and reduce corruption, as well as educate the public toward the Single Tax.[5] Arguing that Johnson's allegiance to these theories would be as dangerous as the ties of his Republican opponent, William J. Akers, to the McKisson faction, the Municipal Association refused to endorse either candidate in the general election.[6] Municipal populists objected to Johnson's career as a street railroad owner: in seeming contradiction to his endorsement of George's views, he had used monopoly tactics to operate lines in Cleveland, Brooklyn, Detroit, and other cities.[7] In an 1899 lecture that was later published, for example, Peter Witt had denounced "Smiling Tom" Johnson for exploiting streetcar passengers and employees to achieve the wealth that had allowed him to build a palatial home on Euclid Avenue.[8]

Johnson did receive support from organizational politicians, most notably Charles P. Salen, who started the "draft Johnson" boom. Johnson won the nomination with the backing of many of the Democratic clubs. By the general election, he was endorsed by most of the party's organizations, although John Farley, the Democratic incumbent, supported Akers.[9] Johnson also received support from business. As he recalled in his autobiography, "Privilege wasn't especially aroused and made no particular fight. Indeed Big Business was rather friendly than otherwise," in the belief that Johnson would give the city "a one hundred thousand dollar man for mayor at six thousand dollars a year." Johnson actively appealed for such support, pledging, "If elected, I would endeavor to give to the people as much of a business administration as is possible under existing statutes."[10] Johnson's endorsement of the Single Tax was less congenial to capitalists, but, as the *Plain Dealer* argued, it was unlikely Johnson would be able to enact this scheme as mayor.[11]

In 1901, then, traditional reformers, municipal populists, organizational politicians, and businessmen behaved much as they had throughout the late nineteenth century. Analysis of 1901 electoral data also suggests that this election followed conventional political patterns, and that it followed these patterns more closely than the election of 1899. Republicans (1900 McKinley voters) had split between Farley and Robert McKisson in 1899 (see Chapter 6), but in 1901 Akers was probably able to claim a plurality of the normally Republican vote, between 40 and 52 percent, whereas the estimate of Johnson's Republican support is from 19 to 48 percent. Democrats supported Johnson over Akers by an even greater margin than they had supported Farley over McKisson: between 48 and 86 percent of the Democratic vote went to Johnson, while between 25 and 40 percent supported Akers.[12] Table 7-1 shows demographic patterns for the election, using ward data from the 1900 census. Johnson was strongest among second-generation whites, Akers among first-generation whites

TABLE 7-1
Voting Behavior by Ethnic Group, 1901

	Akers (Rep.) %	Johnson (Dem.) %
2nd Generation White	30–31	75
Foreign White	7–41	0
Other	45–50	9–50

Note: Suburbanization set at mean value.
$N = 42$.

and among "other" voters, most of whom were native-born whites. Suburbanization, measured as dwellings per family, would later help Johnson against his Republican opponents, but in 1901, the more suburban a ward, the more it favored Akers. Though Johnson introduced the new issues of Henry George into the 1901 campaign, earlier political divisions remained unchanged.

JOHNSON AND THE EXPERTS

Fundamental change in politics and policy did take place after Johnson's election. Despite their support for Johnson's candidacy in 1901, organizational politicians and business elites had limited influence on public policy. Instead, policy was initiated and implemented by experts and quasi-experts who were directly incorporated into Johnson's administration. Charles Salen was appointed director of public works, a position that gave him control over many jobs and contracts. But after Salen became county clerk in 1903, public works were placed under the supervision of William J. Springborn, who sought to eliminate corruption from the department.[13] Johnson accepted the need for cooperation with Salen and other professional politicians in his election campaigns. Yet the patronage demands of the politicians were rebuffed when they came into conflict with the preferences of his expert advisors.[14]

Businessmen organized in the Chamber of Commerce were able to shape educational policy, over which state law gave Johnson little control.[15] The Chamber of Commerce also initiated action for smoke control, toward which Johnson was indifferent, led the movement for public baths, and developed a systematic plan for renaming the streets.[16] In other policy areas, however, business either endorsed experts' initiatives or fought unsuccessfully against the Johnson administration.

Choices in most areas of policy were initiated and carried out by experts appointed to key positions. Not all of Johnson's appointees had graduate degrees and professional affiliations. But even those who lacked the formal trappings of expertise applied some specialized knowledge to policy problems, and took part in national policy debates. One can distinguish, then, between bona fide experts such as Frederic Howe and Edward W. Bemis, who had received professional training, and "quasi-experts" such as Harris R. Cooley, whose ideas were more frequently based on practical experience. But the consequences of each type of appointment were much the same.

Of Johnson's appointees, Edward W. Bemis most clearly had the educational training and professional orientation of an expert; the *Plain Dealer* called him a "figger man." Bemis had received a Ph.D. at Johns Hopkins and helped organize the American Economic Association. In a celebrated academic freedom case, he had been dismissed from the faculty of the University of Chicago after he criticized the conduct of the railroads in the 1894 Pullman Strike. Bemis had also taught at the University of Kansas, worked for the Illinois Bureau of Labor Statistics, and joined John R. Commons to form the Bureau of Economic Research. He was invited to Cleveland in May 1901 as part of Johnson's campaign to increase the taxation of public service corporations. Bemis used statistics to demonstrate that railroad properties were underassessed. His report was not only an important weapon in the battles over taxation at the county and state levels, but an influential work in its field.[17]

Having come to Cleveland to study railroad taxation, Bemis was appointed superintendent of the waterworks, run as a division of Charles Salen's department of public works. Bemis's accomplishments included completion of a water-intake tunnel from Lake Erie, which reduced the typhoid rate from 114 to 12.2 per 100,000 by 1908, and installation of water meters for conservation and more equitable sharing of costs. Bemis fought against patronage in the waterworks; he fired the chief engineer, a Salen appointee, and introduced the merit system. This led to a revolt by party politicians, but Johnson backed Bemis by dismissing two Buckeye Club leaders who had attacked him from their city positions.[18]

While taxation policy brought experts into conflict with business, and the operation of the waterworks brought experts into conflict with organizational politicians, the adoption and implementation of the Group Plan provided an example of the manufacturing of consensus in support of experts' proposals for downtown Cleveland. The idea of a Group Plan for Cleveland's civic buildings, to include the city hall, county courthouse, public library, and federal building, was first formulated in conversations between Frederic Howe and Morris Black, a Harvard graduate who later became a leading anti-McKisson councilman. Each had lived in Germany and wanted a civic center on the model of European capitals. In 1895, Howe and Black convinced the local chapter of the American Institute of Architects to hold a competition for the best plan, and they won the endorsement of the Chamber of Commerce. But city government did not act until Johnson had been elected mayor and gave the Group Plan his enthusiastic support. In 1902, at Johnson's request, Governor George K. Nash appointed a three-member planning commission for the city, composed of three nationally prominent architects: Daniel H. Burnham, John M. Carrère, and Arnold W. Brunner. The architects designed a formal grouping of neoclassical buildings around a public mall, which they hoped would become the center of civic life. Contrary to their expectations, Burnham, Carrère, and Brunner met with little opposition or interference in designing and winning approval of their plan; even the Chamber of Commerce supported the replacement of its earlier conception. Brunner complained about delays and proposals for economy, but all the buildings except a projected railroad terminal were constructed according to the architects' plans, and the three were retained as advisors to the city on the planning of other projects. Cleveland thus became the first major U.S. city besides Washington, D.C., to carry out a plan of downtown development. In Los Angeles, in contrast, experts' plans for a civic center were rejected in favor of a cheaper scheme favored by the Chamber of Commerce.[19]

After Johnson's first health officer was dismissed for altering bills, Martin Friedrich was appointed to the position. Friedrich had received his M.D. from Western Reserve University, studied in Europe for two additional years, then returned to Cleveland as a lecturer on internal medicine and diagnosis at the College of Physicians and Surgeons.[20] Friedrich sought to revise smallpox procedures in accord with his professional observation that no new cases arose from houses that had been sprayed with formaldehyde after they had been identified as sources of the disease. Vaccination, in contrast, had not eliminated the malady and sometimes gave rise to unwanted side effects such as tetanus or swelling. Consequently, Friedrich ended the city's vaccination program and formed two twenty-man squads of disinfectors. The disinfectors, usually medical students, sprayed every room of every house in sections where cases had been identified. Friedrich's success in his first few months led one national magazine to publish an article entitled, "How Cleveland Stamped Out Small-Pox." Unfortunately, an epidemic broke out in the summer of 1902, killing 224 and forcing the health office to resume vaccination.[21]

Unlike Bemis, Howe, or Friedrich, Harris R. Cooley, director of charities and corrections, had a theological rather than an academic background. But Cooley, former pastor of Johnson's church, also had a strong interest in social work that included contact with the British settlement movement; his father had been superintendent of a charity organization, the Bethel Union. Cooley, like those with more formal qualifications as experts, implemented policies in response to ideas rather than patronage needs or demands for economy. Cooley's most famous achievement, construction of the Cooley Farms colony, embodied both the farsighted and the far-fetched aspects of such policies. The colony, located in the countryside surrounding Cleveland, contained a poorhouse for the elderly, a workhouse for prisoners, a tuberculosis infirmary, and a municipal cemetery. Poor, elderly couples, who had previously been separated, were allowed to live together in the Old Couples' Cottage, inscribed with the motto, "To lose money is better than to lose love." If the treatment of the elderly was advanced for its time, Cooley's penal theories seem outlandishly dated today. Prisoners who misbehaved, as Johnson explained, instead of being dealt with by the old brutalizing methods, are bathed and given clean clothes and then sent off by themselves to reflect—not to solitary confinement in dark cells, but to one of the "sun dungeons" originated by Mr. Cooley. These rooms—three of them—in one of the towers of the building are painted white, and flooded with light, sunshine and fresh air. It is part of Mr. Cooley's theory that men need just such surroundings to put them in a normal state of mind when they are feeling ill used or ugly.—"Sending them to the Thinking Tower," he calls it.[22]

Cooley also applied original ideas to running the Boys' Home, located at a second country site. A 1905 Johnson pamphlet defended "Boyville" against charges of waste and extravagance. While the usual "Reform Farm" provided youths with further temptations, it was argued, Cooley's program showed that "good clothes, decent food, healthful work, plenty of play and a sensible school-routine will do as much toward making a good man of the child of the slums as it will for the child of Euclid Avenue."[23]

Johnson's chief of police, Fred Kohler, also acquired expertise through practical experience rather than academic training. Like Cooley, Kohler succeeded in reorienting his department.[24] Before Johnson, stringent vice legislation had allowed police to raid saloons to collect graft and political contributions. Kohler, a McKisson Republican, gained a reputation as an "uncontrollable" raider. Yet he was appointed police chief in 1903 because he was the only officer who understood Johnson's strategy of abolishing raids in favor of "administrative repression" of vice. Under this policy, the patronage of gambling dens and saloons attached to brothels was discouraged by stationing a policeman outside to write down the names of customers. Ministers preferring criminal prosecutions protested against Johnson's approach, but the mayor replied that crusades only scattered vice throughout the city.

Besides continuing to enforce Johnson's administrative repression strategy, Kohler introduced his own "Golden Rule." Juveniles, drunks, and anyone who committed a misdemeanor without malice or forethought were not automatically arrested, but they could be sent home at the discretion of the officer. Drawing on his police experience, Kohler argued that arrest and imprisonment for these crimes hurt both the family and the city. If minor offenses were not prosecuted, policemen would be able to spend more time investigating and preventing serious crimes. Kohler's Golden Rule, like Johnson's administrative repression of vice, replaced an inflexible policy based on moralism with a discretionary policy based on realism about human behavior, reducing opportunities for police corruption in the process. The Golden Rule was debated at the 1908 and 1909 conventions of the International Association of Chiefs of Police, and Theodore Roosevelt at one point described Kohler as the best police chief in the country.

How can Johnson's reliance on experts be explained? The direct incorporation of expertise required that Johnson have the formal capacity to install experts in government, and that experts be available for installation. The Federal Plan gave the mayor the necessary appointment powers. Experts were geographically available, because Cleveland offered economic opportunities and an attractive setting for talented college graduates like Frederic C. Howe and Newton D. Baker.[25] Just as importantly, experts were *politically* available, for they had been only partially incorporated into the traditional reform framework of the Municipal Association.

That Johnson took advantage of the possibility of appointing experts reflected the personal passion for knowledge that led him to study French and philosophy while he was mayor. As Howe recalled, "He liked people with new ideas," and he "deferred to men who had had educational advantages that had been denied him."[26] Johnson also needed experts' skills to carry out policies based on the urban democratic ideology he had developed by way of Henry George. But Johnson's appointment of experts reflected political alignments as well. Policies designed and administered by experts reshaped Johnson's electoral coalition, allowing him to win reelection in 1903, 1905, and 1907. Several of Johnson's officials were even able to win elections on their own, after a new municipal code passed by a hostile Republican legislature placed their service at the pleasure of the voters rather than the mayor.[27] If Johnson's personality and policy preferences explain why he initially brought experts into government, the electoral benefits he derived allowed him to continue to do so.

THE STREETCAR WARS

Transportation policy was an exception to the general pattern by which experts dominated policy making in the Johnson administration. Howe and Bemis backed Johnson in his streetcar battles.[28] But transportation policy was initiated by Johnson himself, not by experts, and his inflexibility was very different from the experts' characteristic emphasis on administrative discretion. Johnson's preferred solution to the transportation problem was municipal ownership, for which he made a political argument. Private control of utilities, he believed, created a class of stockholders who would seek to corrupt government and influence public opinion. Since Ohio law did not permit municipal ownership of streetcar lines, he sought private service at a three-cent fare instead. Johnson claimed to have become convinced of the practicality of the three-cent fare as a streetcar line owner in Detroit. In Detroit, however, Johnson had fought against Mayor Hazen Pingree's efforts to institute a three-cent fare, and the three-cent fare that was established on some lines was subsidized by higher fares on other parts of the Detroit system.[29] Johnson's support for the three-cent fare was not a solution developed through professional training or experience, but an application of the social theories he derived from Henry George.

The goal of the three-cent fare led to a series of conflicts with the existing transit ("traction") companies.[30] As streetcar franchises expired, they were granted to new low-fare companies sponsored by Johnson and his friends. Beyond endorsing these franchise grants, Johnson personally backed the stock offerings of one of the low-fare companies and served as president of a bank formed to finance another. The existing five-cent companies, popularly known as the Big Con and the Little Con (merged into the Cleveland Electric Street Railway Company, or ConCon, in 1903), fought the three-cent lines with injunctions and made limited experiments with low fares of their own.

A temporary settlement to the conflict was reached after negotiations between Johnson, representing the city, and Frederick H. Goff, representing the ConCon, in 1908. The Municipal Traction Company, a holding company for the three-cent line, purchased the stock of the ConCon at an agreed-upon fifty-five dollars per share. Shareholders were to be guaranteed a 6 percent return, and fares were set at three cents. Service deteriorated during a violent strike by employees of the old company, who were granted a one-cent-an-hour raise to bring them up to the pay of workers on the three-cent line but had been promised a two-cent raise if the ConCon franchise were renewed. The strike was supported by newspapers that were normally anti-labor, and Johnson forces charged that it was backed by ConCon interests. To preserve a nominal three-cent fare in the face of the streetcar strike, Johnson and his associates proved willing to reduce or eliminate service on unprofitable lines, introduce a one-cent transfer charge, and raise fares to five cents for trips outside the city limits.

Opponents of the settlement forced a vote on the franchise grant. In the referendum, held on October 22, 1908, the settlement was defeated, 38,249 to 37,643. Streetcar lines then reverted back to the original companies. After the low-fare line went into receivership, the city council approved a new three-cent franchise for Herman Schmidt, a Johnson supporter. The Chamber of Commerce, many of whose members owned ConCon stock, led the referendum fight against the Schmidt grant. *The People's Side*, a pro-Johnson newspaper published during the referendum campaign, pointed out that nine of the twenty-one members of the Chamber of Commerce Street Railway Committee did not live in the city, and that automobile riders were dictating to the streetcar-riding public. One diagram depicted the ConCon at the center of spokes connecting the Chamber of Commerce, the Employers' Association, the railway strikers, and the elite Union Club.[31] Nevertheless, on August 3, 1909, the Schmidt grant was defeated, 34,785 to 31,012.

Both sides then agreed to a settlement by Judge Robert W. Tayler. The ConCon would run all the lines, but the city was to exercise "complete and continuous supervisory control of operation." Shareholders would receive a 6 percent return, based on Judge Tayler's evaluation of the property, while fares would be three cents if possible and no more than five cents or seven for a quarter. After ten years, the city could name a purchaser or, if legal by then, purchase the lines itself. At a referendum held on February 19, 1910, voters approved the Tayler grant, 27,270 to 19,232. Johnson had opposed the Tayler grant, even though the safety clauses he sought had been inserted in the ordinance. In objecting to the continuation of ConCon operations, Johnson underestimated the importance of the supervisory authority granted to the city. Under Newton Baker, the city would take advantage of these regulatory powers to improve service while maintaining fares below those of other cities.

JOHNSON'S SUPPORTERS

Innovative political techniques publicized the Johnson administration's policy record, creating new links between city government and the voters. Tent meetings attracted men and women who did not normally attend political rallies. They could also be held in parts of the city that lacked public auditoriums. Stereopticons were used to project images of the administration's accomplishments, while more traditional campaign weaponry like torches and bands were rejected.[32] During his statewide campaigns in 1902 and 1903, Johnson became one of the first politicians to make extensive use of the automobile, traveling throughout Ohio in a large car called the "Red Devil." Johnson also made early use of newsreels as a campaign tool.[33] The Tax School, formed during the taxation controversy of Johnson's first term, was another method used to inform voters of Johnson's policies. Peter Witt was placed in charge; with employees from the city engineer's office, he developed maps showing the cash and assessed value of lots and buildings. The inequalities discovered by the Tax School were publicized in printed circulars and stereopticon lectures, and new assessments based on W. A. Somers's unit system were proposed.[34]

By publicizing Johnson's policy initiatives, these techniques helped to stimulate electoral change. In the mayoral elections of 1903, 1905, 1907, and 1909, Johnson received more municipal populist support than he had in 1901. Peter Witt, the most prominent municipal populist activist, became director of the Tax School and then city clerk.[35] Beyond Cleveland, Johnson allied with Mayor Edward Dunne of Chicago and was frequently praised by *The Public*, Louis Post's single-tax journal.[36] Traditional reform activists, in contrast, remained ambivalent toward Johnson. The Municipal Association, which had refused to endorse either candidate in 1901, backed Johnson in only one of his four reelection attempts. In 1905, the Association supported Johnson against his McKissonite opponent, William H. Boyd, but in the other elections it endorsed his Republican rivals, Harvey D. Goulder (1903), Theodore E. Burton (1907), and Herman C. Baehr (1909). The Municipal Association *Bulletin* criticized Johnson for building what it considered a political machine, and in particular for seeking party discipline in the city council. Johnson's attitude toward the vice laws and his personal connections to the low-fare companies were also condemned.[37] In 1903, *The Public* responded to the Municipal Association's criticism of Johnson by calling the traditional reform group "professedly a non-partisan civic body, but really a collection of stock investors and Republican tax-dodgers, who feared Johnson's just taxation policy."[38]

"If Big Business was somewhat passive in the campaign of 1901," Johnson recalled, "quite the reverse was true in 1903."[39] With the possible exception of 1905, business actively opposed Johnson in the elections that followed as well. Harvey Goulder, the Republican candidate in 1903, was president of the Chamber of Commerce. In 1907, S. P. Halle of the Halle Brothers department store, Abraham Stern of Stern and Company, S. H. Needs of the Ohio and Pennsylvania Coal Company, and Mortimer Strauss of Williams and Rodgers were among the businessmen who urged Representative Theodore Burton to run for mayor in order to defeat Johnson.[40] Charles A. Otis, an investment banker and a steel manufacturer, bought the *Leader* and the *News* to give the anti-Johnson forces Associated Press franchises. When Herman Baehr defeated Johnson in 1909, Otis later wrote, "I had accomplished my demon and youthful desire to eliminate the first New Dealer, Tom L. Johnson, from Cleveland political and economical society."[41] Johnson did have some business supporters: one contemporary biographer said, "It is an erroneous idea that Johnson had no friends and admirers among the business men of the town. Even in the Chamber of Commerce his friends could be found in goodly numbers. Many of them expressed no opinions, but on election day they cast their ballots for him."[42] The most prominent capitalists, however, remained against Johnson despite his business credentials and his support for the merit system. Their opposition led Lincoln Steffens to argue while campaigning for Johnson that "businessmen don't want a business-like administration but an administration that is to represent their business."[43]

The Socialist party also opposed Johnson. Socialists argued that Johnson's reform measures were only palliatives, designed to postpone working-class victory. They also said that municipal ownership of utilities "merely resulted in a transformation of these utilities from private capitalism to collective capitalism," and that even the three-cent fare was of little value to the man who did not have three cents. Johnson was less hostile toward the Socialists than the Republicans usually were, and he debated some of his Socialist opponents.[44] Like William Randolph Hearst, Johnson was accused of being a Socialist himself, though his support for government ownership was limited to utilities and he preferred working within the existing parties to forming a new one, whether for socialism or the Single Tax.[45] Also like Hearst, Johnson seems to have attracted voters who might otherwise have become Socialist supporters. Despite Cleveland's large German population and the long-standing Socialist affiliation of the Central Labor Union and its newspaper, the *Citizen*, Socialist mayoral candidates running against Johnson never gained more than the 2.0 percent of the vote Tom Clifford received in 1905.[46]

Estimates of transition rates and ethnic voting show both continuity and change in the patterns of support for Johnson in 1903, 1905, 1907, and 1909. Though Johnson's Republican opponents, and some of the issues they raised, varied, Johnson continued to receive support from Austrian, German, Hungarian, and Irish voters, while the Republicans generally did better than Johnson among native-stock voters and Russians. Because Johnson consistently championed lower streetcar fares, an issue of greater importance to commuting suburbanites than to downtown dwellers who could walk to work, suburbanization was associated with support for Johnson in all four of his reelection campaigns. The strength of the relationship between support for Johnson and suburban location, however, varied with the salience of the transportation issue in that year.

THE ELECTION OF 1903

Johnson's opponent in 1903 was Harvey D. Goulder, a lawyer associated with Hanna who was serving as president of the Chamber of Commerce. The Municipal Association said Goulder, unlike Johnson, would give the city a dignified and businesslike administration run according to law. Goulder was also endorsed by various religious organizations and the Ohio Anti-Saloon League, which issued a joint statement condemning Johnson's vice policy. In an effort to attract labor support, the Republicans nominated for vice mayor Sol Sontheimer, president of the Allied Trades and Labor Council. Sontheimer's appeal was diminished when his union withdrew him from the council and when it was demonstrated that he had applied for membership in a Democratic club within the previous year.

Goulder described the three-cent fare as impracticable and associated Johnson with "fads and isms." Johnson pointed out in response that capitalists (he and his allies) had been willing to provide service at three cents but were prevented from doing so by court injunctions. The faddism charge was answered by distributing 150,000 copies of a twenty-page pamphlet citing the accomplishments of Johnson's administration. Besides the traction issue, the pamphlet emphasized the Tax School, the merit system in the waterworks, introduction of the quasi-military "White Wings" sanitation system, the metering of water use, and the pardons granted to prisoners who were jailed because they were too poor to pay fines.[47]

In 1902, Cleveland's wards were reapportioned and reduced in number from forty-two to twenty-six. To estimate the transition rates from 1901 to 1903, therefore, it is necessary to remap the 1903 data onto the earlier wards. The estimated transition rates using this recalculated data suggest that Johnson was able to pick up between 7 and 50 percent of Akers's 1901 supporters while holding on to most of his own 1901 vote (from 50 to 76 percent). At the same time, Goulder received between 27 and 50 percent of Akers's 1901 vote, and none of Johnson's earlier support. Table 7-2 presents estimates of the coefficients of demographic variables, using the recalculated 1903 electoral data and 1900 census data. A comparison of Table 7-2 with Table 7-1, which provided similar estimates for 1901, suggests the sources of voting shifts between the two elections. Goulder, by emphasizing the vice issue and establishing ties to Protestant organizations as well as the Municipal Association, gained traditional reform support from native-stock voters. Johnson lost whatever traditional reform support he had received in 1901, but he was able to maintain a margin of about 6,000 votes by winning more municipal populist support. Johnson's 1903 support came almost exclusively from foreign-stock voters. Goulder, in contrast, did better among "other" (primarily native-stock) voters than Akers had done.

Ethnic patterns of support are better illustrated by estimates based on

TABLE 7-2
Voting Behavior by Ethnic Group, 1903

	Goulder (Rep.) %	Johnson (Dem.) %
2nd Generation White	0	75
Foreign White	38–43	0
Other	50–62	0

Note: 1903 data recalculated onto 1901 wards. Suburbanization set at mean value.

N = 42.

TABLE 7-3
Voting Behavior by Ethnic Group, 1903

	Goulder (Rep.) %	Johnson (Dem.) %
Austrian	13–50	50–51
German	0	0
Hungarian	0	0
Irish	100	100
Native	14–33	0
Russian	50–63	50–60

Note: Suburbanization and illiteracy variables set at mean values.
N = 26.

the original electoral data and the more detailed demographic data of the 1910 census. The 1910 census categories reflected existing national boundaries; hence, "Austrian" and "Hungarian" include many other Eastern European groups, and "Russian" encompasses many Jews and Poles. My classification of "native" combines native-born with native parents, English, and Scottish.[48] Estimates using this data to analyze the 1903 vote are presented in Table 7-3. Goulder did much better than Johnson among native-stock whites, the group to which each candidate belonged. Goulder also did better than Johnson among Russians; Republican ward leaders were influential among the Poles and Jews included in this category. Johnson seems to have been stronger among the ethnic groups of the Austrian Empire, such as Czechs. Unconstrained estimates of the German and Hungarian votes were negative for both candidates and so yield little information. Similarly, estimates for the Irish vote exceeded 100 percent for each candidate; the ratio of the unconstrained estimates suggests Johnson did better among this group by about two to one. Democratic candidates were far more dominant among the Irish in New York, where the Tammany machine was particularly identified with the Irish. Suburban voters were much more likely to support Johnson. According to the unconstrained regression estimates, the predicted Johnson proportion of eligible voters would be 13 percent higher in the most suburban ward than in the least suburban part of the city, while the Goulder proportion would be only 4 percent higher.

THE ELECTION OF 1905

William H. Boyd, the Republican nominee in 1905, was the only one of Johnson's Republican opponents to accept Johnson's challenge to debate. Despite his own ties to McKisson, Boyd accused Johnson of building a machine. He attributed to Johnson "a record that would put to shame Tammany as it exists in New York," including increases in the payroll of the street department at election time and dictatorial control over the county Democratic convention. Johnson was seen as a protector against bossism, Boyd said, but in truth he provided only "such protection as the wolf gives to its prey, and as a lion gives to a lamb; such protection as Russia gave the Jews, and Turkey gives its subjects, and as death gives its victim." His primary piece of evidence for these charges was a copy of Johnson's record book, listing employees and their recommenders. Boyd, who obtained the book from a stenographer, claimed it demonstrated a pattern of political appointments. He agreed to turn it over to the Municipal Association for inspection. Finding no evidence that the book was used to require political activity by appointees, the organization declared Boyd's charges unproven and endorsed Johnson for the only time in his five mayoral campaigns. Two members of the Association, however, filed a minority report criticizing the record book as a political document that served no civic function and suggested that the organization make no endorsement.[49]

Boyd also charged that Johnson's use of political employees had increased expenditures, so that the city was spending $1,194,000 more than in Farley's last year. Everything done by Johnson, Boyd said, cost 25 to 50 percent more than necessary. Boyd was particularly critical of the administration of the workhouse, which he said had earned a profit under Farley but was losing an increasing amount every year under Johnson. Johnson replied that the purpose of the workhouse was not to make a profit, but to improve men; though it had lost money under Cooley, it had taught men arithmetic, the alphabet, and how to spell and make out a bill. More generally, Johnson challenged Boyd to explain in detail where he would economize and argued that "the best way, my friends, to compare the expense of one administration with the same administration at some other time, or another administration, is not to take the cold-blooded dollars— the question is not how many dollars did you pay out, the question is, how much did you get for it."[50] Similarly, Johnson's campaign pamphlet, entitled "The Record of the Past Is the Promise of the Future," said that increased amounts spent on the streets meant they would be cleaned twenty times a year instead of once, and noted that "under the ancient theory and practice of city government, money was saved on the Health Department so that there would be funds to fight epidemics. The modern method is to spend enough money on the Health Department so that there will be no epidemics to fight."[51] The streetcar issue was less prominent in 1905 than it had been in 1903. Johnson continued to fight for a three-cent fare, while Boyd indicated his willingness to accept a settlement at eight tickets for twenty-five cents.[52]

TABLE 7-4
Voting Behavior by Ethnic Group, 1905

	Boyd (Rep.) %	Johnson (Dem.) %
Austrian	10–50	46–50
German	1–50	50–53
Hungarian	0	3–50
Irish	50–76	100
Native	29–32	7–43
Russian	28–50	48–50

Note: Suburbanization and illiteracy variables set at mean values.
$N = 26$.

Johnson received 41,591 votes to 29,466 for Boyd. Estimated transition rates from 1903 to 1905 show that Johnson was able to attract a portion of Goulder's 1903 voters, between 11 and 50 percent, and received between 41 and 51 percent of his supporters from 1903. Boyd, in contrast, failed to attract any voters who had backed Johnson in 1903, while garnering 47 to 59 percent of 1903 Goulder voters. Table 7-4 shows that Johnson probably did better than Boyd among all the ethnic groups listed except the native-stock voters. Even among the native-stock group, Johnson won more support in 1905 than he had won in 1903. Estimates for the native-stock vote suggest that Johnson attracted some of the traditional reform voters who had backed Goulder in 1903.[53] These voters remained hostile to McKisson, with whom Boyd was associated, and were most likely to take seriously the recommendations of the Municipal Association. Goulder had been able to win traditional reform support against Johnson by invoking the vice question, but Boyd made little use of such appeals. Suburbanization was again associated with support for Johnson, although the difference between the coefficients for the two candidates, in keeping with the reduced emphasis on the streetcar issue in the 1905 campaign, was slightly less than in 1903.

THE ELECTION OF 1907

Streetcar issues were more prominently featured in the 1907 campaign.[54] Johnson's opponent was Theodore E. Burton, who had represented Cleveland in Congress since defeating Johnson in 1894. Burton had no interest in municipal affairs but was urged to run by President Theodore Roosevelt and by William Howard Taft and James R. Garfield, two Ohio Republicans in Roosevelt's cabinet. Burton argued for a peaceful settlement of the traction dispute at seven tickets for twenty-five cents; the ConCon cooperated by lowering its fares to this rate until after the election. Burton also called for universal transfers, while Johnson, according to the Republicans, would establish a zone system. The Republicans repeated their 1905 charges that Johnson had been extravagant and was creating a machine. The Democrats denied plans for a zone system, accused the Burton campaign of juggling tax figures, and argued that "there is nothing wrong about a political organization unless it is used for a bad purpose."[55] The Johnson campaign ridiculed Burton's pretensions. When Burton announced his candidacy by quoting, in the original Latin, Julius Caesar's "Jacta alae est" ("the die is cast"), Johnson responded, "Let 'er go Gallagher—we're off!" Burton introduced his speeches by alluding to cities around the world where he had spoken; Witt, campaigning for Johnson, parodied Burton, mentioning Ohio towns where he had had the privilege to speak.[56]

The transition estimates suggest virtually no electoral change from 1905 to 1907: Johnson maintained virtually all his support from his 1905 voters, while Burton won all the 1905 Boyd supporters. A comparison of the demographic analysis of the 1907 vote (Table 7-5) with the comparable estimates for 1905 (Table 7-4), however, does suggest some shifts. Most notably, Johnson lost the native-stock support he had picked up in the previous election. In 1905, the municipal populist pattern of support for Johnson was somewhat blurred by traditional reform antipathy to Boyd. In 1907, with the respectable Burton as the Republican candidate, the distinct municipal populist and traditional reform patterns of support were more pronounced. Burton's self-proclaimed scholarship and statesmanship were appealing to the native-stock upper class and the Municipal Association.[57] But as Johnson and his advisors seem to have recognized, the same traits could be made to work against Burton among immigrant-stock, working-class voters. Russian voters remained fairly evenly divided, with some movement back to the GOP.

Suburbanization was again associated with support for Johnson. The

TABLE 7-5
Voting Behavior by Ethnic Group, 1907

	Burton (Rep.) %	Johnson (Dem.) %
Austrian	18–50	42–50
German	0	50–92
Hungarian	0	9–50
Irish	0	100
Native	42–62	0
Russian	50	45–50

Note: Suburbanization and illiteracy variables set at mean values.
$N = 26$.

streetcar battle was more prominent in this campaign than it had been in 1903 or 1905: one indication was Johnson's campaign pamphlet, which focused more on the traction issue, and less on Johnson's other accomplishments, than those issued in the earlier campaigns. The increased salience of the traction issue would explain why the difference between the unconstrained suburbanization coefficients for Johnson and his opponent was greater in 1907 than in 1905.[58]

THE ELECTION OF 1909

Herman C. Baehr defeated Robert McKisson by a two-to-one margin to win the 1909 Republican mayoral nomination. Baehr, a German brewer serving as county recorder, was associated with Maurice Maschke, a German Jewish politician who had begun his career as a follower of McKisson and would later lead the political machine McKisson had been unable to create. Since Baehr was personally popular but a poor campaigner, Maschke had him avoid speeches or debates in favor of a parlor campaign. The Republicans sought to focus attention on Johnson's traction stand, which had proven unpopular in the two streetcar referenda. Rather than attack Johnson's initiatives in other policy areas, they promised to continue his efforts and argued that more might have been accomplished had the administration not focused on the streetcar question.[59] Johnson, for the first time, sought to deemphasize the traction conflict. The election pamphlet issued by the Democrats claimed credit for the three-cent fares available to many riders, but it gave no more attention to the streetcar fight than to Cooley Farms, water meters, or the other achievements of the Johnson administration. Since a pro-Johnson slate was running for the Board of Appraisers, the campaign gave particular attention to the issue of taxation.[60] Baehr received 41,405 votes to 37,711 for Johnson.

Johnson wrote Brand Whitlock, "The people are probably right."[61] But which people, and what were they right about? The transition estimates from 1907 to 1909 suggest some crossover from $Burton_{1907}$ to $Johnson_{1909}$ (between 3 and 48 percent), and even more in the other direction, from $Johnson_{1907}$ to $Baehr_{1909}$ (between 21 and 43 percent). Johnson, meanwhile, maintained 73 percent of his 1907 support, and Baehr won between 50 and 82 percent of Burton's 1907 vote. Baehr was German, and his occupation as a brewer gave further emphasis to his ethnic identification. Though Baehr's German identity was an important reason Maschke thought he would make a strong candidate, the demographic estimates presented in Table 7-6 suggest that German voters were not particularly responsible for Johnson's defeat. Raw ward totals also suggest that Baehr's attractiveness to German voters was not a major factor in his victory: the

TABLE 7-6

Voting Behavior by Ethnic Group, 1909

	Baehr (Rep.) %	Johnson (Dem.) %
Austrian	17–50	24–50
German	0	50–77
Hungarian	0	6–50
Irish	10–50	100
Native	33–50	0
Russian	46–50	27–50

Note: Suburbanization and illiteracy variables set at mean values.
N = 26.

two most heavily German wards, 6 and 17, both gave pluralities to Johnson. Though Johnson attracted fewer native-stock voters than he had in 1907, this group's estimated support for Baehr was less than it had been for Burton. Despite the endorsement of the Municipal Association, some traditional reform voters may have refused to support a brewer associated with a boss like Maschke.[62]

Once again, suburban location was positively related to support for Johnson. But the difference between the estimates of the suburbanization coefficients for Johnson and Baehr is less than the differences between the estimates for Johnson and his opponents in his earlier reelection campaigns. When other demographic variables are held constant, Johnson's predicted 1909 margin in the most suburban ward is only 2.1 percent greater than in the least suburban ward.[63] This suggests that Johnson's support among suburban voters depended on the traction issue; when the issue became less favorable for him, his suburban support declined. As Michael P. McCarthy has argued, then, suburbanization was associated with support for Johnson in 1903, 1905, 1907, and 1909. But this support for Johnson was based on the single issue of traction policy, rather than the broader array of concerns that McCarthy, following Richard Wade and Zane Miller, has seen as motivating suburban voters.[64]

Though Baehr defeated Johnson for mayor, four of five pro-Johnson candidates, including Frederic Howe, were elected to the Board of Appraisers. With the assistance of W. A. Somers, inventor of the unit method, and Lawson Purdy, who had directed a similar effort in New York, property throughout the city was systematically assessed. The new system did not put Henry George's Single Tax into full effect, but the lower rate of assessment for buildings and other improvements than for land reflected George's principles.[65] The reelection of Newton Baker as City Solicitor was also a victory for the Johnson camp. Even though Baker had been an active partner in the traction fight, he had a broader electoral base than Johnson. While Baker shared Johnson's appeal to municipal populist voters, traditional reform voters saw him as more reliable than Johnson. The Municipal Association praised both Baker and his opponent, Gerhard M. Dahl, as it endorsed Baehr over Johnson. The organization had been even more enthusiastic about Baker in earlier elections: it endorsed him for Solicitor in 1903, 1905, and 1907, though it supported Johnson only in 1905. In 1907, for example, the group had noted Baker's blameless reputation and described him as one of the leading members of the bar.[66]

The absence of a true political machine left more voters available for mobilization by a reform candidate in Cleveland than in New York. By bringing experts into his administration and allowing them to make public policy in most areas, Johnson created the possibility for a progressive coalition between native-stock elites and foreign-stock workers. Municipal populist voters were attracted by sympathetic welfare and penal policies, by health policies that sought to eradicate the diseases to which they were most susceptible, and by parks, baths, and other public works built specifically for their needs. Traditional reform voters might have been attracted as well by Johnson's support for the merit system, by his opposition to Farley and McKisson, and by the civic vision embodied in the Group Plan. The streetcar issue and the Single Tax ideology that surrounded it, however, made it impossible for Johnson to win traditional reform support and create a progressive coalition. Johnson was still able to win reelection to the mayoralty in 1903, 1905, and 1907, in part because suburban voters were attracted by the promise of a three-cent fare. Once the experimental period had shown that lower fares might be accompanied by poorer service, Johnson lost the mayoralty to a candidate sponsored by a machine-building Republican politician. Yet even in 1909, Newton Baker and the Appraiser candidates were able to win election with campaigns based upon the politics of expertise. Baker would again demonstrate his ability to construct a reform coalition broader than Johnson's as a successful candidate for mayor in 1911 and 1913.

CHAPTER 8

Newton Baker's Progressive Coalition

By ADDING traditional reform support to Johnson's municipal populist base, Newton Baker was able to construct a progressive coalition. The Baker administration developed a new consensual ideology of "civitism" and new ties to experts outside the administration. The municipally owned light company and the home rule charter of 1913 reflected Baker's emphases on consensus and expertise. Both of these endured after ethnic conflicts and Baker's retirement caused his electoral coalition to come apart.

Herman Baehr, the candidate of Maurice Maschke's Republican faction, defeated Tom Johnson for the mayoralty in 1909. The Baehr administration gave Maschke Republicans the patronage opportunities they had been denied under Johnson.[1] Policy in most areas, however, followed the directions set by the Johnson administration; few new initiatives were taken. James F. Jackson, general secretary of the Family Service Association, replaced Harris R. Cooley as director of Charities and Corrections. Jackson accepted the position in order to continue Cooley's work, while improving efficiency and increasing cooperation between public and private welfare agencies.[2] Baehr's desire to remove Fred Kohler as police chief was frustrated by civil service protections. Twenty-one charges were filed against Kohler, but all were thrown out, dropped, or rejected by the Civil Service Commission.[3] After the ratification of the Tayler Ordinance in February 1910, the city assumed supervisory powers over the street railway system. Gerhard Dahl, appointed as the first street railway commissioner, was ineffective in the post.[4] Baehr not only accepted the three-cent fare, as enacted by the Tayler Ordinance, but extended the principle by advocating three-cent gas. He did so to the chagrin of Charles Otis, a major financial backer, who recalled that "we certainly had our 'fill' of mayors attacking privately owned utilities."[5]

THE ELECTION OF 1911

After Baehr declined to run for reelection, Frank B. Hogen, his Public Safety Director, won the 1911 Republican mayoral nomination over Miner G. Norton, a member of the party faction led by Robert McKisson.

Newton Baker defeated the organization leader Charles P. Salen in the Democratic primary, receiving 7,118 votes to 3,807 for Salen. Baker and Salen had both claimed leadership of the Democratic party after Johnson's defeat, but Baker was aided when Johnson expressed his preference for him. The Baker-Hogen contest was relatively issueless. Both, for example, advocated approval of a $2 million bond issue to build a municipal light plant. The Municipal Association had by this time adopted a policy of not endorsing mayoral candidates, though it had commented favorably on Hogen's administrative performance in May 1911. Baker was elected over Hogen, 46,214 to 28,376. Both Baker and the *Plain Dealer* interpreted the results as a tribute to the recently deceased Johnson.[6]

Cleveland's ward map was redrawn before the 1911 election. To estimate transition rates from 1909 to 1911, therefore, it is necessary to map the new wards onto the old and calculate adjusted 1911 data. The estimated transition rates using this adjusted data show that Baker not only retained between 50 and 98 percent of Johnson's 1909 support, but drew 26 to 50 percent of the 1909 Baehr vote. Hogen retained 69 percent of the Baehr vote, but made no inroads among Johnson supporters.

The results of the 1920 census were aggregated by the wards created in 1911. This census data can thus be used in estimates of equations showing the impact of demographic variables in the 1911, 1913, and 1915 elections. The ethnic categories of the 1920 census followed postwar boundaries. Hence, the behavior of Czech and Polish voters can be estimated, while the variables for Germans, Hungarians, and Russians have more limited meaning than in estimates using 1910 census data.[7] Table 8-1 presents estimated behavior by ethnic group. Baker, like Johnson, received ethnic support: Czech, German, Hungarian, Irish, and Russian voters all favored him over Hogen.[8] Hogen won more native support, but Baker

TABLE 8-1
Voting Behavior by Ethnic Group, 1911

	Hogen (Rep.) %	*Baker (Dem.) %*
Czech	41–50	100
German	0	100
Hungarian	0	10–50
Irish	100	100
Native	19–25	6–31
Polish	11–50	30–50
Russian	20–50	35–50

Note: Suburbanization and illiteracy variables set at mean values.

$N = 26$.

came closer to winning a plurality of this group than Johnson had ever done. The estimated suburban coefficient is greater for Hogen than for Baker, but the difference is slight, in keeping with the reduced salience of the traction issue following the approval of the Tayler Ordinance.

BAKER AS MAYOR

The policies of the Baker administration reflected a new relationship of experts to city government. During the McKisson period, experts had been part of the traditional reform opposition; under Johnson, they had been directly incorporated into city government. While Baker retained or reinstated some of Johnson's appointees, he also developed ties to independent organizations in which experts played important roles. As mayor, Baker resumed or continued many policies developed under Johnson. Baker's approach to the utility problem, however, eschewed Johnson's long-range political goals for immediate service improvements. Moreover, Baker abandoned the Single Tax as an ideological framework for reform, replacing it with his own conception of "civitism." The less conflictual character of reform under Baker made it possible for his administration to rely heavily on the business-based Cleveland Foundation in its response to unemployment and to ally with the reorganized Municipal Association in the fight for a home rule charter.

Baker's social welfare policies extended approaches taken under Johnson. Cooley was brought back as director of charities and corrections.[9] Kohler was retained as police chief until February 1913, when Baker reluctantly suspended him after he had been named as third party in a divorce suit.[10] Municipal dance halls represented a new application of the practical approach to social problems associated with Cooley and Kohler. The municipal dance halls offered a "wholesome" alternative to private dance halls that served liquor, and they charged only three cents for a five-minute dance, compared with the five cents charged for three minutes by the private sector.[11] Johnson's emphasis on expertise in the administration of public works was continued in the department of public service, where "all the division heads are trained and experienced specialists, [and] the engineering bureau has one of the best staffs in the country."[12]

Baker's utility policies, like Johnson's, aimed at eventual municipal ownership, but for different reasons. Johnson's argument for municipal ownership was political: private utilities would corrupt government. Baker's argument for municipal ownership was economic. For him, municipal ownership was a means to cheaper and more efficient service. Concluding in 1917 that Cleveland had made "successful and profitable" progress toward a solution of the electricity problem, Baker wrote, "Whether it be effective regulation in the interest of the consumer, or consolidation of the two plants under municipal ownership, matters not."[13] Johnson, in contrast, had said, "Regulation by city or commission will not correct these evils. The more stringent the regulation, the more bitter will be the civic strife."[14]

Peter Witt was appointed as Baker's street railway commissioner. Despite his radical background, Witt made more effective use of the supervisory powers of his position than had his predecessor, Gerhard Dahl. To increase speed and reduce accidents, he developed a skip-stop system that won 80 percent approval in a referendum vote. Witt also introduced safety education for school children, improved the power system and repair shops, and added trailers to cars during rush hours. In cooperation with John J. Staley, president of the railway company, he even invented his own "Pete Witt car," which was adopted by other cities as well as by Cleveland. Witt's extension of the transit lines onto Euclid Avenue, against the protests of its wealthy residents, and his attempt to reduce fares to two tickets for five cents under the Tayler Ordinance formula were more in keeping with Johnson's approach to the traction issue. Witt was not a transportation expert when he was appointed street railway commissioner, but he became one in office and later served as a transit consultant to Philadelphia, Seattle, and Boston.[15]

During the Johnson administration, Cleveland acquired two small municipal lighting plants by annexing neighboring villages. Under Baker, the city built a large municipal lighting plant that had been authorized in a November 1911 referendum.[16] Municipal light rates were to serve as a yardstick for the private Cleveland Illuminating Company, which continued to supply electricity to most residents. The private company's rates of six to seven cents per kilowatt hour were forced down, first by competition with the municipal three-cent rate, and then by a city ordinance setting three cents as the maximum rate for privately produced power. The municipal lighting plant was run without the inefficiencies, labor conflict, or apparent conflict of interest that had plagued the semipublic Municipal Traction Company under Johnson. Baker, moreover, declined to begin an all-out war between the city and the Illuminating Company. He approved the company's application to supply heat to downtown buildings, for example, arguing that it would be many years before the city could provide the heat itself, and that the city should not throttle private development because it might someday occupy the field. Though he disapproved of the company's high rates and political activities, Baker said, he was not willing to cripple the city or business in the contest. In defense of his position, he cited Johnson's extension of Cleveland Railway grants as evidence of a similar attitude.[17]

The new meaning of municipal ownership under Baker fit with a trans-formation of reform ideology. Johnson had understood reform within the context of the Single Tax. Baker had never been as enthusiastic an adherent of the theories of Henry George.[18] He endorsed the Single Tax as a member of Johnson's cabinet, but as mayor he emphasized instead his own conception of "civitism." This was the equivalent of patriotism at the municipal level. As explained by Baker's biographer, "Baker believed that the greatness of a city did not depend on its buildings, either public or private, but rather on the intensity with which its citizens loved the city as their home. Such a pervasive feeling would inevitably produce beautiful parks, cleaner streets, honest government, and widespread adherence to justice as the ideal of its social and economic life."[19] The cultural dimension of civitism was illustrated by the appropriation of ten thousand dollars for a municipal orchestra, including three thousand for the salary of its German conductor. This expenditure was controversial.[20] But as an ideology, civitism was consensual. No particular group was threatened, and none was excluded from the broad political coalition implied in Baker's vision. Baker even opposed the racial segregation of municipal recreational facilities, at a time when the nation's leading intellectuals endorsed the spread of Jim Crow.[21]

THE CLEVELAND FOUNDATION AND THE CIVIC LEAGUE

By moderating conflict over municipal ownership and inventing the ideology of civitism, Baker made it possible for the administration to work with outside experts without either traditional reformers or municipal populists feeling betrayed. He thus created an environment in which the Cleveland Foundation could be formed and the Municipal Association reshaped into the Civic League. Both organizations were designed for cooperation and consensus, with financial and governmental structures that fit the democratic mold. Although the Cleveland Foundation and the Civic League preferred to portray themselves as belonging to the whole community, they remained particularly dependent on business support. Staff members with professional training and orientations, working closely with the Baker administration, were nonetheless able to shape the agendas of these organizations.

The Cleveland Foundation was organized in 1914 by Frederick H. Goff, who had represented the ConCon in negotiations with Johnson. Goff was president of the Cleveland Trust Company, which, together with city officials, appointed the board of the Cleveland Foundation. This arrangement gave the organization a semipublic character, as did its decision to appeal to the entire community, and not just wealthy industrialists, for support. Baker praised the Cleveland Foundation for preaching the "gospel of opportunities, rather than wealth"; Witt and Cooley were also very favorable. Throughout the nation, the Cleveland Foundation replaced the older, self-perpetuating board as a model of the charitable trust.[22]

The new Foundation played a central role in Cleveland's response to the nationwide depression of 1914–15. In November 1914, the Cleveland Labor Exchange and the City Council Committee on Labor collected data estimating that 61,000 workers were unemployed.[23] In December, the Cleveland Foundation's survey committee, directed by Allen T. Burns, a social worker, criticized outdoor relief and other aspects of the city's welfare system. Baker responded by appointing a Citizens' Relief Commission, with Goff as chairman and Burns as secretary. In its "Hire-a-Hand" campaign, the Commission urged employers to create jobs. But it also went further, raising eighty-six thousand dollars for work relief through a highly publicized appeal. Burns, Goff, and the Commission pursued their appeal despite the protests of private charities who feared that their applications would increase and that their own fund-raising efforts would suffer. Under the work relief program, the unemployed were offered five days work, at five hours a day and seventeen and a half cents an hour.

As in New York, immediate relief was emphasized over long-term solutions. Yet there were important differences between the Citizens' Relief Commission in Cleveland and the Mayor's Committee in New York, discussed in Chapter 5. Though far below prevailing wages in both cities, the rate of pay was higher in Cleveland than in New York. Public works were subsidized in Cleveland, and Baker authorized an excavation project that had not been planned until spring; in New York, Comptroller William A. Prendergast had blocked the release of public works funds. Finally, Goff, unlike Judge Elbert Gary of the New York committee, admitted that the response to unemployment had been inadequate.

During the Baker administration, the Municipal Association was reorganized to give freer reign to expertise. The changes began in 1910, before Baker's election, when Mayo Fesler was hired as the organization's first permanent full-time secretary. Fesler did graduate and undergraduate work in political science and history at the University of Chicago and taught political science at Indiana University for one year. He then served as secretary to the Civic League of St. Louis. Under Fesler, the Municipal Association stopped endorsing candidates for mayor, citing "the practice of the leading non-partisan associations of the country," and the availability of many other sources of voter information. The *Bulletin of the Municipal Association* had been issued irregularly, usually at election time; it was replaced by a quarterly *Municipal Bulletin* that included administrative studies by Fesler and other experts, local and imported. In

1913, the organization adopted a new constitution that replaced the self-perpetuating fifty-member general committee with an elected executive board of twelve. A new dues structure, varying by ability to pay, was established. The new constitution also changed the name of the organization to the Civic League. As Fesler explained, the original name was often shortened to "Muny," causing confusion with the many municipally owned projects. Moreover, the work of the group had come to encompass county as well as city affairs. All of these changes were pushed by Fesler, at times against the opposition of some members. In April 1912, for example, he urged that the *Bulletin* provide only a statement of facts about the upcoming county nominations but was instructed to prepare the usual preprimary endorsements.[24]

Though its new policy prevented it from making endorsements, the Municipal Association was sympathetic to Baker after 1911. In a 1914 report, for example, it largely absolved him of blame for Cleveland's dangerous financial condition. Baker was criticized for failing to maintain the city's sinking funds and for not liquidating debts as they came due. The Civic League, however, accepted the administration's claims that Cleveland spent no more than comparable cities, that further retrenchment was impossible, and that the real cause of the crisis was the stringent limit on local taxation imposed by state law.[25]

CHARTER REFORM

Fesler and his organization worked closely with Baker in winning home rule for Cleveland and in drafting and passing the actual charter. The Municipal Association Constitutional Home Rule for Cities Committee began seeking changes in the state constitution in 1910. The committee originally included Baker and was chaired by Augustus R. Hatton, the Marcus A. Hanna Professor of Political Science at Western Reserve University. In January 1912, the Municipal Association sponsored a Conference of Ohio Municipalities, which called for passage of a home rule amendment at the state Constitutional Convention that was to meet that month. The conference established a permanent Ohio League of Municipalities, with Baker as president and Fesler as secretary. Baker lobbied for home rule at the Constitutional Convention, and the Convention approved an amendment that Baker, Fesler, and Hatton had presented at a meeting of the League of Municipalities. The amendment allowed cities to choose between mayoral (Federal Plan), commission, or council-manager government in drafting their own charters, although the state continued to restrict cities' fiscal autonomy. The home rule amendment, along with the forty-seven other amendments approved by the Convention, was then submitted to the voters. Baker campaigned for the amendment throughout the state. The Civic League made no recommendations on most of the amendments but endorsed home rule and the merit system. The home rule amendment, approved statewide, carried Cleveland by a vote of 52,287 to 7,744 and won a large majority in every ward.[26]

For the city to enact a charter under the home rule amendment, it was necessary that the voters both authorize the selection of a charter commission and elect its members. After the state home rule amendment had been enacted, Baker appointed a nominating committee to select a slate of fifteen candidates for the charter commission. The nominees, known as the Non-partisan slate, included Baker and Hatton. No Socialists were named, but otherwise the slate was broadly representative. Nonetheless, a second slate was nominated by the Progressive Constitution League. The League adopted a detailed platform calling for nonpartisan elections; initiative and referendum votes; recall of elected and appointed officials; the Federal Plan of government; and a council of no more than nine members, elected at large. Five members of the Non-partisan slate who agreed to these provisions were included on the League's list. The remaining members of the Non-partisan slate refused to be bound by the platform. Baker himself accepted four of the League proposals but disagreed with changing the form of the council and believed that only elected officials should be subject to recall. The Socialist party proposed its own slate, but it was rejected by the board of elections on technical grounds. The Socialists were the only organized opposition to the authorization of a charter commission: they claimed that the charter was a "businessmen's deal." At the election, held on February 4, 1913, establishment of the charter commission was approved, 19,125 to 5,218. All fifteen members of the Non-partisan slate, including the five jointly nominated by the Progressive Constitution League, were elected.[27] Mayo Fesler, nominated by Baker, was elected secretary of the charter commission by a 9–4 vote. Four League nominees voted against Fesler; the fifth was absent. Fesler, drawing upon his connections with the national movement for urban reform, provided the commission with tables showing charter provisions in other cities and with the results of questionnaires sent to municipal officials throughout the country.[28]

The influence of Fesler and Baker probably explains why city-manager government, then coming into vogue, was given little attention by the charter commission. In a speech given before the Cleveland Council of Sociology in October 1912, Fesler outlined four general principles of municipal government: a clear distinction between political and administrative functions; broad and direct representation; fixed responsibility in the administrative departments; and expert and permanent service. He was less critical of the city-manager form than of commission government but believed that the Federal Plan of mayoral government was closest to the four principles. "I do not mean to say," Fesler told the council,

that this form of government as outlined is going to be the cure-all. No form will be. It is only the machinery which must be operated by an intelligent and active public opinion. All that I claim for the form is that it has the fewest possible number of levers and brakes to manipulate and it has the self sparking attachment which will not require the operator, the people, to get out and crank it up every time there is a lull in its speed.

Baker also opposed city-manager government: city officials, he believed, were more directly responsible to the people under the mayoral system. The key resolution establishing the Federal Plan, empowering the mayor to appoint the directors of departments, was approved unanimously by the charter commission.[29]

The major debate within the charter commission was between advocates of a small council, elected at large, and members who wanted a large council elected by ward. (Under the existing system, twenty-six wards each elected one councilman, and six more were elected at large.) Proponents of a small, at-large council claimed that members would be less parochial and less susceptible to domination by ward bosses. The Chamber of Commerce was among the groups endorsing these arguments. Defenders of the ward system responded that at-large elections were contrary to the principle of the short ballot and would deprive minorities of representation. Michael P. Mooney, for example, argued that Catholics, though one-third of the city, would not be able to elect any members of an at-large school board. D. C. Westenhaver, a close associate of Baker, argued that at-large elections would exclude the growing number of Socialists, increasing their class consciousness, distrust, and misunderstanding, while representation would soften their views through close contact and better acquaintance with the majority. Baker consistently voted in favor of a large ward council, while Fesler had argued in his Council of Sociology address that a small, at-large council violated the principle of representation. Fesler recognized that such a council was modeled on the private corporation but pointed out that "the advocates forget that there is a distinct difference between the two forms of corporation—one is financial, the other political—the one is for profit, the other for service." After a number of shifts, the commission voted 8–5 in favor of Daniel E. Morgan's proposal for a twenty-six member council elected by ward; the six at-large seats were abolished.[30]

There was little disagreement within the charter commission over the nonpartisan ballot, which had been endorsed by both slates in the commission election. The majority, Baker argued, wished to vote for a party in national elections but for individuals at the local level. Hence, elections should be separated. The commission unanimously approved nonpartisanship, but it was opposed by both the Democratic and the Socialist parties. Parties, the Socialists argued, represented class interests, and class interests were at stake in local as well as national elections; only social revolution would eliminate class conflict. Preferential voting for mayor and council, introduced by Hatton, aroused more controversy within the commission but was approved, 13–2. Under the new system, voters would mark their first three choices. If no candidate had a majority of the first-choice votes, second-choice votes would be added to the totals. The candidate with the highest total would then be elected, if the combined total was more than 50 percent of the first-place votes cast for all candidates. If no candidate had a majority on the second ballot, third-choice votes would be counted in the same way. Only if no candidate had a majority on the third ballot could a candidate be elected without the approval of more than half the voters. Proponents argued that this system provided the truest representation of popular opinion, but W. Burr Gongwer, chief clerk of the board of elections, complained that it was designed to give "high-browed political scientists" a chance to try out their own "cloister-made notions of political government."[31]

Baker and Fesler led the fight for approval of the proposed charter.[32] Baker won the Democratic party's endorsement for the charter despite its nonpartisan provisions. The Civic League also endorsed the charter, and Fesler wrote twenty articles explaining it for the *Plain Dealer*. Opposition to the charter was led by Robert McKisson, who said it would make the mayor more powerful than an absolute monarch. (He would have known: as discussed in Chapter 6, McKisson, while mayor, had tried to use the centralized authority of the earlier Federal Plan to build a citywide machine.) On July 1, 1913, the charter was approved, 24,083 to 12,090. In August 1914, voters approved a charter amendment withdrawing laborers from civil service, 17,149 to 16,582, but rejected an amendment that would have restored partisan nominations and elections, 16,691 to 17,324. The Civic League had opposed both amendments.

The 1913 City Charter, then, embodied Baker's alliance with Fesler and the Civic League, just as the city's unemployment policies embodied Baker's ties to Burns and Goff. The new relationship between experts and city government was institutionalized in the City Club, formed in 1912 for nonpartisan discussion of public issues. Fesler, who had organized such a club in St. Louis, initiated the proposal and served as secretary. Hatton was an early supporter; the Chamber of Commerce, in contrast, was initially unenthusiastic. Baker was a charter member of the City Club and used its forum to defend appropriations for the municipal orchestra. The most important discussions on the city charter also took place at the Club.

The City Club demonstrated its independence from business by allowing Socialists to speak from its platforms despite protests from some of its members.[33]

THE ELECTION OF 1913

The mayoral elections of 1913 and 1915 showed the impact of these new arrangements, and the policies they generated, on voting patterns. The election of 1913 was the first held under the new, nonpartisan preferential voting system.[34] Baker's major opponent was Harry L. Davis, a Maschke protégé. Davis's campaign, Baker later complained, showed little regard for accuracy in its figures or remarks. Davis focused on the condition of the streets, Baker's intellectualism, and the Democratic party's alleged control by an Irish machine. Baker received a first-choice plurality with 41,286 votes to 36,126 for Davis but was only elected when second-choice votes were counted. The closeness of the election was a surprise to Baker and other observers, including the oddsmakers who had predicted that Baker would be elected by six to eight thousand votes on first-choice votes alone.

According to Frederic C. Howe, Baker's margin of victory was less than in 1911 because of defections by Democratic politicians opposed to the nonpartisan charter. Wards considered Democratic, the *Plain Dealer* reported, voted for Davis, while wards considered Republican voted for Baker. Estimated transition rates from 1911 to 1913 first-choice votes suggest that Davis did attract between 17 and 39 percent of Baker's 1911 supporters, as well as 50 to 75 percent of the Hogen vote. Baker offset this loss by winning 20 to 50 percent of 1911 Hogen voters, while retaining 45 to 65 percent of his 1911 support. This pattern of electoral change might reflect abstentions by partisan Democrats or the difficulty working-class voters faced in making choices without the partisan cues to which they were accustomed.

Following his election, Baker thanked Czech, German, Greek, and Jewish community leaders or newspaper editors for their backing, and Table 8-2 shows that he received ethnic support in 1913. Baker did better than Davis among Czech, German, Hungarian, Irish, and possibly Russian voters, although Davis received more Polish support.[35] The abolition of party labels may have encouraged native-stock voters to support Baker, since they could now do so without voting Democratic. He did better among native-stock voters than he or Johnson had done in earlier elections, and may have even won a plurality of their vote. He can thus be said to have constructed a progressive coalition that combined ethnic and

TABLE 8-2
Voting Behavior by Ethnic Group, 1913

	Davis %	Baker %
Czech	36–50	50–68
German	0	100
Hungarian	0	9–50
Irish	100	100
Native	14–24	22–28
Polish	24–50	16–50
Russian	19–50	23–50

Notes: Suburbanization and illiteracy variables set at mean values. First-choice votes for both candidates.
N = 26.

native-stock support.[36] As in 1911, suburbanization was more strongly associated with support for Baker's opponent than for Baker, but the difference was small.

THE ELECTION OF 1915

In December 1914, Baker announced that he would not seek reelection.[37] Despite the opposition of organizational politicians, Witt won the endorsement of Baker and the Democratic party. Six other candidates appeared on the 1915 ballot. Harry L. Davis and Miner G. Norton represented the Maschke and McKisson factions of the Republican party; efforts to convince one or both to drop out in order to unify the Republican vote were unsuccessful. Charles Salen, the former organizational Democrat who had been appointed deputy tax commissioner by a Republican governor, and Charles Ruthenberg, the local Socialist leader, also sought the mayoralty.[38]

In his campaign pamphlets and in debates with Norton and Davis, Witt defended the record of the Baker and Johnson administrations. Like Johnson, he responded to demands for economy by pressing his opponents to specify the cuts they would make.[39] Witt refused to debate Ruthenberg, who demanded immediate municipal ownership of streetcar lines. Witt and his supporters defended the Tayler Ordinance (which Witt had originally opposed), pointed out that existing state laws would add 600,000 dollars per year to the cost of a takeover, and criticized the Socialists for hypocrisy in demanding municipal ownership after they had ridiculed

Johnson's traction battles as irrelevant to the needs of the working class.[40] Witt also rejected demands from Georgeites that he base his campaign upon the Single Tax.[41]

Though Witt emphasized his own background as a molder, some unions opposed him because of his ambivalent attitude toward city workers: he had gone against the motormen in speeding up the transit schedule and wrote a fireman that he opposed service pensions unless they could be granted to all members of the industrial army.[42] Witt undercut his own efforts to draw support from a variety of ethnic groups when he told a German audience that he was against war, but if he had to choose sides he would favor the Kaiser. These remarks were criticized in much of the Slavic press.[43] Witt expected victory and many supporters congratulated him in advance.[44] He received 39,835 first-place votes to 36,841 for Davis, 14,271 for Norton, 6,014 for Ruthenberg, and 5,801 for Salen. Fatally, however, Witt had told the public he wanted only first-choice votes.[45] He received fewer second- and third-choice votes than the four other major candidates and Davis was elected on the third choice, with a total of 47,697 to 44,912 for Witt. Neither candidate obtained a majority of the total vote. Witt's view was that he "was beaten by a progressive idea, the preferential ballot law. . . . Being of our own creation, I must not criticise very much."[46] Baker privately emphasized the impact of Witt's remarks about the war on Eastern European voters.[47]

Table 8-3 gives the estimated transition rates from 1913 to 1915. Estimates are shown for the 1915 Witt, Davis, Norton, and Salen first-choice votes. Davis was able to attract part of Baker's 1913 vote; Witt, in contrast, received none of the 1913 Davis vote. Norton drew about as large a share of the 1913 Davis vote as Davis himself did, suggesting that a large proportion of the Republican electorate, which had had only one candidate in 1913, was still sympathetic to McKissonites. As Witt predicted, Salen's candidacy probably drew more votes from Davis and Norton than it did from him.[48]

TABLE 8-3
Transition Rates, 1913–1915

1913	1915			
	Davis %	Norton %	Salen %	Witt %
Davis	34–50	40	8–12	0
Baker	31–45	0	4–7	48–96

Note: First–choice votes for each candidate.
N = 26.

TABLE 8-4
Voting Behavior by Ethnic Group, 1915

	Davis %	Norton %	Salen %	Witt %
Czech	100	0	0	21–50
German	0	0	4–35	100
Hungarian	0	4–50	3–30	31–50
Irish	100	0	35–50	100
Native	21–25	10–13	0	10–27
Polish	35–50	7–50	0	19–50
Russian	27–50	0	0	8–50

Notes: Suburbanization and illiteracy variables set at mean values. First-choice votes for each candidate.
$N = 26$.

Witt's comments about the war seem to have been the source of the shift in reform support from 1913 to 1915. Table 8-4 presents estimates of ethnic group voting for the four leading candidates. Czech and possibly Russian voters preferred Baker over Davis in 1913, but both groups voted for Davis over Witt in 1915. Davis's margin among Polish voters was greater in 1915 than in 1913, and he probably also regained a plurality of the native-stock vote. German, Hungarian, and Irish voters, all sympathetic to the Central Powers, were strong for Witt. The estimate of the suburbanization coefficient for Witt was greater than that for Davis, but suburbanization was most strongly associated with support for Norton and Salen.

Like Mayor John Purroy Mitchel in New York, Baker showed that traditional reform and municipal populist opposition to organizational politics could be brought together. Baker, moreover, was able to expand his coalition while in office and win reelection in 1913. Baker's approach to policy, based on civic idealism and expert knowledge, differed from that of Johnson, with its ideological commitment to municipal ownership. But Baker's approach also differed from the business emphasis on economy implemented by Mitchel. Both Baker's and Mitchel's electoral coalitions ultimately dissolved, but the reasons for Witt's defeat in 1915 seem incidental rather than intrinsic to Baker's politics. In Cleveland, as in New York and Chicago, the First World War made coalition formation more difficult by creating new conflicts among groups who could previously ally. Cleveland politics was further complicated by the peculiar preferential voting system. Under single-ballot voting, Witt would have been elected in 1915. Instead, the election of 1915 marked the end of the reform succession and the dissolution of the progressive coalition constructed under Baker.

THE PERSISTENCE OF MUNICIPAL POPULISM

Municipal populism survived Peter Witt's defeat in the election of 1915 to continue as an independent force in Cleveland politics. Witt's failure to preserve Newton Baker's progressive coalition, however, meant that municipal populists and traditional reformers would fight their fiercest battles against each other, with each side calling upon its own set of experts. The persistence of municipal populism in Cleveland contrasts with its disappearance in New York and Chicago. The municipal populist revolt against machine politics in New York ended with the defeat of John Purroy Mitchel. The ethnic, working-class voters who had supported William Randolph Hearst and other municipal populist candidates were eventually incorporated into Fiorello La Guardia's rebuilt progressive coalition with the help of experts whose political learning dated back to the Mitchel era. In Chicago, as the next part of this book shows, experts allied with traditional reformers and never developed an institutional base independent of those reformers' political fortunes; that city's municipal populist vote was ultimately absorbed by a newly consolidated Democratic machine.

Witt remained the leader of Cleveland's municipal populists until his death in 1948. As local manager of Robert La Follette's 1924 presidential campaign, he carried the city for the third-party candidate. The next year, Witt began his "town meetings," at which paying customers heard him "skin the skunks," denouncing all whom he considered enemies of the people. Like Frederic C. Howe, but unlike Newton Baker or Toledo's Brand Whitlock, Witt became a fervent New Dealer.[49] Witt was also the foremost member of the "Soviet Table," a core group of municipal populists that met for lunch at the City Club. The Soviet Table worked against city-manager and metropolitan government, opposed construction of the Union Terminal and the Municipal Stadium, and fought plans for development of the waterfront. Mayo Fesler of the Civic League, which had been renamed the Citizens League, criticized the group as defeatist and irreconcilable. Jack Raper, a member of the Soviet Table, replied by describing the League as "a tool of privilege, without the confidence of the great mass of voters[,] and its pronouncements are without influence except among the fawning and the gullible." Two distinct lines of thought, Raper wrote, had emerged, "one line represented by the Citizens' League and Chamber of Commerce and the other by those whom Mr. Fesler calls 'political mal-contents.'"[50]

The conflict between the traditional reform views of Fesler and the Citizens League and the municipal populism of Witt, Raper, and the Soviet Table contributed to a pattern of instability exemplified by Cleveland's experiment with the city-manager system. Though Harry Davis imitated Tom Johnson by issuing pamphlets detailing his policy achievements, the main effect of his election as mayor over Witt in 1915, and his reelection in 1917 and 1919, was the restoration of patronage politics under Maurice Maschke's Republican organization.[51] Fesler and the League responded by supporting a shift to the city-manager system they had opposed in 1913; Witt also supported the switch. A city-manager charter written by Augustus Hatton was finally approved in 1921, making Cleveland the largest city to adopt the manager plan.[52] Designed to rid Cleveland of bossism, city-manager government was in fact dominated by the combination of Maschke, as leader of the Republicans, and W. Burr Gongwer, who had emerged as leader of the Democrats: William R. Hopkins, the first city manager, took office after Maschke and Gongwer agreed to a 60–40 division of patronage. Witt became the leading opponent of Hopkins and the city-manager plan. In 1931, two members of the Soviet Table—Saul Danaceau, a former student of Hatton, and Edward Doty, a member of the 1913 charter commission—joined with Davis, who had broken with Maschke, to win repeal of the city-manager plan despite its continued support by traditional reformers. Davis regained the restored mayoralty in 1933.[53]

The somewhat delayed effect of the New Deal was to stabilize Cleveland politics. Beginning with the election of Frank Lausche in 1941, a series of ethnic Democrats served as mayor, remaining in office until they moved up to state or national positions, when they were replaced by their law directors. The Republican party ceased to be competitive in municipal politics.[54] This New Deal system of city politics lasted until the civil rights revolt of the 1960s, to which can be traced the election of Carl Stokes, Cleveland's first black mayor, in 1967; of Ralph J. Perk, a conservative Republican backed by white ethnics, in 1971; and of Michael White, chosen over George Forbes in the black-versus-black mayoral election of 1989.[55]

The mayoral administration of Dennis J. Kucinich, who defeated Perk in 1977, showed that for all the changes wrought by the New Deal and the 1960s, municipal populism remained a factor in Cleveland politics. In many ways, Kucinich's administration paralleled that of Tom Johnson.[56] Each was elected by an initial coalition that followed earlier political cleavages, then introduced policies that triggered electoral change. Each depended upon white ethnic support. Johnson had been indifferent to black voters; Kucinich made racial appeals directed against them. Both mayors granted authority to experts and quasi-experts with training outside business or government.[57] Johnson tried to prevent private interests from controlling downtown development by supporting the Group Plan; Kucinich, by opposing tax abatements. Kucinich's efforts to preserve

MUNY Light, the municipal light company that was itself a survival from the Progressive Era, resembled Johnson's battle with the ConCon. Johnson's fight for the three-cent fare had led to a disastrous street railway strike; Kucinich's rejection of bankers' demands that the city sell MUNY Light brought Cleveland into default. Kucinich himself laid a wreath at Johnson's statue after voters approved retention of the light company in a referendum.

Of course, there are limits to the parallels. Johnson, unlike Kucinich, won the mayoralty after personal economic success that gained him some business support. Johnson also achieved more electoral success than Kucinich, who narrowly survived a recall vote only to lose to George Voinovich in the regular election of 1979. Blacks, about 1.5 percent of Cleveland's population in Johnson's day, were 38 percent of the city in Kucinich's.[58] And no Newton Baker was able to broaden Kucinich's municipal populist base.

But the conflict between municipal populists and traditional reformers, each allied with their own experts, that characterized both the pre–New Deal years and the Kucinich administration can only be understood as a consequence of the politics of the Progressive Era. It was during that period that experts were incorporated into the political system. It was during that period as well that a reform coalition which built upon the role of experts in policy formation was both constructed and torn apart. A Dennis Kucinich as mayor, consciously challenging the supposed imperatives of economic growth, would be an unlikely political aberration in New York, Chicago, or most other American cities. In Cleveland, however, he was only a reminder of the ways the outcomes of the Progressive Era have influenced subsequent politics and policy.

Part IV

CHICAGO: THE FAILURE OF PROGRESSIVISM

It was to be expected that the big Standard Oil university at
Chicago, founded by Rockefeller, would soon begin to bear fruit
after its kind. Whatever the Rockefeller employes [*sic*] down there
may know about other subjects, they certainly know the value of
special privileges and have well digested the moral to be drawn
from a careful study of the crooked course of the Standard Oil
serpent. This so-called university is but an outpost of plutocracy,
scientific humbugery and general total depravity. Its main business
is to send forth shafts of impenetrable darkness and to obscure and
to blot out the few Jeffersonian stars which still twinkle, during the
eclipse of democracy, in our intellectual firmament.
W. F. *Cooling*, The Chicago Democracy

DIFFERENCES BETWEEN reform outcomes in New York and Cleveland are
dwarfed by the contrast between either city and Chicago. Between 1896
and 1917, Cleveland was governed by reform administrations for twelve
years, New York for six. During the same period, it was only in the two-
year term of Edward F. Dunne that Chicago had a mayor elected by a
reform constituency. In New York and Cleveland, John Purroy Mitchel
and Newton Baker fused traditional reform and municipal populist support to form a widely inclusive and winning progressive coalition. No such
coalition captured any Chicago mayoral election. The politics of the Progressive Era in New York made possible the bureaucratization of the New
Deal. In Cleveland, a municipal populist tradition survived the Progressive Era to ally with a newer urban liberalism during the 1930s. The New
Deal did not make Chicago either radical or bureaucratic. It became instead the epitome of the machine city, both in political science and in
popular belief.

Underlying these contrasts are similarities that make it possible to explain why politics turned out so differently in Chicago both in the short
and the long run. Like New York and Cleveland, Chicago had identifiable
traditional reform and municipal populist constituencies during the Pro-

gressive Era. Dunne and John Peter Altgeld can be compared to William Randolph Hearst or Tom Johnson, who also relied on municipal populist support in New York and Cleveland, respectively. Similarly, John Maynard Harlan, the frequent candidate of Chicago's traditional reform voters, can be compared with New York's Seth Low or William Ivins and Cleveland's Harvey Goulder or Theodore Burton. Political cleavages in Chicago, as in New York and Cleveland, were more fluid than those portrayed in most studies of the Progressive Era.

In Chicago as in the other two cities, patterns of electoral support were linked to the incorporation of experts into city politics. Settlement social workers campaigned against ward bosses, professors conducted investigations, and a municipal research bureau was organized. The incorporation of expertise culminated in 1911 with the nomination of Charles E. Merriam, a University of Chicago political scientist, as the Republican candidate for mayor. Like Mitchel or Baker, Merriam sought to broaden the pattern of reform support by combining the municipal populist constituency with adherents of traditional reform.

Still, Mitchel and Baker won their initial elections by wide margins, while Merriam was defeated by Carter Harrison II. Merriam's inability to construct a winning electoral coalition reflected the pattern of organizational party politics and the incorporation of expertise. The fragmentation that characterized Chicago's major parties meant that Merriam was more vulnerable to the defection of ward leaders than his counterparts in other cities. And while experts did enter Chicago politics in new roles, reform politics was not transformed as completely as in New York or Cleveland.

Chicago political history has often been treated as a teleology, with all events leading to the inevitable domination of Anton Cermak and Richard J. Daley. Yet to perceptive observers of the Progressive Era, Chicago was the model for reform success.[1] As of 1897, Chicago's party organizations were weaker, and the reform opposition stronger, than in New York or Cleveland. Chicago party organizations were able to draw upon foreign-stock support, but ethnic and governmental fragmentation prevented them from consolidating their power. Hence, the Chicago organizations were more decentralized than those of the other two cities: ward leaders, not a citywide machine or even factional blocs, were sovereign. Cohesion among Chicago's economic elite allowed its members to form a series of traditional reform organizations, culminating with the establishment of the Municipal Voters' League in 1896. Since Chicago was a young city, its elite was not divided between old and new money as in New York. The Chicago elite was also less tied to the national Republican party than the Cleveland elite of Mark Hanna. Chicago's municipal populists had never waged an electoral campaign as threatening to the elite as the Henry George campaign in New York, but they had been more organized than their counterparts in Cleveland. In New York, Tammany had incorporated Irish George voters into its clubs, but municipal populist traditions continued among the Chicago Irish. Together, municipal populist and traditional reform voters could have overwhelmed the fragmented party organizations.

A Chicago mayoral candidate backed by such a coalition might have won election by as wide a margin as Mitchel did in New York and held power for as long as Johnson and Baker did in Cleveland. The policies of a progressive mayor might have drawn on the concentration of experts around the University of Chicago. With bases of support among all classes and ethnic groups, Chicago reform might have even been able to survive the aggravation of ethnic tensions by the First World War. Postwar machine builders would not have been able to draw support from the new-stock ethnic groups, for these voters would have been incorporated into the reform coalition. Had it been possible to construct a progressive coalition, Chicago might have remained the paradigm of the reform city, rather than become the paradigm of the machine. The main question of the next three chapters, therefore, is, why was it not possible to form a progressive coalition in Chicago? Why are the above scenarios hypothetical rather than historical? Table IV-1 summarizes the elections covered.

Parts II and III of the book explained the shifting electoral patterns of

TABLE IV-1
Chicago Mayoral Elections, 1897–1911

Year	Traditional Reform	Municipal Populist	Progressive Coalition	Organization Candidates	Socialist Party
1897	Harlan			**Harrison** Sears Hesing	
1899		Altgeld		**Harrison** Carter	
1901				**Harrison** Hanecy	Hoyt
1903		Cruice		**Harrison** Stewart	Breckon
1905	Harlan	**Dunne**			Collins
1907		Dunne		**Busse**	Koop
1911	Merriam			**Harrison**	Rodriguez

Note: Winning candidate in **bold**.

New York and Cleveland in terms of the incorporation of expertise and explained the incorporation of expertise in terms of the behavior of individuals who wanted to be mayor as they confronted particular patterns of organizational politics. Carter Harrison II was as important to the course of reform in Chicago as Robert McKisson was in Cleveland or George McClellan was in New York and more successful than either: Harrison served as mayor from 1897 to 1905, and again from 1911 to 1915. Chapter 9 explores Harrison's relationships with experts and with ward leaders in the context of Chicago's class and ethnic conflicts and its fragmented party politics. In tracing the patterns of electoral support for Harrison, I pay particular attention to the elections of 1897, when he defeated Harlan, and 1899, when he defeated Altgeld. Harrison was replaced by Dunne in 1905; Chapter 10 analyzes Dunne's electoral support and the policies of his administration, including the demand for municipal ownership and the drafting of a home rule charter. Dunne was defeated in 1907 by Fred Busse, during whose administration Merriam became a major political actor. Chapter 11 relates the course of reform under Busse to patterns of support in the election of 1911. I conclude my discussion of Chicago reform by examining the linkages between reform outcomes and the developments that gave Chicago politics its modern form: the rise of William Hale Thompson within the Republican party and the formation of a citywide Democratic machine.

CHAPTER 9.

Carter Harrison versus Reform

LIKE NEW YORK and Cleveland, Chicago during the Progressive Era had party organizations, traditional reform, and municipal populism. Two key differences during this period were that Chicago party organizations could not be consolidated, and that traditional reform and municipal populist voters could not be brought together to form a progressive coalition. The connection between these two characteristics can be located in the person of the most successful politician of Progressive Era Chicago, Carter Harrison II. Edward R. Kantowicz aptly describes Harrison, the winner in five of the seven mayoral elections held from 1897 to 1911, as a master practitioner of "the politics of balance."[1] In the context of Chicago's fragmented organizational politics, the constant formation of new coalitions of ward bosses was a more important component of Harrison's balancing strategies than the incorporation of expertise. Because Harrison did not bring experts into city politics, they could not provide the link between traditional reform and municipal populism that had made progressive coalitions possible in New York and Cleveland.

PARTY FACTIONALISM AND BOODLE

Power within the Chicago party system was decentralized. Efforts to consolidate control were frustrated by governmental fragmentation: Cook County, the Sanitary District, the Lincoln, South, and West Park Boards, and, until 1901, townships responsible for tax assessment remained outside the control of City Hall, giving refuge and patronage to defeated politicians.[2] Alliances among the factions changed rapidly, frequently (though usually surreptitiously) crossing party lines. Within the Democratic party, ward leaders such as John Powers of the Nineteenth Ward and "Bathhouse" John Coughlin and Michael "Hinky Dink" Kenna of the "flophouse" First Ward were independent of external control, providing allegiance to whatever city or county slate seemed likely to help them maintain their own political strength and economic interests.[3] Carter Harrison I, elected mayor five times between 1879 and 1893, used personal popularity and ethnic appeals to aggregate support, but he did not create a durable organization. Conflict among Democratic ward leaders resumed during Harrison's temporary withdrawals from electoral competition, and after his assassination.[4] Organizational support for Carter Harrison II was also unstable. By 1905, the younger Harrison had split with most of his early allies, including Robert E. Burke and Joseph S. Martin, who had been crucial to his 1897 nomination. Usually opposed to the Harrisons was the West Side organization of Roger Sullivan and John Hopkins.[5] As Gold Democrats, the Hopkins-Sullivan faction bolted the party in 1896 and ran their own ticket in the municipal election of 1897. The Republicans were organized into more cohesive factions, but none could expand beyond its territorial base. Thus, during the 1900s, William Lorimer was dominant on the West Side, Fred Busse on the North Side, and Charles S. Deneen on the South Side.[6]

Organizational aldermen, termed "gray wolves" by their opponents, occupied most of the city council seats until the late 1890s. The most common forms of "boodle" were systematized, with one hundred dollars charged for an alley ordinance and twenty-five thousand for a railway franchise. Powers organized these activities and distributed the money received among the aldermen. Along with the Harrisons' intraparty opponents, Sullivan and Hopkins, Powers also participated in "sand bagging," by which they awarded franchises to their own fictitious companies with little compensation to the city. The existing utility monopolies would then be forced to buy out the new firms or face competition.[7]

TRADITIONAL REFORM AND MUNICIPAL POPULISM

The gray wolves' control over the city council was ended by the Municipal Voters' League, the most electorally oriented of a series of traditional reform associations. The Citizens' Association was formed in 1874 in response to an insurance embargo of the city, which remained flammable even after recovery from the Great Fire of 1871. The Association succeeded in enacting a citywide ban on wooden buildings and reorganizing the fire department to the satisfaction of the insurance companies. It then turned to charter reform and the prevention of electoral fraud; in the view of the Association's president, Franklin McVeagh, universal male suffrage in municipal elections was "an immoderate fancy."[8] The Union League Club, formed in 1879 to promote a third term for President Ulysses Grant, also became involved in electoral regulation. Its political action committee lobbied for stricter registration and offered rewards for the apprehension of illegal voters.[9] The Civic Federation of Chicago was organized by William T. Stead, an English journalist, in 1893. During his visit to the United States, Stead also wrote *If Christ Came to Chicago*, a wide-ranging exposé that revealed boodle practices, criticized the dangerous conditions on Charles Yerkes's street railways, blamed prostitution on the low wages paid women workers, and called for "a firm fighting alliance [between] the forces of organized labor and the forces of organized Christianity." Stead's book helped to publicize the Civic Federation, but the organization soon took a narrower approach to social problems, focusing on the drive for civil service.[10]

In January 1896, after the city council had approved sand-bag ordinances for the Cosmopolitan Electric and Ogden Gas companies, the political action committee of the Civic Federation invited representatives of other reform groups to a conference. A committee of fifteen, appointed to consider alternative courses of action, rejected proposals for a third party in favor of establishing the Municipal Voters' League. Like the Citizens' Union in New York and the Municipal Association in Cleveland, the Municipal Voters' League issued recommendations for aldermanic elections based on questionnaires distributed to the candidates. In 1896, the League opposed twenty-six of the thirty-four aldermen up for reelection. Sixteen of the twenty-six were not renominated, while another four were defeated in the general election. In 1897, twenty-four of the twenty-seven aldermen opposed by the League were defeated. By 1899, a majority of the city council had been elected with League endorsement; by 1900, only five of the original gray wolves remained in office.[11]

Chicago's leading capitalists supported earlier traditional reform efforts but came into conflict with the Municipal Voters' League. Marshall Field, owner of the department store and an investor in Yerkes's railways, and Philip D. Armour, head of the city's largest meatpacking firm, were active in the Citizens' Association, the Union League, and the Civic Federation. But each had also developed close ties to organizational politicians, who could provide the air rights, franchise grants, and police protection of strikebreakers that they required. Hence John Coughlin could boast of his relationship with Field, while Armour was close to William Lorimer. Field criticized the Municipal Voters' League, claiming that it discouraged investment. Armour endorsed a Republican customs appointee opposed by the League's William Kent and Walter Fisher.[12] The leaders of the League were not magnates like Field and Armour, but second-level or second-generation businessmen. George Cole, the first president, ran a moderately successful stationery business. Charles Crane and William Kent, Cole's successors, were sons of major industrialists. Crane's father owned a manufacturing company; Kent's father founded a packing firm and acquired large real estate holdings.[13] Among the experts active in the Municipal Voters' League were Allen Pond, an architect; John Henry Gray and William Hill, professors of political economy; and Jane Addams and Graham Taylor, settlement workers. Like others in the League, they focused on campaigning rather than policy development.[14]

Overall, League endorsements usually favored businessmen, Protestants, and native-born candidates over saloon keepers, Catholics, and the foreign-born. Yet the ward-by-ward endorsements of the League allowed adaptation to local ethnic rivalries. In the Ninth Ward, for example, the League helped a Bohemian defeat a native-stock organizational politician. Jane Addams and the staff of her Hull House settlement sought to displace John Powers in the Nineteenth Ward. Powers, they argued, had enriched himself while ignoring the needs of his constituents. The Italian press joined the campaign, accusing Powers of insulting Italians as well. These charges helped win Italian support for a series of losing reform candidates, but Addams was frustrated by her inability to defeat Powers and withdrew from ward politics. Graham Taylor and his Chicago Commons settlement house made similar appeals to the Seventeenth Ward, with more success. Among the candidates backed by Taylor and the Commons were a Norwegian, a Pole, and William E. Dever, an Irish lawyer who later became mayor. Aldermen of both parties were elected with the support of the Municipal Voters' League and the Commons. When one Seventeenth Ward alderman elected as a reformer voted contrary to their views, he was replaced.[15]

The response to Addams's and Taylor's efforts, like the popularity of William Travers Jerome on Manhattan's Lower East Side, demonstrated that class and ethnic appeals could mobilize immigrant-stock workers as municipal populist opponents of the party organizations.[16] Ward leaders of both parties depended on ethnic support. Poles, Jews, and Italians, among other groups, were often represented by organizational politicians who provided recognition, patronage, and services such as payment for the funerals of the indigent. Coughlin and Kenna performed similar favors for their dispossessed constituents in the First Ward.[17] At the same time, as Italian newspapers opposed to Alderman John Powers pointed out, the schools were overcrowded and the streets were dirty.[18]

Many ward leaders, moreover, were Irish, while their constituents belonged to other ethnic groups. The newer groups often felt the Irish were depriving them of their fair share of offices and keeping the better patronage positions for their own kind. Resentment of the Irish contributed to Italian support for Powers's electoral opponents; Germans, Swedes, Poles, and Bohemians expressed similar hostility toward the Irish politicians who governed them.[19] Jews, who supported "personal liberty" (that is, loose enforcement of state laws on saloons and on Sunday closings) but received little patronage from either party, voted Democratic in local elections and Republican in national ones. In 1902, the heavily Jewish Seventeenth District elected Clarence Darrow, running as an Independent, to the Illinois House of Representatives; it was one of many municipal populist campaigns in which Darrow participated.[20]

Even among the Irish, a politics of municipal populism survived, winning particular support from the middle class. The vitality of Irish municipal populism in Chicago, and the related absence of a centralized Irish machine, contrasts with the situation in New York, where Irish municipal populism was manifest in the 1886 vote for Henry George, but diminished with the establishment of the Democratic clubs and the consolidation of Tammany.[21]

HARRISON'S COALITIONS

Traditional reform and municipal populist voters could join together at the ward level, but not in citywide mayoral elections. The Municipal Voters' League and the native-stock elite provided traditional reform support for John Maynard Harlan, who was defeated as an independent in 1897, failed to win the Republican nomination in 1903, and lost as the Republican candidate in 1905. Washington Hesing, in 1897, and John Peter Altgeld, in 1899, received municipal populist support for their independent mayoral candidacies, but they too were defeated.

The winning candidate in 1897, 1899, 1901, and 1903 was Carter Harrison II, who remained in office by organizing shifting coalitions of ward leaders. Though Harrison was elected to his first term with more votes than his rivals combined, his continued political success required that he survive the return of the Hopkins-Sullivan faction to the Democratic party and win support from the electoral constituency of either Harlan or Hesing. Within the Democratic party, Harrison was able to maintain power by allying with Kenna, Coughlin, and a shifting set of other ward leaders. Kenna and Coughlin were early backers of Harrison's mayoral aspirations and remained his allies through his first four terms. Harrison received large majorities in their First Ward, and Kenna and Coughlin supported him in his council battles against Yerkes. For the two aldermen, alliance with Harrison assured a lenient vice policy. Alliance with Harrison also helped Kenna and Coughlin in their fight for council supremacy over John Powers.[22]

Other early Harrison supporters included Bobbie Burke, head of the Cook County Democratic Marching Club; Joseph S. Martin, a gambler; Thomas Carey, of "Carey's Indians"; and William Loeffler, a Bohemian Jewish ward leader. Each of these machine Democrats broke with Harrison by 1905. Burke felt Harrison had abandoned him after he was indicted for pocketing oil inspection fees. Martin backed Altgeld, his political mentor, over Harrison in 1899. Carey supported Hearst for president in 1904, when Harrison also had national ambitions. Loeffler, Harrison believed, had secret connections with Yerkes. Harrison's loss of these sources of support led to his defeat by Hopkins and Sullivan in many of the contests for control over the county and state party organizations.[23] With the backing of Kenna and Coughlin, however, he was able to retain the party's mayoral nomination.

Harrison's alliances with organization politicians required patronage. It was necessary, therefore, that he interpret the civil service laws loosely. This aroused traditional reform opposition, particularly when Harrison fired two Republican civil service commissioners in order to reinstate Democratic policemen dismissed by his Republican predecessor.[24] Harrison, in turn, was always critical of the Municipal Voters' League, accusing it of partisanship, dictating to aldermen, and even helping utilities get favorable terms from the city.[25]

Harrison's war to end Yerkes's control of the city's surface transportation, however, was supported by traditional reformers. Yerkes was distrusted by other businessmen, even his own partners: after investing in Yerkes's lines to get connections to his store, Marshall Field concluded that "Mr. Yerkes is not a safe man." Harrison's vague commitment to future municipal ownership, moreover, did not seem to threaten private property. Harlan, Cole, the Municipal Voters' League, and the Union League found themselves allied with Harrison, Coughlin, and Kenna in defeating bills to extend Yerkes's franchises for fifty years.[26]

Harrison's traction positions attracted traditional reform voters, but they were repelled by his hostility toward civil service and his ties to politicians like Coughlin and Kenna. Nonetheless, Harrison was able to obtain enough traditional reform support to win reelection in 1899, 1901, and 1903. Without Republican support in these elections, he later wrote, he would have been defeated.[27] What won Harrison traditional reform support was not his mixed policy record, but his opposition. In 1899, he ran against Altgeld, seen as a radical. In 1901 and 1903, he ran against candidates associated with Lorimer and Yerkes. The unpopularity of these candidates gave Harrison enough traditional reform support to win reelection. Harrison made few concessions to municipal populist voters, and many of them remained indifferent to his candidacies.[28]

THE ELECTION OF 1897

In 1897, John Maynard Harlan, a lawyer and the son of Supreme Court Justice John Marshall Harlan, ran as an independent traditional reform candidate. The regular Republican, Judge Nathaniel C. Sears, had been chosen by the Lorimer faction, which was held in disrepute by reformers because it had supported generous traction franchises for Yerkes. Harrison, the Democratic nominee, was also viewed unfavorably because of his opposition to civil service. Harlan was encouraged to enter the race by the support of Victor Lawson's *Record* and *News*. Harlan's platform emphasized the traction issue, hinting at the possibility of municipal ownership. He also opposed political corruption. Though the formal policy of the Municipal Voters' League was to make recommendations only for aldermanic races, Cole wrote a letter urging members to support the candidate with the best chance of defeating Harrison. To the Yerkes-controlled *Inter-Ocean*, the League was the "tail of the little Harlan kite." Particularly attracted to Harlan were young reformers like Harold Ickes, who was then a student at the University of Chicago. The fourth candidate in 1897 was Washington Hesing, nominated as an independent by the Hopkins-Sullivan Gold Democrats. Hesing's candidacy was ostensibly a response to Harrison's endorsement of Bryan in 1896, but it also continued the factional rivalry between the Hopkins-Sullivan and Harrison groups: Hesing had lost the 1893 nomination to the elder Harrison. Hesing was popular among his fellow Germans and had controlled patronage as postmaster under President Grover Cleveland. Despite his resources, support for his candidacy declined as it became apparent he could not win.[29]

Harrison was elected with 148,880 votes to 69,730 for Harlan, 59,542 for Sears, and 15,427 for Hesing. Table 9-1 presents estimates for voting behavior according to the categories given in the 1900 census, which provides ward data for nativity by generation, but not by ethnic group. Dwellings per family was used as a measure of suburbanization.[30] According to Table 9-1, Sears was more popular among the "Other" group, which includes blacks and native-born whites, than among foreign-born or second-generation whites. Harrison most likely received his strongest support from foreign-born whites. Reflecting his narrowly German base, Hesing did best among second-generation whites. Harlan did well among "Other" voters, reflecting his support among native-born whites. Harlan was also strong among second-generation whites, which may indicate sup-

TABLE 9-1
Voting Behavior by Ethnic Group, 1897

	Sears (Rep.) %	Harrison (Dem.) %	Harlan (Ind.) %	Hesing (Ind.) %
2nd Generation White	11–14	28–34	16–40	4–13
Foreign White	12–17	42	0	0
Other	17–26	16–50	18–30	3–7

Note: Suburbanization set at mean value.
$N = 34$.

TABLE 9-2
Partisan Sources of Support, 1897

	Sears (Rep.) %	Harrison (Dem.) %	Harlan (Ind.) %	Hesing (Ind.) %
Republican	16–29	0	38	8
Democratic	7–17	84	0	0

N = 34.

port from Scandinavians, who voted for traditional reform candidates in later elections.[31] As the candidate who most emphasized the traction issue, Harlan received suburban support beyond what would be predicted by national origins. Holding other variables constant, Harlan's percentage of the vote would be an estimated 3.0 percent greater in the most suburban ward than in the least suburban ward, while Harrison's proportion of the vote would fall by an estimated 16.4 percent from the least to the most suburban ward.[32]

Table 9-2 shows the impact of partisanship, as measured by transition rates from the 1896 presidential election to the 1897 mayoralty contest.[33] Both Harlan and Sears drew more support from Republicans than Democrats, and Harlan's share of the Republican vote is greater than that of Sears, the party nominee. Harrison's vote is closely associated with that for Bryan. Hesing, a Gold Democrat, did better among McKinley Republicans than among Bryan Democrats.[34]

THE ELECTION OF 1899

In 1899, Harrison was opposed by Zina Carter, an organizational Republican, and by Altgeld, the former Democratic governor of Illinois, running as a Municipal Ownership candidate. Altgeld had helped to engineer Harrison's nomination but broke with him in December 1898. Altgeld supporters charged Harrison with betrayal for appointing Gold Democrats to city positions and issuing city bonds payable in gold; for campaigning for Tammany's Robert A. Van Wyck against Henry George in the New York mayoral campaign of 1897; and for slighting Altgeld at the state convention.[35] Altgeld's platform called for free silver and municipal ownership. He opposed political employment and contracting, though his own candidacy drew upon the resources of machine politics: he was backed by Mike McDonald, an organizational ally of Carter Harrison I, and by "Foxy" Ed Cullerton, who had lost his council seat to a Municipal Voters' League candidate. Altgeld, moreover, had inherited a one-eleventh share in the sand-bag Ogden Gas Company from his cousin and business associate, John W. Lanehart. Harrison and Altgeld accused each other of accepting funds from Yerkes.[36]

Altgeld's gubernatorial pardon of the surviving Haymarket anarchists, together with his devotion to free silver, led Chicago's elite and their newspapers to consider him a radical. His proposals for municipal ownership were also more developed than those of Harlan or Harrison. Altgeld turned down William Kent's request that he and his slate withdraw in favor of candidates backed by the Municipal Voters' League, and the traditional reform voters who had rallied behind Harlan in 1897 ignored or opposed Altgeld's candidacy. George Cole endorsed Harrison. Twenty-five-year-old Harold Ickes viewed Harrison's reelection as certain.[37]

Altgeld's activists came instead from a core group of municipal populists who had supported a Populist-Labor slate in 1894 and would later back Edward Dunne's mayoral campaigns. "Day after day," recalled Clarence Darrow, who played a major role in the campaign, "his headquarters were crowded with weird-looking idealists and worshippers—the poorly clad, the ill-fed, the unemployed, the visionaries gazing off toward the rainbow espying something further on than the very stars themselves." Darrow also remembered that Altgeld's meetings attracted "a large proportion of students, lawyers, scientists, who appreciated what he had to say, and knew that he was right." But Altgeld does not seem to have attracted the experts who had enthusiastically backed Harlan in 1897. The University of Chicago had been a source of volunteers for Harlan. For W. F. Cooling, like Darrow an Altgeld advisor, the university was instead a great enemy of the Jeffersonian democracy Altgeld represented.[38]

Harrison won the election with 148,496 votes. Carter received 107,437, Altgeld only 47,169, though a *Chicago Chronicle* poll a month earlier had shown Altgeld ahead. Altgeld's supporters claimed fraud, but no recount was held.[39] Both Cooling and the Harrison-affiliated *Times-Herald* emphasized the transfer of Republican votes to Harrison in explaining the outcome.[40] Table 9-3, which shows estimated transition rates from the 1896 presidential election to the 1899 mayoral election, suggests the extent of this transfer. Harrison's 1897 share of the 1896 McKinley vote was estimated in Table 9-2 as zero. Table 9-3 suggests that in 1899, Harrison received at least 28 percent of the McKinley vote. Table 9-3 also suggests that, contrary to Cooling's claims, most Bryan Democrats stayed with Harrison: a minority voted for Altgeld, while none switched to Carter. Altgeld, then, was unable to win acceptance as the heir to Bryan and Jefferson.[41]

Table 9-4, showing estimated transition rates from the 1897 to the 1899 mayoral election, provides more information about vote transfer patterns. These estimates suggest that the McKinley transfer to Harrison came

TABLE 9-3
Partisan Sources of Support, 1899

	Carter (Rep.) %	Harrison (Dem.) %	Altgeld (Mun. Own.) %
Republican	29–50	28–41	8–13
Democratic	0	78–84	13–17

$N = 34$.

from Republicans, not from Gold Democrats returning to their party. In 1897, almost four times as many voters had backed Sears as backed Hesing, and in 1899, Harrison won a larger percentage among the Sears$_{1897}$ voters than among the Hesing$_{1897}$ voters. Carter took the largest share of the 1897 Harlan vote, though Harrison also did well and about one-third went to Altgeld. Some traditional reform voters, then, could also support a municipal populist candidate, but others voted Republican or backed Harrison as the less dangerous alternative to Altgeld. The overlap between traditional reform and municipal populism was too small to secure a plurality for Altgeld, particularly in an election with possible fraud. In the New York election of 1905, similarly, some voters who had previously supported Seth Low shifted to Hearst, while others rallied behind George McClellan as the only candidate who could prevent a municipal populist victory.

The estimates in Table 9-4 show a strong association between support for Hesing in 1897 and support for Altgeld in 1899, even though Hesing was a Gold Democrat and Altgeld a prominent Silverite. This suggests that the Altgeld vote, like that for Hesing, was predominantly German.[42] Table 9-5, showing voting behavior by ethnic group, supports this inference. Altgeld's support, like that for Hesing, was limited to the category

TABLE 9-4
Transition Rates, 1897–1899

1897	1899		
	Carter (Rep.) %	Harrison (Dem.) %	Altgeld (Mun. Own.) %
Sears (Rep.)	100	27–50	0
Harrison (Dem.)	0	50–81	16–17
Harlan (Ind.)	43–50	30–50	31–34
Hesing (Ind.)	0	8–50	100

$N = 34$.

TABLE 9-5
Voting Behavior by Ethnic Group, 1899

	Carter (Rep.) %	Harrison (Dem.) %	Altgeld (Mun. Own.) %
2nd Generation White	25–26	31–34	22
Foreign White	12–31	26–42	0
Other	23–47	33–50	0

Note: Suburbanization set at mean value.
N = 34.

of second-generation whites. According to the 1910 census, 26.8 percent of second-generation whites were Germans.[43] Harrison did well among all three nativity categories. Estimates for the impact of suburbanization show the strongest positive effect for Carter, though his campaign stressed civil service while Harrison spoke of his victory over Yerkes and Altgeld demanded municipal ownership.[44]

THE ELECTION OF 1901

In 1901, Harrison was reelected with 156,756 votes to 128,413 for Elbridge Hanecy, a Lorimer Republican. Hanecy was defeated despite support from Altgeld and, Harrison claimed, from Hopkins-Sullivan Democrats.[45] Table 9-6 gives estimates for voting by ethnic group. These estimates use 1910 census data and the 1901 vote, each tallied by the city's thirty-five redrawn wards. Coefficients estimated for Austrian, German, Irish, Italian, and Russian voters combine first- and second-generation

TABLE 9-6
Voting Behavior by Ethnic Group, 1901

	Hanecy (Rep.) %	Harrison (Dem.) %
Austrian	3–50	0
German	4–50	31–47
Irish	29–50	50–68
Italian	3–50	27–50
Native	17–48	27–40
Russian	12–50	15–50
Scandinavian	27–50	0

Note: Suburbanization and illiteracy variables set at mean values.
N = 35.

totals. Coefficients for native represent native-born with native parents plus first- and second-generation English and Scottish. Coefficients for Scandinavian represent first- and second-generation Swedish, Norwegian, and Danish. Dummy variables for illiteracy are used to divide the wards into three groups: upper class ($Ill_1 = Ill_2 = 0$), middle class ($Ill_1 = 1$, $Ill_2 = 0$), and lower class ($Ill_1 = Ill_2 = 1$). As before, suburbanization is measured as dwellings per family.

The estimates in Table 9-6 show the ethnic breakdown of support when neither a traditional reform candidate nor a municipal populist candidate was on the ballot. Hanecy, it was discovered during the campaign, was an Irish Catholic who had changed his name from Hennessey and converted to Methodism.[46] Irish voters still gave him at least 29 percent support. The revelations, together with his ties to Lorimer, may have hurt Hanecy among native voters, who gave roughly equal support to him and to the blue-blooded Harrison. Germans backed Harrison, but Scandinavians and Austrians gave him little support. Suburbanization was associated with voting for Hanecy.

THE ELECTION OF 1903

Harrison's Republican opponent in 1903 was Graeme Stewart, a grocer associated with Fred Busse's North Side organization.[47] Lorimer, usually in conflict with Busse, accepted Stewart's nomination to block Harlan. During the campaign, Stewart strengthened his ties to Lorimer: when Democrats demanded a recount of the vote that had sent Lorimer to Congress, Stewart expressed his approval of the injunction upholding the result. Traditional reform leaders once again shifted to Harrison. Victor Lawson and William Kent endorsed him. Even Harold Ickes, who had become publicity manager for Stewart after running Harlan's campaign, recalled that after he discovered Stewart's links to Yerkes, "my loss of confidence in Stewart was so great that I simply could not bring myself to vote for him."[48] Harrison received 146,208 votes to 138,548 for Stewart. Daniel L. Cruice, running as an Altgeld candidate on the Independent Labor ticket, received only 9,947 votes. Darrow, who had turned down the Independent Labor nomination, supported Harrison.

As in 1901, traditional reform voters' distaste for the Republican nominee allowed Harrison to win reelection despite defections by Hopkins-Sullivan Democrats.[49] Table 9-7 shows estimated behavior by ethnic groups. Once again, Harrison did about as well among the native vote as his Republican opponent. Harrison also won likely pluralities among the Germans, Irish, Italians, and Russians; Scandinavians favored Stewart as they had favored Hanecy. Suburbanization is again associated with sup-

TABLE 9-7
Voting Behavior by Ethnic Group, 1903

	Stewart (Rep.) %	Harrison (Dem.) %
Austrian	4–50	1–50
German	9–50	27–50
Irish	20–50	50–51
Italian	5–50	25–50
Native	29–43	33–45
Russian	11–50	18–50
Scandinavian	27–50	0

Note: Suburbanization and illiteracy variables set at mean values.
$N = 35$.

port for the Republican candidate. Stewart was personally ignorant about the traction issue, but his published statements, written by Ickes, incorporated Harlan's positions.[50]

HARRISON AND THE EXPERTS

Traditional reform support for Harrison's reelection attempts did not hinge upon the incorporation of experts into his administration. For Harrison, as for most politicians of the period, expertise was inferior to practical experience. Experts claim to have figured things out, Harrison told the Conference of Mayors in 1914, but

> the expert . . . fails to take into consideration the human equation. And there is a human equation to be considered in this as well as in all phases of human life.
>
> This argument is most unscientific I am constrained to admit. The citizens, however, are more interested in good service and cheap rates, than they are in the securing of these benefits by methods of scientific accuracy. Results are what the people are after, not a scientific method of regulation, approved of by the up-to-date expert which exhausts itself in red tape, and leaves rates high and service poor.[51]

Harrison did establish a Bureau of Statistics, which published an annual *City Manual*, and started the Municipal Reference Library, which remains in existence today. Yet the "Bureau" and the "Library" had no office space until the administration of Edward Dunne, Harrison's successor, gave them two rooms in City Hall.[52]

The best indication of Harrison's attitude toward experts is how little impact they had on his policies. Harrison's solution to the utility problem was mayoral responsibility. State regulatory commissions, he argued, divided responsibility; advisory boards were not necessary for a well-equipped executive and would not help an executive who was not equipped. Harrison's traction proposals took the form of the "Tentative Ordinance" defeated in a referendum vote in April 1905. The Tentative Ordinance, opposed by Hearst, Dunne, and other advocates of immediate municipal ownership, would have granted a franchise extension to the City Railway. The railway company was required to waive rights to the ninety-nine year franchise, granted under a state law then being challenged in court; to set a five-cent fare with universal transfers; and to make specific improvements. Settlement would depend on the state's passage of legislation allowing eventual municipal ownership. Like Harrison's scheme, the traction settlement approved in 1907, discussed in Chapter 10, provided for continued private ownership. The 1907 settlement, however, established a more important regulatory role for transportation experts than Harrison conceived for them.[53]

The limits of Harrison's commitment to expertise were also shown by his education policy. William Rainey Harper, president of the University of Chicago, had been appointed to the board of education by Mayor George B. Swift in 1896. In December 1897, Harrison named Harper to a special education commission and consulted him on the other appointments. Harper was elected chairman of the commission, which based its conclusions upon research and discussions with university educators. The commission urged that the powers of the superintendent be increased; that the size of the school board be reduced; and that teachers be more systematically selected and promoted. Harrison did not endorse the commission report. Instead, he accepted the objections of teachers and politicians who saw the recommendations as elitist proposals to allow the University of Chicago to control the school system. Bills based upon the report failed, and Harper was not reappointed to the school board. E. Benjamin Andrews, the former president of Brown University who had become superintendent with Harper's support, then resigned. Harrison installed Edwin Cooley as his replacement, but Cooley soon complained about Harrison's attempts to influence personnel decisions. Harrison's school board appointees fit the usual pattern of businessmen primarily concerned with fiscal responsibility.[54]

Like George McClellan of New York, Harrison confronted traditional reformers, municipal populists, and organizational opponents within his own party. Both mayors sought national office.[55] But McClellan's electoral strategy was based on the incorporation of expertise and Harrison's was not. One difference was in the strength of municipal populist opposition: Hearst had almost won the 1905 New York election, while Altgeld's appeal to non-German voters was weak. McClellan had to ally with experts to assert his independence from Tammany. In the more factionalized politics of Chicago, Harrison could instead seek the support of particular ward leaders against the Hopkins-Sullivan faction. Chicago experts, moreover, had not experienced the limitations of a traditional reform administration like that of Seth Low, which may have made New York experts more available for alliance with an organizationally connected politician.

McClellan's approach was less effective than Harrison's: McClellan's political career was over by 1909, while Harrison enjoyed continued electoral success. Neither attained any office above the mayoralty. Beyond Harrison's individual fortunes, what was significant for Chicago politics about his approach was that at the end of Harrison's first four administrations, experts remained within the roles of traditional reformers. Traditional reform and municipal populist constituencies, consequently, remained distinct. They could come together to oppose a boodle alderman or a Yerkes franchise, but could not ally in support of a common electoral alternative to organizational politics. In the election of 1905, the two reform constituencies were instead in direct opposition.

CHAPTER 10

Edward Dunne: Municipal Populism and Party Factionalism

EDWARD DUNNE, elected as a Democrat in 1905, was the only reform mayor of Chicago during the Progressive Era. Dunne was a Cook County judge with close ties to the Municipal Ownership clubs, to the Hearst press, and to the wing of the Democratic party associated with William Jennings Bryan and John Peter Altgeld. An Irish Catholic active in both nationalist and religious organizations, Dunne became the leader of a municipal populist Irish network that also included William O'Connell and William Dever and received its strongest support from the Irish middle class.[1] Unlike his municipal populist counterpart and ally in Cleveland, Tom Johnson, Dunne was unable to construct a coalition that could last longer than one election; he was defeated by Fred Busse in 1907. Dunne's defeat reflected both the continuing isolation of municipal populism from academic experts active in city politics and the shifting patterns of factional alliances within both Chicago parties.

THE ELECTION OF 1905

Dunne's mayoral candidacy was sponsored by municipal populist organizations and accepted by Mayor Carter Harrison, the various ward leaders, and the party faction led by John Hopkins and Roger Sullivan.[2] The Municipal Ownership League named Dunne as its candidate in November 1904, but he said he would not run on a third-party ticket. In January 1905, Judge Murray F. Tuley of the League announced a draft of Dunne as a Democratic candidate. William Prentiss of the Chicago Federation of Labor said he would run if the Democrats did not nominate Dunne. The Socialists, who had done well in the 1904 presidential vote, said they would not run a candidate if Dunne were nominated.[3] Dunne's strongest supporters were Bryan-Altgeld Democrats like Clarence Darrow, J. Hamilton Lewis, and Samuel Alschuler. His candidacy was endorsed by the Hearst press and by Louis Post's municipal populist journal, *The Public*. The core of Dunne's campaign was a network of voluntary groups organized by ward or profession and assisted by the existing municipal ownership organizations. These groups provided an alternative to the Harrison-controlled county committee. Harrison eventually endorsed Dunne, but he took no part in the campaign and strongly objected to Dunne's demand for immediate municipal ownership of traction lines. Hopkins and Sullivan, though they also disagreed with Dunne's position on municipal ownership, supported him as a move against Harrison. Among the ward leaders, John Powers and Thomas Carey also backed Dunne, while Ed Cullerton, Edward Lahiff, and Stanley Kunz dissociated themselves from Dunne's campaign. "Bathhouse" John Coughlin and Michael "Hinky Dink" Kenna of the notorious First Ward were early Dunne supporters; Dunne reciprocated by endorsing Kenna for reelection.

Dunne's Republican opponent was John Maynard Harlan; it was the only time Harlan obtained the Republican mayoral nomination. The core of Harlan's campaign, like Dunne's, was a group of long-time reform activists. Harlan's key supporters included Harold Ickes, Raymond Robins, William Kent, and Graham Taylor. They had been as consistent in their support of Harlan's earlier campaigns and other traditional reform efforts as Darrow or Tuley had been in support of Bryan and Altgeld and frequently cited Dunne's support for Kenna against Dunne. Harlan was also backed by most of the press and by such business figures as Harry Selfridge, Alexander H. Revell, Julius Rosenwald, and Marshall Field. Organizational Republicans were no more enthusiastic about Harlan's candidacy than they had been in the past. William Lorimer's West Side organization failed to back Harlan: Harlan had refused to allow Lorimer candidates to run on his city ticket, and he was identified with Governor Charles Deneen, nominated over a Lorimer candidate in 1904. Fred Busse's North Side Republican organization also did not support Harlan.[4]

The 1905 election thus set a Democrat long identified with municipal populism against a Republican long identified with traditional reform. The main issue of contention between the two reform camps was municipal ownership of traction lines; Dunne succeeded in making this the main issue of the campaign as well.[5] In accepting the mayoral nomination, Dunne announced that his platform would be immediate municipal ownership (IMO) under Illinois's 1903 Mueller Law. Comparing Chicago's private traction system to the municipal traction of European cities, and to Chicago's own municipal light and water systems, Dunne argued that municipal ownership would bring more efficient service, lower fares, and increased wages. Municipal ownership would also be a blow against J. P. Morgan, who had recently acquired majority ownership of the Chicago City Railway, in which Marshall Field and Philip Armour held minority shares. When combined with civil service, moreover, municipal ownership would end political corruption.

Harlan claimed that Wall Street wanted Dunne because his approach would lead the city to pay too much to acquire the traction system. His own approach, he said, would allow municipal ownership when the city was ready for it. Victor Lawson, a publisher active in traditional reform causes, argued Dunne's program would result in endless litigation; William Kent of the Municipal Voters' League called the immediate municipal ownership campaign demagoguery and a front for corruption. Harlan criticized Dunne for his willingness to begin municipal ownership without a referendum; Dunne said the voters had already shown their support for municipal ownership in the traction referenda of 1902 and 1904. Harrison continued to favor the Tentative Ordinance and a more gradual transition to municipal ownership, but his approach was rejected by Dunne, Harlan, and the traction companies.[6]

Dunne was elected with 163,189 votes; Harlan received 138,671. Harrison's Tentative Ordinance granting a franchise to the Chicago City Railway was rejected, 150,785 to 64,391. On the more general question, "Shall the City Council pass any ordinance granting a franchise to the Chicago City Railway Company?," the vote was 60,020 for, 151,974 against. "The public in anticipatory greed," Harrison wrote later, "was already licking its chops at the prospect of a public seizure of the rich traction properties; irresponsible I.M.O. yawpers were promising an economic millennium, no taxes, vast revenues pouring into the public treasury, high wages for the traction employees, new jobs for political loafers and the always present army of unemployed; the voters were just about crazed with the alluring prospect unfolded to their hungry gaze."[7]

Many contemporary observers traced Dunne's victory to the reluctance of Republican leaders to support Harlan. Others saw the municipal ownership issue as crucial: *Collier's*, for example, accused Dunne of making an emotional appeal to the "blind hatred of capital."[8] The estimates of transition rates and voting behavior by ethnic groups suggest that the electoral patterns of 1905 were not as different from those of 1903 as these views implied. The estimated transition rates from 1903 to 1905 demonstrate electoral stability from both Stewart$_{1903}$ to Harlan$_{1905}$ (virtually 100 percent) and from Harrison$_{1903}$ to Dunne$_{1905}$ (50 to 95 percent). At the same time, Harlan received none of the 1903 Harrison vote, while Dunne picked up 10 to 50 percent of Stewart's 1903 support. Table 10-1, showing estimates of voting support by ethnic group, also suggests that neither Harlan's traditional reformism nor Dunne's municipal populism produced immediate electoral shifts. Table 10-1 can be compared with Table 9-7 for the 1903 election, since both sets of estimates are based on 1910 ethnic data. As a candidate who strongly identified himself with his fellow Irish, Dunne improved the Democratic vote among that group. Harrison and Dunne each divided the native-stock vote about evenly with his Republican opponent. Like Harrison in 1903, Dunne in 1905 won likely pluralities among German, Italians, and Russians, while losing heavily

TABLE 10-1
Voting Behavior by Ethnic Group, 1905

	Harlan (Rep.) %	Dunne (Dem.) %
Austrian	4–50	2–50
German	13–50	29–50
Irish	13–50	50–72
Italian	1–50	30–50
Native	25–43	26–50
Russian	7–50	24–50
Scandinavian	38–50	0

Note: Suburbanization and illiteracy variables set at mean values. $N = 35$.

among Scandinavians. In 1903, the Democrats gained 6.4 percent in moving from the upper-class to the middle-class wards, and an additional 1.5 percent in moving to the lower-class wards.[9] In 1905, the Democrats gained 7.0 percent from the upper-class to the middle-class wards, and an additional 0.2 percent from the middle-class to the lower-class wards. The decline in the Democratic edge among the poorest (most illiterate) wards suggests reduced participation by some of the ward organizations, but otherwise class patterns were similar in the two elections. Suburbanization favored the Republican candidate in both elections, by about the same margin. This difference translates into an estimated Republican advantage of 5.8 percent from the least to the most suburban ward in 1903, and 5.3 percent in 1905. Though Dunne had made traction the dominant issue of the campaign, the issue does not seem to have reshaped voting patterns among suburban residents, for whom transportation would be most crucial.[10]

DUNNE AS MAYOR

Dunne's initial candidacy did not reshape electoral patterns. Dunne's attempts to construct a municipal populist administration did produce electoral change, but the shifts were not in his favor. During his two years as mayor, Dunne sought to make appointments that would retain his municipal populist support while constructing ties to traditional reformers and organizational politicians. Dunne's cabinet included such longtime municipal populists as Clarence Darrow, special assistant corporation counsel for traction affairs; J. Hamilton Lewis, the regular corporation counsel; Peter Bartzen, building commissioner; and James Medill Patterson, commissioner of public works. But Dunne's advisors also included Raymond

Robins and Graham Taylor, social workers who had supported Harlan for mayor. Comptroller Lawrence McGann was a holdover from the Harrison administration, and many Harrison men remained entrenched in the city agencies.[11] Dunne's record in traction, education, charter reform, and other policy areas also suggests an effort to combine municipal populists, traditional reform, and organizational Democratic support. But by 1907, electoral support for Dunne was more narrowly limited to municipal populist voters than it had been in 1905.

Elected on a promise of immediate municipal ownership, Dunne searched fruitlessly for a solution to the traction problem that could attract support from both municipal populists and traditional reformers while winning the approval of a city council that was still dominated by organizational politicians who preferred franchise extensions negotiated with individual companies. Twice, Mayor Dunne sought a compromise along the lines favored by supporters of Harlan, then rejected his own administration's proposals in favor of a renewed commitment to immediate municipal ownership.[12] Shifting from his campaign position of IMO, Dunne initially proposed the "Contract Plan," under which the city was to grant a twenty-year franchise to a private firm willing to raise funds for modernization; net receipts would go into a sinking fund for eventual purchase by the city. Dunne's shift endangered his municipal populist base. The mayor was forced to deny that he had abandoned the cause of municipal ownership, and his appointees, Darrow and Patterson, were expelled from the Municipal Ownership League for supporting the Contract Plan. All this was for naught: the council voted down the plan, and also rejected Dunne's appointment of A. B. DuPont, a business and political associate of Tom Johnson, as a special traction consultant. Darrow resigned as traction counsel in November 1905, denying rumors of a split with Dunne.

Dunne responded to the failure of the Contract Plan and to Darrow's departure by again advocating immediate municipal acquisition through condemnation. With the support of boodling aldermen unhappy about the amounts the traction companies had offered them for opposition, Dunne was able to win council approval for a bond referendum. In the April 1906 votes, majorities approved the issue of the certificates and the decision to proceed with municipal ownership rather than franchise extensions. Though a majority also voted yes on the question, "Shall the city of Chicago proceed to operate street railways?," this was not enough, for the proposal did not receive the three-fifths approval required for municipal operation under the state's Mueller Law.

Dunne then shifted again, appointing Walter L. Fisher, a Republican and a former president of the Municipal Voters' League, to Darrow's former position as special traction counsel. Fisher, the author of the Mueller Law, accepted the position only after Dunne agreed that municipal ownership need not be immediate. Fisher drafted the "Settlement Ordinances," setting new terms for private operation under twenty-year franchises. Dunne first praised the ordinances, but changed his position after it was attacked by Hearst and municipal ownership advocates. Dunne then announced that he would not support the ordinances unless they were revised to guarantee the city's share of profits and to ease the conditions for eventual municipal acquisition. Traditional reformers, in contrast, endorsed the Settlement Ordinances; *The Outlook* called them the "single brilliant achievement of [Dunne's] administration."[13] Fisher "pointed out that the only solid opposition to his compromise came from eminently impractical University of Chicago intellectuals, who lived where 'municipal ownership is a little god.'"[14] The council disregarded Dunne's objections and passed Fisher's bill, then overrode a mayoral veto. In April 1907, the voters approved Fisher's settlement, 167,367 to 134,281, at the same time that they elected Fred Busse mayor over Dunne; a *Tribune* poll indicated that voters believed a settlement would mean better service.

Educational policy also produced conflict between municipal populists and traditional reformers, but within this policy area Dunne was more consistent. During the administration of Mayor John Purroy Mitchel, New York educators tried to reorganize the classroom according to the Gary Plan; in Cleveland, a business-dominated board of education supported centralization and introduced vocational and commercial programs to better meet business needs.[15] Chicago School Superintendent Edwin Cooley shared the approach of Cleveland's school administrators, while Jane Addams expressed concerns similar to those later voiced by experts in New York. Except for Addams, however, Dunne's school board pursued a third agenda that emphasized improved conditions for teachers, to be financed by business through taxes and rents on school lands.[16] Each year, the mayor could appoint one-third of the board of education to three-year terms. Harrison and his predecessors had favored business appointees. Dunne's seven June 1905 appointees, in contrast, included Jane Addams; John C. Harding of the Typographical Union; and Emil W. Ritter, a former teacher. Only one of the previous incumbents was reappointed. In June 1906, Dunne gained a majority of the board by appointing five new members while renewing two appointments. The new 1906 appointees included Raymond Robins; Louis Post; John J. Sonsteby of the Garment Workers Union; Wiley Wright Mills, a Single Taxer; and Philip Angsten, a municipal ownership activist. Most of the new members were approved by Margaret Haley of the Chicago Teachers' Federation, which had fought the board over salary demands and the union's affiliation with the Chicago Federation of Labor.

Even before the second group of Dunne appointees had joined the board, it voted to raise teachers' salaries. After Dunne gained a majority, the board adopted reforms in the promotion system that weakened the powers of Superintendent Cooley and gave teachers the rights to obtain their evaluations and to appeal dismissals. In February 1907, the board approved a preliminary plan for district teachers' councils. To pay for its proposals, the Dunne board went to court to force the *Tribune* and the *Daily News* to pay higher rents on the downtown property they leased from the school system. The *Tribune* called the Dunne appointees "freaks, cranks, monomaniacs, and boodlers" and publicized Nicholas Murray Butler's speech to the Commercial Club, in which he praised Superintendent Cooley, criticized the board, and urged that all members of teachers' unions be fired.[17]

Though Jane Addams described her fellow appointees as "for the most part adherents to the new education," the description seems to apply more to her than to her colleagues. Addams voted for the new promotion system, but promised to propose amendments later. She wrote that she "was seldom able" to follow the suggestions of the Teachers' Federation and could not convince the union to allow nonmembers to share the proceeds when it won a suit for withheld wages. Yet Addams was also critical of the type of business efficiency embodied by Cooley, which "dangerously approximated the commercialistic ideal of high salaries only for the management with the final test of a small expense account and a large output." Under the Dunne board, she recalled, efforts, presumably her own, to mediate between existing arrangements and proposals for change "were looked on as compromising and unworthy, by both partisans."[18]

In public health, the Dunne administration, led by Dr. Charles A. Whalen, introduced meat and dairy inspections. The Building Department, under Peter Bartzen, canceled permits and closed down violators, including Marshall Field's department store. But Dunne was unable to gain effective control of other departments. Police Chief John M. Collins, a family friend, faced a rebellion in the ranks. Fire Marshal John Campion had to be dismissed for disobedience over fire engine specifications. Joseph Medill Patterson resigned from public works and became a registered Socialist. He expressed disillusionment with the inefficiency and graft of his department.[19]

CHARTER REFORM

The Chicago Charter Convention of 1906–7 was marked by continued conflict between traditional reformers associated with the city's elite and municipal populists allied with Dunne; though experts participated in the process, their proposals did not serve to unite the two reform camps. The

Citizens' Association and the Civic Federation had long sought to consolidate Chicago's fragmented government and had succeeded in abolishing
tax assessment townships within the city in 1899. But Chicago still was
governed by the state's 1872 City and Villages Act, rather than by a charter of its own. From 1902 to 1904, traditional reform groups joined with
the Chicago Federation of Labor and settlement workers to draft a home
rule amendment and win its approval by the state legislature and the city
electorate. The successful home rule measure authorized a convention to
draft a charter that would be submitted to the state legislature and then to
Chicago voters. Before the convention met, the charter revision movement also won legislative approval of a four-year term for the mayor, city
clerk, and city treasurer, and of the replacement of justices of the peace
by a municipal court.[20]

The Convention began in November 1906 and approved a charter in
March 1907. The seventy-four delegates included representatives of the
state legislature, the Cook County Board of Commissioners, the Sanitary
District, the city council, the three independent park boards, the library
board, and the board of education, as well as fifteen members chosen by
Governor Charles Deneen and fifteen chosen by Mayor Dunne. Patterson, Post, Robins, William Dever, and Graham Taylor were among the
delegates associated with the Dunne administration. George Cole and
Walter Fisher were among the delegates who had been active in traditional reform activities. Charles Merriam, professor of political science at
the University of Chicago, was an active delegate. Carter Harrison,
though a delegate, was inactive and often absent. The overall composition
of the Convention overrepresented Republicans and business while under-
representing foreign-stock ethnic groups.[21] The issues debated at the Convention included election of the mayor by the voters or the council; use of
an office or party block ballot; the number of wards and number of aldermen per ward; terms for the mayor and aldermen; petition requirements
for referenda; and the nature of the board of education. Some votes set
reformers against organizational politicians. Others set traditional reformers and municipal populists against each other.

Merriam sought to make the comparative study of municipal government the basis for charter reform and often discussed the experiences of
other cities in his speeches at the convention. Augustus R. Hatton, a
Merriam student who was later a member of the Cleveland Charter Commission, prepared a 351-page *Digest of City Charters*, organized by topic
and covering Berlin, Glasgow, London, Manchester, Melbourne, Paris,
Sydney, Toronto, and Vienna, as well as the largest U.S. cities.[22] Other
delegates were often unconvinced by such evidence. For example, Walter
Fisher argued that administrative competence and the short ballot required election of the mayor by the city council, citing the view of the

Russian scholar, Moisei Ostrogorski, that Congress needed to elect the president if the national government were to be effective. Similarly, Merriam invoked the authority of James Bryce and said that no successfully governed city in the world had a popularly elected mayor. Robert R. McCormick of the *Tribune* family responded that he was not looking for lessons in government from Russia; Ostrogorski's book was possibly useful for schools, but not for the teaching of politicians "who would rather vote in accordance with their own experience and their experience with the city, than according to the views of the most learned academic school or municipal government teachers." By a vote of 40–8, the motion for a mayor selected by the council was tabled.[23]

Fisher and Cole offered the usual traditional reform arguments for nomination by petition, rather than party nomination: the national parties, they said, were irrelevant to municipal issues. Their position was rejected by the Convention, most of whose delegates were elected officials chosen under the partisan system. The delegates did approve a direct primary in place of the existing, organization-controlled nominating system. The party ballot was retained despite Merriam's discussion of the desirable impact of the Australian ballot in fifteen states and Robins's warning that party voting paved the way for the Socialists, "a party organization more compact than your own; more unreasoning than your own; more passionate than your own; more certain to vote for the principle, as they say, than for the man; tremendously enthusiastic on the principle." Party symbols were removed from the ballot.[24]

Traditional reform arguments were also made in favor of a smaller council that retained the existing thirty-five wards but elected only one member from each instead of the then-current two. The Convention voted to keep the council large, with one member from each of seventy wards. Alexander Revell, a wealthy Republican furniture manufacturer, sought to write at-large elections into the charter on the grounds the council needed men as large as the city. His effort was defeated. The Convention did approve a four-year term for both the council and the mayor, with the council elected in the middle of the mayor's term. Louis Post called this change a step toward council oligarchy, making the aldermen masters of the people rather than servants. The inability to rule through elections, he said, would lead to revolution.[25]

Debate over referenda focused on the percentage of voters who had to sign a petition to force a vote. The Convention initially set the requirement at 25 percent, but lowered it to 10 percent toward the end of its session. Merriam described a requirement of 10 to 15 percent as in accord with general principles and praised the decision of the Convention to limit referenda to franchise grants.[26] The Convention voted to more closely integrate the board of education with city government. Members would still be appointed rather than elected and would continue to serve without compensation. Post argued for an elected board. Robins voted for paying salaries of $2,500; Merriam and Taylor voted against this measure.[27]

Rather than allow either supporters or opponents of Sunday drinking to defeat the charter, the Convention postponed decision on the issue as long as possible. It finally voted to send the legislature a separate measure permitting home rule on this question.[28] A similar provision for a separate woman suffrage bill was defeated.[29] With these issues excluded, the charter was approved, 32–0; nine members, including Post, were present but not voting, and thirty-three were absent.[30] The Republican-controlled state legislature then made several changes in the Convention's charter. District boundaries that favored the Republicans and could not be altered until 1920 were written into the charter. Party symbols were restored to the ballot. The liquor home rule bill was defeated in committee, leaving the city subject to the state Sunday closing law. Merriam, the Civic Federation, and most of the press still favored the charter, but the new version was opposed by Robins, Post, the Democratic party, the South Park Board, the Chicago Federation of Labor, and the United Societies, a coalition of wet ethnic groups. In September 1907, the charter was defeated, 121,479 to 59,581. Merriam argued that the original version of the charter would have been easily approved. Realtors, however, would still have objected to the higher tax ceiling approved at the Convention.[31]

THE ELECTION OF 1907

Dunne was not able to create a continuing faction within the Democratic party to rival those of Harrison or Hopkins-Sullivan. To secure his political base, he discharged Harrison appointees, established closer ties to Hearst, and set up a personal organization based on municipal ownership clubs and friendly aldermen like Dever and William O'Connell. Yet Harrison and Sullivan successfully allied against Dunne at the 1906 judicial convention and passed a resolution condemning Dunne's administration. In 1907, Dunne needed the support of John Powers, and ultimately of Roger Sullivan, to win renomination; Coughlin and Kenna supported Harrison's "passive candidacy."[32] Dunne's Republican opponent was Fred Busse, a German coal and ice dealer who headed his own North Side organization and had recently become postmaster of Chicago. Busse ran on a platform of a clean city, a businesslike administration, a qualified school board, and a "practical civil service system." He endorsed Fisher's traction settlement, up for approval at the same election; the city, he said, needed more common sense and less theory. Fisher and Harlan endorsed Busse; Harlan even shared a campaign platform with his political enemy,

William Lorimer.[33] Busse was elected with 164,702 votes to 151,779 for Dunne.

The Arena, Louis Post, and J. Hamilton Lewis blamed Dunne's defeat on Morgan and other New York financiers who, they charged, had contributed to Busse's campaign in order to prevent municipal ownership. Sullivan and *The Outlook* both commented that Dunne lost because the voters rejected his traction policies.[34] Was traction policy the cause of Dunne's defeat, as these diverse actors agreed? If so, was it because Dunne's municipal populism alienated traditional reformers, or because organizational politicians abandoned him in order to preserve their relationships with the traction companies? Transition estimates from 1905 to 1907 show that, as Harlan's own endorsement suggests, Busse was able to retain virtually all of Harlan's 1905 voters. Dunne, in contrast, retained between 47 and 63 percent of his 1905 voters. Dunne, then, lost the 1907 election because he was unable to either hold on to the usual Democratic vote he had received in 1905, or to attract enough of Harlan's traditional reform support to compensate for Democratic defections: he received between 14 and 50 percent of Harlan's 1905 support, while Busse captured from 3 to 50 percent of the 1905 Dunne vote.

Table 10-2 gives estimates for the vote of each major ethnic group. Compared with his 1905 vote (Table 10-1), Dunne did better among Austrians and ran about the same among German, Irish, Italian, Russian, and Scandinavian voters. His biggest losses came among native-stock voters, who had given him substantial support in 1905 and had done the same for Harrison in 1901 and 1903. Estimates for the effects of class also suggest a different pattern than in 1901, 1903, and 1905.[35] In the three previous elections, the Democratic margin increased from the upper- to the middle-class wards and increased again from the middle- to the lower-class wards. In 1907, however, the Democratic margin increased 3.7 per-

TABLE 10-2
Voting Behavior by Ethnic Group, 1907

	Busse (Rep.) %	Dunne (Dem.) %
Austrian	0	12–50
German	17–50	28–50
Irish	8–50	50–70
Italian	0	27–50
Native	31–50	11–50
Russian	4–50	18–50
Scandinavian	36–50	0

Note: Suburbanization and illiteracy variables set at mean values.
$N = 35$.

cent from the upper- to the middle-class wards but fell by 0.8 percent from the middle-class to the lower-class wards. The falloff among the lower-class wards supports reports of "knifing" by ward leaders. Coughlin and Kenna, for example, openly supported Dunne, but their First Ward gave him the smallest margin for any Democratic mayoral candidate since they had gained ascendancy.[36]

With class and ethnicity controlled, the more suburban a ward in 1905, the greater the Republican advantage. But in 1907, suburbanization benefited Dunne, whose predicted margin would be 6.5 percent higher in the most suburban ward than in the least suburban ward.[37] These estimates suggest that Dunne's traction policies evoked a positive response from suburban voters. The direct impact of Dunne's demand for immediate ownership, then, was to *help* his reelection candidacy; the suburban voters to whom the issue was most important were most likely to support him when other demographic variables are held equal. But the indirect effect of Dunne's traction stands was to alienate ward leaders whose support Dunne still needed to win election.

Unlike Tom Johnson, with whom Dunne frequently conferred, Dunne could not gain mastery over local party organizations and use them to consolidate a winning municipal populist electoral coalition. Johnson also won election along the usual partisan lines and within two years reshaped electoral patterns by his policy initiatives. Support for municipal ownership led to suburban support for both candidates. Johnson, however, could gain control of city government and use public agencies to appeal directly to the voters and to gain control of the Democratic party. Chicago's more fragmented governmental structure prevented Dunne from doing the same. He could not, for example, reorient the park system toward popular recreation, as Johnson was doing, since the Chicago parks were under the control of independent boards.[38] Perhaps even more importantly, fragmented government gave Harrison and Sullivan Democrats continuing bases of resistance.

The alternative path to electoral success was that of Newton Baker: incorporation of traditional reform voters into a progressive coalition through the mediation of policy experts. Dunne did draw upon the network of politically active settlement workers who had previously been involved in traditional reform organizations and campaigns. Jane Addams was appointed to the school board. Raymond Robins, also appointed to the school board, investigated Democratic candidates for Dunne and campaigned for Dunne's traction policies. Graham Taylor headed a commission of inquiry appointed to settle the teamster strike against Montgomery Ward.[39] The settlement workers shared the background and worldview of a Frederic Howe or Henry Bruère, but they played a marginal role in the Dunne administration. They did not change Dunne's ideology or rhetoric, nor did they control particular policy areas. After Dunne's defeat, Charles Merriam led another group of experts as they formed an autonomous research organization modeled after the New York Bureau of Municipal Research and played a different role in their city's politics.

CHAPTER 11

Busse, Merriam, and the
Bureau of Public Efficiency

As EDWARD DUNNE'S administration in Chicago paralleled that of Tom Johnson in Cleveland, the administration of Fred Busse, who defeated Dunne in 1907, paralleled that of Herman Baehr, who defeated Johnson in 1909.[1] Busse and Baehr were each German Republicans. Each ran for mayor with a quiet campaign that required little personal exposure. Once in office, each sought to install "sound" methods that appealed to business as alternatives to municipal populism. Each restored systems of organizational politics, but with less overt corruption than expected.[2] Each declined to run for election to a second term. Busse also presents parallels to two New York Democrats, George McClellan and William Gaynor.[3] Like Busse, McClellan and Gaynor attained the mayoralty by defeating a municipal populist, William Randolph Hearst. And like McClellan and Gaynor, Busse allowed municipal experts to develop a new role as investigators, and to institutionalize this role in an autonomous research organization.

These similarities, however, highlight a crucial difference between Busse's administration and those of Baehr, McClellan, and Gaynor. After Baehr, Newton Baker was elected mayor of Cleveland with the support of a progressive coalition; after McClellan and Gaynor, John Purroy Mitchel was elected mayor of New York with the support of a progressive coalition. Both Baker and Mitchel were linked to municipal experts, whose participation allowed them to expand their coalitions beyond the support they had inherited from Tom Johnson and Seth Low, respectively. Charles E. Merriam, nominated by the Republican party to succeed Busse in 1911, was himself the foremost municipal expert in Chicago politics. Yet Merriam was unable to construct a progressive coalition and was defeated by Carter Harrison.

BUSSE AND THE EXPERTS

During the 1907 campaign, one realtor told the sympathetic *Tribune* he was going to vote for Busse because his election would "settle for many years the question as to whether the long haired men and short haired women are going to rule and ruin this town."[4] The role of experts in the Busse administration can be seen in transportation policy, in education, in city planning, and in the development of investigative research. Chicago's 1907 traction ordinance became a national model, influencing the settlement in Cleveland as well as in many other cities. Under the Chicago ordinance, regulatory authority was given to the city council, but its regulations were reviewed by the Board of Supervising Engineers, including a representative from the city, a representative from the companies, and an impartial chair. Bion J. Arnold, the first chair, was a transportation expert who believed engineers should control the system. Yet he also accepted the company position that franchises and other intangibles should be included in valuations, and he sided with central business-district merchants in favoring a downtown subway over a neighborhood system. Willard B. Herely, the Busse administration's traction official, was criticized by the Merriam Commission on City Expenditures for his ties to the traction companies; the Commission found his office to be a complaint bureau only. Supervised by Arnold and the Board, the traction companies introduced new equipment, granted universal transfers, and built extensions as required by the council. The Board did not solve the problems of car overcrowding or Loop congestion, and could not prevent the overcapitalization encouraged by the financial provisions of the 1907 settlement. In 1913, the Illinois legislature placed all public utilities under state regulation, superseding city control. In 1915, the Board of Supervising Engineers ended its transportation research.[5]

Busse sought to change educational policy by removing Dunne's appointees from the school board. In May 1907, Busse sent letters of resignation to twelve board members, including Louis Post and Raymond Robins, but not Jane Addams. Ten of Busse's replacements had business backgrounds. None were educators. The new board reelected the business-oriented Edwin Cooley as superintendent and adopted his promotion plan over the plan favored by Post and the Teachers' Federation. Post, Robins, and five other dismissed members fought to retain their positions. They were upheld by the Illinois Supreme Court and reinstated in January 1908. "I found myself belonging to neither party," Jane Addams later wrote of the removal controversy; her strongest complaint was that it became impossible to consider classroom reforms on their merits. Busse, however, did not reappoint her to the board when her term expired in July 1908.[6]

In 1909, Busse took a different approach to the school board. The mayor reappointed a Dunne appointee who had opposed the purge, and added a reformist Catholic priest and a lawyer who had earlier turned down an appointment by Dunne. When Otto C. Schneider, a Busse appointee, was unable to win reelection as president of the board, the mayor convinced him to withdraw. Cooley resigned as superintendent following a dispute over the granting of credits under the teacher promotion plan. Ella Flagg Young, principal of the Chicago Normal School, was chosen as his replacement, though Busse wanted a male superintendent from outside Chicago. Young shared John Dewey's approach to education. She introduced vocational education, higher salaries, school lunches, and hygiene classes.[7]

The Plan of Chicago was commissioned by the Merchants Club in 1906 and prepared by Daniel Burnham, who had presided over construction of the "White City"—the World's Columbian Exposition, held in Chicago in 1893.[8] Burnham's Plan emphasized the redevelopment of the central business district, the extension of Michigan Avenue across the Chicago River, and the relocation of railroad and port terminals. A forty-square block civic center, with a huge domed administration building in the middle of it, would symbolize order and unity. Housing needs were not addressed in the Plan, and public transportation received less emphasis than the improvement of streets for automobile use. The Plan was promoted by the Merchants Club and the Commercial Club, which merged in 1907. In 1908, Busse appointed a harbor commission to consider proposals made in the Plan and alternatives favored by real estate interests and army engineers. Among the appointees were Frederic Delano and Charles Norton, both of whom had sponsored the Plan of Chicago as members of the Merchants Club; Charles Merriam served as secretary. The commission endorsed Burnham's harbor proposals. In November 1909, the Commercial Club officially presented Burnham's Chicago Plan to Busse, who then appointed a 328-member Plan Commission to mobilize public support and named another early Merchants Club sponsor, Charles Wacker, as chairman. Wacker found new ways to publicize the proposals, including development of an eighth-grade city-planning course for the public schools.

Much of the Chicago Plan was eventually implemented, beginning with the Michigan Avenue extension. The civic aspects of the Chicago Plan, however, were never realized.[9] As Busse told the city council when he appointed the Chicago Plan Commission, "This plan is not to be considered as the embodiment of an artist's dream or the project of theoretical city beautifiers who have lost sight of everyday affairs and who have forgotten the needs and interests of the mass of people. On the contrary, the men who produced the Chicago Plan are all hard-boiled business men."[10] Burnham had collaborated on the Group Plan for downtown Cleveland's public buildings, and plans for both cities reflected the monumental neoclassicism of his later work. But unlike the Chicago Plan, the Cleveland proposals, implemented by Johnson and Baker, grew out of the theoretical project of Frederic Howe and Morris Black and emphasized civic idealism over business concerns.[11]

In transportation, education, and planning, then, experts gained some influence over policy under the Busse administration. Elton Lower also developed new methods of personnel management for the Civil Service Commission, and Dr. W. A. Evans introduced school examinations, infant care education, and more effective disease control as head of the Department of Health.[12] Busse did not believe in expertise per se; commenting on Merriam's aldermanic candidacy, he said, "I do not favor anyone from the University of Chicago. They are all Socialists out there. There's too much damn Hull House in it for me."[13] Yet incorporation of experts kept municipal populists out, while meeting business demands for effective government. In education, Ella Flagg Young was an alternative to Louis Post and the "longhairs"; in transportation, B. J. Arnold was an alternative to Dunne and municipal ownership. Burnham's City Plan was sponsored by downtown businessmen who implemented its most commercially salient aspects.

As in New York and Cleveland, municipal populist electoral mobilization in Chicago led to the incorporation of experts by a mayor more closely associated with party organization than with earlier reform efforts. In New York, McClellan and Gaynor's desires to dissociate themselves from organizational politics shaped an expert agenda different from that of big business. Neither Baehr nor Busse had the New York mayors' desire for independence or their presidential ambitions. Busse's experts, like Baehr's, pursued agendas compatible with those of business leaders, though sometimes in conflict with those of particular business sectors such as traction companies, real estate interests, or textbook manufacturers.

THE BUREAU OF PUBLIC EFFICIENCY

The development of municipal investigation by the Merriam Commission, and then by the Bureau of Public Efficiency, fit business leaders' conception of reform and was encouraged by Fred Busse despite his distrust of expertise.[14] In June 1909, the city council approved a resolution by Merriam, elected alderman from Hyde Park that year, to create a commission to investigate expenditures. The Commission's findings, Merriam argued, would help to win electoral approval of an upcoming bond issue. Busse, expecting the Commission would report favorably on his administration, named Merriam as chair. He also discussed the commission's findings with Merriam, though the mayor did say, "I can't be too familiar with the son of a bitch or they'd think I was a reformer."[15]

The Commission began its investigations in October 1909, borrowing Herbert R. Sands, an accountant from the New York Bureau of Municipal Research, to examine budgetary practices. The Commission did not accuse Busse of personal corruption, but discovered laxity, inefficiency, and dishonesty in the administration of city government. Cast-iron work went to a firm of Busse associates despite competitive bidding requirements. Rock purchased as shale was found to be soft clay. Meat and fish inspections were superficial. Building and fire escape inspectors were unqualified. The City Statistician was termed too old for his job and had "obtained a mark of 50 on a simple examination in arithmetic"; his work was actually done by his assistant.[16] The city, Merriam concluded, lost more through poor business methods than through the actual looting of the treasury. The Commission's work led to the development of a classified budget, based on itemized department receipts. Various economies and improved methods were introduced, and a division of efficiency was set up within the civil service commission. The commissioner and deputy commissioner of public works resigned, and three other high officials were discharged by the civil service commission. Sixteen persons were indicted as a result of the investigations, but none were convicted, for which Merriam blamed the indifference of the State's Attorney.

Organizational politicians on the city council sought to hinder the Commission's investigations. Stanley Kunz ridiculed its expenditure of one dollar for a valet. The council voted to hold meetings on the Commission's findings in private to avoid "unpleasant publicity" and declined to publish the Commission's last four reports. These reports were published instead by the Chicago Bureau of Public Efficiency.[17]

The Bureau of Public Efficiency was organized in June 1910 to support the Merriam Commission. Julius Rosenwald, president of Sears, Roebuck, served as first chairman and was a major donor and initiator. Merriam and Walter L. Fisher were also on the board of trustees. Herbert R. Sands was director and George C. Sikes was secretary.[18] The organization listed its purposes as follows:

1. To scrutinize the systems of accounting in the eight local governments of Chicago.

2. To examine the methods of purchasing materials and supplies and executing construction contracts in these bodies.

3. To examine the payrolls of these local governing bodies with a view of determining the efficiency of such expenditures.

4. To make constructive suggestions for improvements in the directions indicated under 1, 2 and 3, and to co-operate with public officials in the installation of these improved methods.

5. To furnish the public with exact information regarding public revenues and expenditures, and thereby promote efficiency and economy in the public service.[19]

Martin J. Schiesl observes that even though it was "designed to be an agency for the 'rigid scrutiny of all the complicated schemes of local government,' the bureau narrowed its perspective in the hope that better results would come from focusing upon specific problems."[20] As its name suggests, the Bureau of Public Efficiency did not reassess the city's policy needs but examined the methods used to achieve existing goals. Its focus was administrative improvement, not policy development. The Bureau's first report, issued in January 1911, discussed "Methods of Preparing and Administering the Budget of Cook County, Illinois." Later topics included the purchase of voting machines, street paving methods and materials, and the offices of the county recorder, treasurer, coroner, and sheriff. The Bureau also published the Merriam Commission's reports on the waterworks system, the bureau of streets, the civil service commission, and special assessment practices. It endorsed governmental consolidation in reports on the park boards and what it called "the nineteen local governments in Chicago." The Bureau did not endorse candidates but urged the voters to reject two municipal court propositions that would have increased salaries and shortened hours.[21]

The Merriam Commission's investigations and the founding of the Bureau of Public Efficiency marked the introduction of expert analysis of administration and expenditure into Chicago municipal government. In New York, the formation of the Bureau of Municipal Research and the accomplishments of the Fusion Board of Estimate allowed John Purroy Mitchel to develop new electoral appeals and construct a progressive coalition combining the earlier followers of Seth Low and William Randolph Hearst. In Chicago, construction of such a coalition would have meant bringing supporters of John Peter Altgeld and Edward Dunne together with those of John Maynard Harlan and the Municipal Voters' League council candidates. In the election of 1911, Merriam sought to construct such a coalition. He maintained his traditional reform base and added the support of municipal populist leaders, but he could not capture the municipal populist electorate.

THE ELECTION OF 1911

Under Illinois law, 1911 was the first Chicago mayoral election with nominations decided by direct primary. Merriam entered the Republican primary after Walter Fisher declined to run. Busse did not seek reelection; he believed he could defeat Merriam but would then lose to a Democrat. With Busse's withdrawal, the Republican organizations divided in their opposition to Merriam. Busse and William Lorimer, the Republican leader on the West Side, backed John R. Thompson, while Governor Charles Deneen and his South Side organization backed John F. Smulski. The Merriam campaign was chaired by Charles R. Crane and managed by Harold Ickes. Crane, Rosenwald, William Kent, Cyrus McCormick, and Victor Lawson were among the major contributors. A Young Men's Republican League, organized in support of Merriam, enrolled 15,000 by primary day. The Chicago Federation of Labor also endorsed Merriam for the Republican nomination. To the surprise of the Republican organizations, Merriam was nominated with 53,089 votes to 26,406 for Thompson and 23,138 for Smulski.[22]

The Democratic primary was also a three-way contest. Former mayors Harrison and Dunne sought to regain the office, while Andrew J. Graham ran as candidate of the party faction headed by John Hopkins and Roger Sullivan. The Chicago Federation of Labor endorsed Dunne, but Hearst, who had backed Dunne in 1905 and 1907, supported Harrison to further his own presidential ambitions. Harrison won the nomination with 55,116 votes to 53,696 for Dunne and 38,578 for Graham. Dunne and Merriam supporters pointed out that Harrison's margin came from the corrupt First Ward of "Bathhouse" John Coughlin and Michael "Hinky Dink" Kenna, which gave him 2,979 votes to 521 for Dunne and 570 for Graham. Harrison countercharged that to stop his candidacy, Sullivan Democrats had thrown their support to Dunne.[23]

Merriam's general election campaign emphasized honesty and efficiency as issues that would bring Dunne Democrats and Merriam Republicans together. Speakers at the Merriam mass meeting on April 1, 1911, included two self-proclaimed Democrats, Thomas O'Shaughnessy and Charles A. Alden. Both Alden and Merriam noted that if it had not been for the suspect First Ward vote, the Democrats would have nominated Dunne. Clifford J. Roe, involved in the fight against the "white slave trade," criticized Harrison's vice policies and traced them to Harrison's First Ward support. Merriam cited the opportunity to reclaim the millions of wasted tax dollars through honest, efficient, and economical methods. He also promised to break the First Ward system of vice. Merriam and Raymond Robins each described Harrison as looking backward while Merriam looked forward.[24]

Harrison's campaign tried to raise class and ethnocultural issues that would keep the two reform constituencies from joining in support of Merriam. The Harrisonites attacked Merriam as a dry: he had supported the Hyde Park Protective Association's efforts to keep liquor dealers out of that neighborhood under the local option provisions that accompanied Hyde Park's annexation. He was also falsely accused of running for office in Iowa, his home state, as a Prohibitionist. Merriam's response was to deny that personal liberty was an issue and affirm his commitment not to interfere with Sunday drinking or other activities. The United Societies, representing various wet ethnic associations, endorsed Harrison, but by only an 11–6 vote. Merriam, who like Harrison had received part of his education in Germany and could speak some German, was endorsed by the *Abendpost* and the *Staatszeitung*.[25]

The Harrison campaign also attacked Merriam as an enemy of the workers. Workers were asked to vote against Merriam because the Merriam Commission, in its report on the Building Department, had found mechanics unqualified to be building inspectors and recommended a new code excluding union men from the position. "RESULT!," a Harrison pamphlet, predicted that "the Building Inspectors would come from the University of Chicago."[26] Harrison, like many of Merriam's opponents, made a point of referring to Merriam as "Professor" throughout the campaign. Nonetheless, the Chicago Federation of Labor again gave Merriam its mayoral endorsement, as did 224 of its 240 member unions.[27] Each candidate was a Protestant married to a Catholic; each campaign launched similar accusations, disowned by the candidates themselves, that the opponent's wife had not been practicing and that the children had not been properly raised in the faith.[28]

Organizational politicians on both sides gave secret support to the candidate of the opposite party. "The organizations," Merriam recalled,

> were turned topsy-turvy. Two of the three Democratic factions supported the Republican nominee; and two and a half of the three Republican organization factions supported the Democratic, not openly of course, for this would be contrary to principle, but in effect. Harrison was really better off, but he was frankly independent of the regular organization and they of him; while part of the regular organization really supported me in good faith and all of them nominally.[29]

Ickes held conversations on a train with Roger Sullivan, George Brennan, and John P. Hopkins, while Busse and Lorimer Republicans threw their support to Harrison.[30]

Merriam counted Dunne's supporters among the two Democratic factions supporting him, and he did win over many of the Dunne leaders. Raymond Robins, Charles Alden, and Clarence Darrow all participated in the general election campaign after working for Dunne's nomination. Robins headed an auxiliary organization of Dunne Democrats for Merriam. The Chicago Federation of Labor, which had endorsed both Dunne and Merriam in the primaries, backed Merriam over Harrison. Harrison blamed the "Dunne die-hards" for introducing the religious issue into the campaign against him. Dunne himself made no endorsement, and Hearst continued to support Harrison.[31]

Despite the endorsement of the Dunne leaders, Merriam was defeated, receiving 160,672 to 177,997 for Harrison. Estimated transfer rates from 1907 to 1911 suggest that at the mass level, Merriam was not able to construct a progressive coalition combining his own traditional reform vote with Dunne's municipal populist support.[32] The estimated zero transition rate from $Dunne_{1907}$ to $Merriam_{1911}$ suggests that Merriam could not capture even a portion of the Dunne vote. The Harrison esti-

TABLE 11-1
Transition Rates, 1911 Primaries and General Election

Republican Primary	General Election	
	Merriam (Rep.) %	Harrison (Dem.) %
Merriam	100	0
Thompson	50–93	50–65
Smulski	50–94	50–65
Democratic Primary		
Harrison	2–50	100
Dunne	0	50–66
Graham	1–50	50–86

$N = 35$.

mates suggest a similar conclusion: despite the divisive primary, Harrison was able to win between 50 and 79 percent of the Dunne$_{1907}$ vote. Harrison was also able to attract 22 to 50 percent of the Busse$_{1907}$ vote, presumably from voters mobilized by the Republican organizations hostile to Merriam, although Merriam did manage to receive between 50 and 62 percent of the 1907 Busse vote.

Table 11-1 presents transition rates from the 1911 primaries to the 1911 general election as evidence about the behavior of specific subgroups within each party.[33] As would be expected, the highest transition rates were from Merriam$_p$ (Merriam primary) to Merriam$_e$ (Merriam general election), and from Harrison$_p$ to Harrison$_e$. Transition rates from the primary vote for Thompson, the Busse candidate, and Smulski, the Deneen candidate, are similar; they suggest that most, but far from all, of the supporters of the two defeated Republicans went to Merriam in the general election. Harrison did much better with intra-party opponents: the estimates suggest that none of the Dunne primary vote, and relatively little of the Graham (Hopkins-Sullivan) vote, was transferred to Merriam. Since the 1907 general election vote for Dunne included some support from Harrison and Hopkins-Sullivan Democrats, Table 11-1's estimates for the behavior of the 1911 Dunne primary vote in the 1911 general election provide a purer test of municipal populist voting than do the 1907–11 transition rates presented above. But the estimates in Table 11-1 suggest the same conclusion: Merriam was unable to capture the Dunne vote. The estimated transition rate from Dunne$_p$ to Harrison$_e$, while lower than the transition rate from Harrison$_p$ to Harrison$_e$, still suggests that Harrison received the support of most of the Dunne primary voters.

Dunne supporters who would not back Harrison seem to have abstained or voted Socialist rather than switch to Merriam.[34]

Table 11-2 presents estimates for voting behavior by ethnic group.[35] Merriam, these estimates suggest, won pluralities of the Austrian and probably the Russian votes. The proportion of Germans or Irish voting for Merriam was probably lower than that for the four previous Republican mayoral candidates, Hanecy (1901), Stewart (1903), Harlan (1905), or Busse (1907). Merriam did no better than Busse had done among Italians and won a smaller share of the Italian vote than Hanecy, Stewart, or Harlan. Each of these last three groups had been mobilized against organizational candidates in previous elections: Dunne had a strong Irish following, Germans had backed Altgeld, and Italians had rebelled against John Powers's control of the Nineteenth Ward. Merriam's poor showing among these groups suggests again his inability to attract municipal populist support. Since these three ethnic groups were wet, Merriam may not have succeeded in defusing the temperance issue among the mass electorate. Merriam did, however, hold on to the traditional reform base of native and Scandinavian voters. Harrison's claim that, in this campaign alone, he received a strong minority of the Scandinavian vote is not borne out by the estimates.[36]

Suburbanization, which might be expected to favor Hyde Park's Merriam, shows an advantage for Harrison equivalent to a 15 percent difference between the most and least suburban wards. Since both Harrison and Merriam had opposed the traction interests, and since the 1907 settlement was in force, the traction issue was less prominent than in previous elections, but this would not explain the size of Harrison's advantage. Perhaps the variable reflects padded totals for Merriam in inner-city Hopkins-Sullivan wards. Coefficients for the illiteracy dummies suggest another surprising conclusion: Merriam's predicted vote is high-

TABLE 11-2
Voting Behavior by Ethnic Group, 1911

	Merriam (Rep.) %	Harrison (Dem.) %
Austrian	50–51	21–50
German	0	38–50
Irish	3–50	50–55
Italian	0	18–50
Native	50–56	24–50
Russian	17–50	13–50
Scandinavian	100	0

Note: Suburbanization and illiteracy variables set at mean values.
N = 35.

est among the lower-class wards with the most illiteracy. This may reflect organizational switching or fraud.

WHY MERRIAM FAILED

Why wasn't Merriam able to combine the voters who had earlier followed Dunne and Harlan into a progressive coalition like those formed by Mitchel and Baker? First, the potential institutional basis for such a coalition, the Chicago Bureau of Public Efficiency, was less suited for this role than were the New York Bureau of Municipal Research or the Cleveland Civic League. Mitchel's initial electoral coalition was constructed by experts from the Bureau of Municipal Research and based on the Bureau's investigative record and policy proposals. Baker was able to realize "civitism" through cooperation with Mayo Fesler and the restructured Civic League. Though Merriam as an alderman was not officially connected with the Chicago Bureau of Public Efficiency, the Bureau was closely associated with his mayoral campaign. It had developed from his commission on city expenditures, and Julius Rosenwald was the largest donor to both the Bureau and the campaign. But the Bureau of Public Efficiency did not play the same political role as its counterparts in the other two cities. It had only been formed in August 1910, eight months before the election, so it could not build up the analytical and political skills that could best lend themselves to an electoral campaign. The diffuse governmental structure of Chicago meant that many of the Bureau's battles would be fought over issues outside the scope of mayoral authority. And, as suggested above, the Bureau of Public Efficiency was organized around a more narrowly conceived and less electorally salient mission than research bureaus in New York or other cities.

Second, the ethnocultural attitudes of the Merriam camp were in some ways still those of traditional reformers. In New York, the new emphasis on municipal research not only developed new policy proposals but transformed traditional reformers' ethnocultural attitudes. Mitchel himself was an Irish Catholic. Anecdotal evidence suggests that in Chicago, this transformation was incomplete. At Merriam's mass meeting in the Auditorium Theatre, the obviously Irish Thomas O'Shaughnessy made a speech and others issued direct appeals to primary voters for Dunne, whose Irish identification was strong. Yet at the same meeting, two speakers, Clifford J. Roe and Charles Alden, told stereotypical Irish jokes.[37] In a later book, Merriam told a story, meant as humorous, that nonetheless suggests the kind of appeals his campaign thought attracted working-class support: "In my inner headquarters hung one of those dreadful lithographs that usually deface the landscape during electoral struggles. It was impressive in its dimensions, but seemed to me a terrible distortion of my features. My managers flaunted it before me, and labeled it 'Nitro Charley, the Yegg-man's Friend,' assuring me it would win many votes in the tougher districts of the city. Perhaps it did, but not enough."[38]

Third, partisanship was a greater barrier to coalition formation in Chicago than in Cleveland or New York. In national elections, traditional reformers were typically Republicans and municipal populists were typically Democrats; partisan allegiances continued to be shaped by the election of 1896. If a progressive coalition was to be formed, national party ties had to be made less binding. In New York, the Hearst campaigns served as a halfway point for Democrats who might not have been ready to immediately adopt the party of McKinley. By 1913, they could vote for Mitchel, who ran as both a Fusion candidate and a Republican; again, it was not necessary to vote Republican to vote against Tammany. Mitchel, moreover, was a Wilson Democrat in national politics. In Cleveland, the adoption of the nonpartisan preferential voting system also worked to unbind voters from national party ties. In the election of 1913, Republicans who had earlier backed Theodore Burton could vote for Baker without adopting the party of William Jennings Bryan. In Chicago, neither third parties nor balloting systems worked to overcome the divisive impact of national partisanship. Like New York's Hearst, Chicago's Altgeld had received municipal populist support in his independent mayoral candidacy, but Altgeld won a lower share of the Chicago vote in 1899 than Hearst won in New York in either 1905 or 1909. Moreover, the interval between the election(s) in which the independent municipal populist candidate had run and the election in which significant efforts to construct a progressive coalition were made was longer in Chicago than in New York—1899 to 1911 for Chicago, 1905 and 1909 to 1913 in New York. Thus, time had likely done more to erode the antiparty effects of Altgeld's 1899 candidacy on 1911 support for Merriam in Chicago than it had to erode the antiparty effects of Hearst's prior candidacies on 1913 support for Mitchel in New York. Proposals for a nonpartisan system of nomination by petition, which might have had the same effects on electoral behavior as Cleveland's preferential voting, had failed at the Chicago Charter Convention of 1906–1907.

Finally, Merriam's academic affiliation, constantly emphasized by the Harrison campaign, may have made him a less acceptable expression of progressive politics than Mitchel (in 1913) or Baker. University-trained experts were as unpopular in New York or Cleveland as in Chicago. But in the other two cities, the mayoral candidates were not themselves professors. The experts' role could thus be behind the scenes. Merriam, it should be noted, did not think his academic credentials a handicap to his political career. "For one thing," he later wrote, "among many of the foreign-born groups a professor is a person of some importance, and it turned out to be an unfortunate choice of an epithet."[39]

Merriam's own explanation for his defeat was that the property interests were not ready for change. "They were willing," he wrote later, "to have an administration which would wipe out grafting, which would economise the tax payer's money, which would give an efficient and progressive administration, but they were doubtful as to my attitude towards labor and towards what they call the radical movement. They decided that it would be better not to attack graft: it would be better to continue waste of funds, and slipshod government rather than to take any chances on a new man."[40] Louis Post also complained that business "shied at Merriam like an unbroken horse at a haystack on fire."[41] Yet Rosenwald and other leading businessmen had financed the campaign. Earlier, moreover, the Municipal Voters' League had elected a majority of the city council despite the ties of many business leaders to the traction companies. And in New York too, many businessmen had economic and political ties to Tammany or rival political organizations.[42] Even if Merriam had obtained more business support, it would not have stimulated support for him among municipal populist voters. Mitchel's defeat in the New York election of 1917 suggests increased identification with leading capitalists might actually have hurt Merriam.

Given the alleged extent of organizational betrayal and business indifference, Merriam might not have won the 1911 election even with the support of Dunne voters. His inability to construct a progressive coalition, however, is important both for comparison with the New York and Cleveland cases and for understanding the later course of Chicago politics. Dunne could not do what Baker was to do in Chicago: add traditional reform support to a municipal populist base. Nor could Merriam do what Mitchel was to do in New York: add municipal populist support to a traditional reform base. The incorporation of experts into city politics had not restructured city politics. In Chicago, the concept of efficiency suggested neither social welfare, as in Mitchel's New York, nor civic pride, as in Baker's Cleveland. For the Bureau of Public Efficiency, it meant only saving money through administrative methods. Merriam could rebut Harrison's class and ethnic appeals or respond in kind, but he could not change the language of political debate to a tongue more appropriate to his electoral needs.

MACHINE POLITICS: CHICAGO MODEL

All who study American urban politics know Chicago as the big city in which machine control extended the furthest and lasted the longest. As his counterparts elsewhere vanished into memory, Richard J. Daley endured as mayor, party boss, and even, for most of his mayoralty, kingmaker at Democratic National Conventions. The consolidation of authority that built a centralized Democratic machine from a chaotic politics of ward organizations occurred against the efforts of Chicago reformers and reflected their inability to build enduring electoral coalitions during the Progressive Era. A progressive coalition linking traditional reform and municipal populist challenges to machine politics became even more difficult to construct after Charles Merriam's defeat in the election of 1911: experts shifted their attention from local to national affairs, and World War I made it easier for politicians to stimulate ethnic antagonisms than to overcome them. The ethnic, working-class voters who had backed municipal populist candidates like Edward Dunne were eventually absorbed into the Democratic machine. Merriam and other traditional reformers continued to oppose the party organizations, but as marginal protesters rather than as competitors for political power.

"Big Bill" Thompson, not Merriam, became the dominant figure in the Chicago Republican party after 1911. He did so by practicing ethnocultural politics in ways that were fervently inconsistent but took advantage of the local animosities triggered or exacerbated by international conflicts. In 1915, Thompson distributed the pro-German handbill his Democratic opponent had used in the primary, with pictures of Kaiser Wilhelm and Emperor Franz Joseph, in anti-German Czech and Polish neighborhoods. During the war, however, he was pro-German and won support from that group in 1919. After sitting out the 1923 election for health reasons, Thompson defeated the Democratic incumbent, William Dever, in 1927 by opposing prohibition (though he had enforced Sunday closing in 1915) and by attacking Britain in his "America First" campaign. Textbooks adopted by the board of education, Thompson claimed, were ignoring Polish, German, French, and Irish heroes and presenting a pro-British version of the American Revolution. He also threatened to "kick the snoot of King George out of Chicago." In 1931, Thompson tried to arouse Irish jealousy of the Czech Democrat, Anton Cermak, whom he called "pushcart Tony." The sole consistency in Thompson's politics was his reliance on heavy black support.[43]

Merriam's political career could not survive the new tactics introduced by Thompson. In 1917, Merriam lost his aldermanic seat, counted out by a Thompson judge. In 1919, Merriam ran again for mayor. "When they hired a theater for a rally," according to Barry Karl, "Thompson supporters filled the seats and boo'd and heckled Merriam into a shouting, white-knuckled rage." Merriam finished third in the Republican primary. In 1935, Paul H. Douglas tried to interest the Roosevelt administration in supporting a fusion ticket headed by Merriam, as it was supporting La

Guardia in New York. Roosevelt, however, remained allied with the Democratic organization and Merriam did not run. Though the Roosevelt administration would not support him for the mayoralty, Merriam became a New Deal intellectual, serving on the National Resources Planning Board and the Brownlow Committee on Administrative Management.[44]

Following his withdrawal from Chicago politics, Merriam pioneered in the creation of a new political science oriented toward foundations and grant proposals rather than candidates and elections.[45] As John G. Gunnell has argued, Merriam's ideas were the link between the historicism of his teachers at Columbia, William A. Dunning and John W. Burgess, and the behavioralism of his students at Chicago, such as Harold Lasswell, Harold Gosnell, V. O. Key, and David Truman.[46] Merriam's scientistic break with the previous study of politics did not represent a discontinuity in substantive content but in the organization and method of inquiry and the identification of its intended audience. During the debates over the founding of what became the Social Science Research Council, William H. Allen, formerly of the New York Bureau of Municipal Research, recognized this when he "accused Merriam of having 'put the soft pedal upon one of the most important aspects of political research, namely, putting the research virus into the lay mind.'"[47]

In his second mayoralty of 1911–15, Carter Harrison II remained hostile to expertise and considered the Bureau of Public Efficiency part of a Merriam machine.[48] "As far as genuine, blown-in-the-bottle nonpartisanship and freedom from personal ambitions is concerned," Harrison wrote, "the Bureau of Public Efficiency is . . . about as innocent as an Apache warrior of the frontier days with a belt full of white men's scalps." He was particularly angered by the Bureau's opposition to his plan for a comprehensive subway, which was also opposed by Bion J. Arnold and the Board of Supervising Engineers and was voted down in a 1914 referendum.

Harrison tried to win traditional reform support, but through a crackdown on vice, rather than through alliance with experts. In his first series of administrations, he had followed a lenient vice policy. After 1911, however, Harrison closed many of the large brothels, citing the report of the Vice Commission appointed by Busse and a Rockefeller study of European conditions. He was particularly strict in closing down brothels that had moved into upper-class neighborhoods. The new policy brought him into conflict with the First Ward leaders Kenna and Coughlin, and Harrison supported Judge John Owens as Owens removed names from the First Ward voters' lists and fired the First Ward election clerks and judges. Harrison calculated that his loss of First Ward support would be outweighed by votes from women, who would vote in their first mayoral election in 1915. In the 1915 Democratic primary, however, the women's vote divided equally between Harrison and his opponent, Robert Sweitzer; and Sweitzer, a Hopkins-Sullivan candidate who had the support of most ward leaders, defeated Harrison, 183,249 to 104,063.[49] Sweitzer, who claimed to be of German descent, was able to win German votes with nationalistic appeals to show support for the Fatherland by electing a Teutonic mayor. Harrison never sought electoral office again. With his defeat, the Hopkins-Sullivan faction, headed by George Brennan after Sullivan's death in 1920, emerged dominant within the Democratic party.[50]

Like Harrison, William Dever, a staunch Dunne supporter during Dunne's mayoral administration, failed in his efforts to expand his political coalition by anti-vice campaigns that would appeal to the forces of traditional reform. Elected mayor in 1923 with the support of the Hopkins-Sullivan organization, Dever attempted to enforce prohibition and fight organized crime. His efforts won him the support of Merriam, Harold Ickes, Graham Taylor, and the traditional reform press, but cost him reelection in 1927 by alienating the wet ethnic groups who were the basis of a municipal populist electoral constituency.[51]

Merriam's failure to attract working-class, ethnic voters, Dever's inability to keep them while appealing to traditional reformers, and Harrison's loss of political balance allowed the Hopkins-Sullivan-Brennan Democratic organization to construct its own winning coalition by combining its core supporters with the very groups that had supported municipal populism. After Brennan died in 1928, Cermak became the Democratic leader by combining support from some Irish ward leaders with support from Czechs, Poles, Jews, and Germans unhappy with the Irish domination under Brennan. Dunne and Harrison returned to the Democratic organization under Cermak's auspices, while ward leaders like Coughlin and Kenna lost their autonomy. With Cermak's victory over Thompson in 1931, the Democrats became the citywide majority party again. Merriam, Ickes, Julius Rosenwald, and the leaders of the Municipal Voters' League and other traditional reform organizations endorsed Cermak out of antipathy toward Thompson.[52]

Though Cermak died in 1933, the Democratic organization remained intact under the successive leadership of Edward Kelly and Patrick Nash, Martin Kennelly and Jacob Arvey, and Richard J. Daley.[53] The programs of the New Deal, and later the War on Poverty, were used to consolidate the Democratic majority.[54] The nearly complete shift of blacks to the Democratic party eliminated the possibility of recreating the Republican coalitions that had elected Thompson. From 1931 to 1979, organization Democrats won every mayoral election, despite primary splits in 1955, 1977, and 1979. Native-stock Protestants and upper-middle-class Jews with traditional reform concerns organized the Independent Voters of Illinois (IVI), but it was effective in only a few wards and had little impact on citywide races.[55] Any possibility that experts could remake Chicago politics ended with the merger of the Chicago Bureau of Public Efficiency into the older, traditional reform Civic Federation in 1932. Chicago municipal research, never as independent from business as in New York or Cleveland, moved even closer to it after the merger: a 1940–42 administrative survey of Chicago city government was jointly sponsored by the Civic Federation and the Association of Commerce.[56]

Division of the organization vote between incumbent Jane Byrne and Richard M. Daley (the son of the late mayor) in the 1983 Democratic primary permitted the nomination of an insurgent candidate, Harold Washington. Washington then became Chicago's first black mayor by winning the general election over a Republican who had the support of more than three-quarters of the white Democratic voters—and of most of the white Democratic ward leaders. The electoral patterns of the 1983 vote recalled those of insurgent candidates in Chicago and other cities during the Progressive Era. Washington's core support came from black voters unhappy with their group's subordinate position under the Democratic machine. These voters can be considered contemporary municipal populists: they had backed Richard Newhouse in 1975 and Washington in 1977. Just as middle-class ethnics had supported earlier municipal populists, opposition to the machine was especially strong among middle-class blacks. Washington won the general election by adding to the black vote he had mobilized in the primary a majority of the Hispanic vote and, critically, support from some white "lakefront liberals." These last voters, located in Hyde Park as well as in the Lake Shore wards, can be considered traditional reformers; they had been the basis for the IVI and had supported Robert Merriam (Charles Merriam's son) in 1955 and William Singer in 1975.[57]

The dynamics of such coalitions during the Progressive Era suggest that it is easier to create coalitions while in opposition than to consolidate them while in power; that they must be consolidated to survive the reformation of organizational alliances; and that the role of experts in city government shapes the possibilities for consolidating initial electoral coalitions through the formulation and implementation of public policy. The history of the Washington coalition illustrates these lessons. Professional planners were particularly important among the experts Washington incorporated into city government; their efforts at community-oriented planning helped to forge ties with neighborhood activists. Like Edward Dunne, the only reform mayor of Progressive Era Chicago, Washington was hampered by a city council dominated by his organizational rivals. Unlike Dunne, Washington met the first test for the consolidation of a reform regime: he won reelection in April 1987, defeating

Byrne in the primary and winning the general election over Edward Vrdolyak, an organization Democrat turned independent candidate who was a more significant opponent than Donald Haider, the Democrat who became the Republican nominee.[58] Washington's personalistic style, and then his sudden death by heart attack in November 1987, prevented him from meeting a second test of regime consolidation: achievement of a smooth transition to a designated successor.[59]

The factional conflicts, independent candidacies, and cross-party alliances of Chicago in the 1980s were reminiscent of the city's politics during the Progressive Era. So was the politician who ended up on top. William J. Grimshaw sums up the administration of Richard M. Daley, who became mayor in 1989, as "machine politics, reform style."[60] The same label could have been applied to Carter Harrison II, Chicago's mayor from 1897 to 1905 and from 1911 to 1915. Both Harrison and Daley were second-generation mayors, whose fathers had become identified with the city. And like the younger Harrison, the younger Daley has proven to be adept at the politics of balance, maintaining his organizational base while doing just enough to attract the reform support needed to stay in power.

Part V

CONCLUSIONS

What happens in politics *depends on the way in which people are divided* into factions, parties, groups, classes, etc. The outcome of the game of politics depends on which of a multitude of possible conflicts gains the dominant position.

E. E. Schattschneider, The Semisovereign People: A Realist's View of Democracy in America *(emphasis in original)*

Progressivism, Electoral Change, and Public Policy

THE ANALYSIS OF REFORM presented in this book illustrates many of the themes that are emphasized in the growing literature on urban political economy. During the Progressive Era, New York, Cleveland, and Chicago were very much part of a national polity and a national economy. Within the common constraints imposed by larger forces, the politics of reform could produce different outcomes in each of the three cities. Economic and ethnic cleavages were significant, but not completely determining, for political leadership and political strategy could bring together (or keep apart) alternative reform coalitions.

Reform outcomes in New York, Cleveland, and Chicago also suggest the need to revise the analysis of reform politics, just as political scientists and historians have revised their analysis of machine politics in recent years. My findings can be summarized in the form of four specific points:

1. Patterns of reform support varied, by city and by candidate, and can be classified as traditional reform, municipal populist, or progressive. No particular ethnic group or social class should be exclusively identified with reform.

2. Reform support was not a function of suburbanization per se. Any association between suburban location and support for reform candidates resulted from either the residential patterns of particular social groups or the salience of transportation issues in particular campaigns.

3. The role of experts was determined by the way they were incorporated into the politics of each city. Where and when experts were both autonomous from business and linked with reform politicians, their proposals could provide the basis for a progressive electoral coalition that cut across existing social divisions.

4. The success or failure of experts and politicians in constructing and maintaining this coalition had short-term and long-term effects on a city's political development. Experts' ideas influenced policies; policies influenced voting behavior.

The sections below elaborate on each of these statements.

PROGRESSIVISM, ETHNICITY, AND CLASS

The fierce antagonism between the two camps notwithstanding, ethnocultural and Marxist analysts share a tendency to treat electoral cleavages as socially determined. They simply disagree on which basis of social division, ethnicity or class, is determining. Thus, immigrants (especially the Irish) or workers are portrayed as natural supporters of machine politics, while native-stock voters (or business owners, or the middle class) are portrayed as reformers. This kind of analysis leaves little room for different patterns of reform support in different cities, or for changes over time.[1] The analysis presented here suggests that electoral cleavages should be seen instead as fluid. This does not mean that they will change, but that they can change. It is important, therefore, to understand how change takes place. My argument has been that the incorporation of expertise can lead to the reformulation of political appeals, which in turn can produce electoral change and policy innovation.

Chapters 3 through 11 presented my findings on electoral behavior in New York, Cleveland, and Chicago. Table 12-1 summarizes patterns of reform support by the largest ethnic groups in each of the three cities. For each city, ethnic groups are listed in order of their support for traditional reform, municipal populist, and progressive candidates. A group was categorized as supporting the reform candidate if the unconstrained ecological regression estimates indicate that candidate received a plurality of its vote.[2] Figures in parentheses next to each group show the number of times the group supported this type of reform candidate (numerator) and the number of elections studied in which this type of reform candidate ran (denominator). Only elections that could be analyzed with the ethnically specific 1910 and 1920 censuses are included. Since different categories are used for the 1910 and 1920 Cleveland census data, fewer elections are included for Austrians (1910 only), Czechs (1920 only), and Poles (1920 only) than for other Cleveland groups.

Table 12-1 suggests that it is simplistic to categorize particular ethnic groups as pro- or anti-reform.[3] Different groups were mobilized by different types of reform appeals. If no group was hostile to all reform candidates, each group was also willing to vote for organization candidates to stop reformers it disliked. Native-stock voters are most strongly associated with support for traditional reform candidates and opposition to municipal populism. Germans rejected traditional reform candidates but supported municipal populists. The Irish, often identified with machine politics, backed Tom Johnson, Newton Baker, and Peter Witt in Cleveland and Edward Dunne in Chicago. New York's Jews supported William Randolph Hearst in 1909 and John Purroy Mitchel in 1913 but rejected Mitchel in 1917 as they had rejected Otto Bannard in 1909. Cleveland's

TABLE 12-1

Patterns of Reform Support, by Ethnic Group

	New York	Cleveland	Chicago
Traditional Reform	Native (2/2)	Native (2/2)	Scandinavian (2/2)
	German (0/2)	Russian (2/2)	Austrian (2/2)
	Irish (0/2)	Austrian (0/2)	Native (1/2)
	Italian (0/2)	German (0/2)	Russian (1/2)
	Jewish (0/2)	Hungarian (0/2)	German (0/2)
		Irish (0/2)	Irish (0/2)
			Italian (0/2)
Municipal Populist	German (1/1)	German (5/5)	German (2/2)
	Jewish (1/1)	Hungarian (5/5)	Irish (2/2)
	Irish (0/1)	Irish (5/5)	Italian (2/2)
	Italian (0/1)	Austrian (4/4)	Russian (2/2)
	Native (0/1)	Russian (1/5)	Austrian (1/2)
		Native (0/5)	Native (1/2)
		Czech (0/1)	Scandinavian (0/2)
		Polish (0/1)	
Progressive	German (1/1)	Czech (2/2)	
	Jewish (1/1)	German (2/2)	
	Native (1/1)	Hungarian (2/2)	
	Irish (0/1)	Irish (2/2)	
	Italian (0/1)	Polish (1/2)	
		Russian (1/2)	
		Native (0/2)	

Notes: Candidates and elections included:

New York:
Traditional Reform: Bannard$_{1909}$, Mitchel$_{1917}$
Municipal Populist: Hearst$_{1909}$
Progressive: Mitchel$_{1913}$

Cleveland:
Traditional Reform: Goulder$_{1903}$, Burton$_{1907}$
Municipal Populist: Johnson$_{1903}$, Johnson$_{1905}$, Johnson$_{1907}$, Johnson$_{1909}$, Witt$_{1915}$
Progressive: Baker$_{1911}$, Baker$_{1913}$

Chicago:
Traditional Reform: Harlan$_{1905}$, Merriam$_{1911}$
Municipal Populist: Dunne$_{1905}$, Dunne$_{1907}$
Progressive: [None]

Hungarians, Czechs, and Poles supported Johnson and Baker but split according to First World War alignments in the election of 1915. Chicago's Scandinavians supported traditional reform, though they became organizational Republicans with the rise of "Poor Swede" Fred Lundin, the patron of Mayor "Big Bill" Thompson, as political boss.[4] With the exception of the Scandinavians, foreign-stock voters were not going to support candidates who wanted to stop them from drinking, Protestantize their schools, and tell them as often as possible that they were inferior. But that did not mean foreign-stock voters felt their needs were met by machine politicians who became rich at public expense and were often themselves from other ethnic groups.

Table 12-1 also suggests the importance of differences among cities. New York, Cleveland, and Chicago were all large, economically and ethnically diverse Northeastern cities. Yet different patterns of class and ethnic mobilization during the nineteenth century produced different patterns of politics during the Progressive Era. In New York, where the Irish controlled Tammany Hall, they opposed any kind of reform. But the Irish in Chicago and Cleveland, who did not control dominant party machines, could be mobilized by municipal populist or progressive candidates. Native-stock support for traditional reform was more consistent in New York or Cleveland than in Chicago, where native-stock voters backed Dunne over John Maynard Harlan in 1905. In Cleveland, Austrians favored municipal populism and Russians traditional reform, but in Chicago, Russians favored municipal populism and Austrians traditional reform. Italians were hostile to all reform candidates in New York but supported municipal populism in Chicago. A better understanding of ethnic politics in American cities requires more research into such city-specific patterns of political incorporation.

Class is notoriously difficult to measure, and it becomes even more so if one seeks to operationalize the subjective definitions of class that social historians have found more useful than objective categorizations.[5] It is also hard to separate the effects of class from those of ethnicity or, for more recent political eras, race. Ira Katznelson has contributed the important insight that in the United States, a separation developed between work (the shop or factory), where people organized into class-based unions, and home (the neighborhood), where people organized into ethnically based parties. This contrasts with the development of other industrial societies, where either class or ethnicity became the basis of organization at work *and* at home.[6] The separation of home and work, however, was never complete. Katznelson himself argues that the black militants of the 1960s crossed this divide; Richard Oestreicher suggests other examples.[7] Even when and where class and ethnicity are independent at the level of organizations, they are usually intercorrelated at the level of individuals. As Amy Bridges says of antebellum New York, "The class structure exhibited a marked cultural division of labor."[8]

For this study, I used census data on illiteracy as a measure of social class. The 1910 and 1920 censuses present this data by ward for Cleveland and Chicago, and by Assembly District (AD) for New York. Illiteracy rates were functions of ethnicity as well as class; according to the 1910 census, for example, the heavily Italian Nineteenth Ward had the highest illiteracy level in Chicago, more than three times the rate for the city as a whole.[9] When we include illiteracy variables in ecological regression equations along with census variables for ethnicity, we can expect that the illiteracy measure will pick up the separate effects of class. Illiteracy rates were converted into dummy variables to test for curvilinear patterns by which middle-class wards (as measured by intermediate illiteracy levels) demonstrated more support for certain reform candidates than either upper-class (low illiteracy levels) or lower-class (high illiteracy levels) wards. Table 12-2 summarizes the results. A candidate was categorized as receiving upper-class votes ("Yes") if he showed a statistically significant decrease in support between upper-class and middle-class wards. A "No" indicates a statistically significant increase in support between upper-class and middle-class wards. Similarly, a "Yes" for "Middle Class?" indicates a statistically significant decrease in support in going from middle-class to lower-class wards and a "No" indicates a statistically significant increase in support in going from middle-class to lower-class wards. Variables that were not significant at the .05 level are omitted from the table.

The categorization scheme used in this book suggests that traditional reform candidates would enjoy support from the upper-class wards, but not from the middle- or lower-class wards ("Upper Class?" = "Yes," "Middle Class?" = "No"); that municipal populist candidates would enjoy support from the middle-class wards, but not from the upper- or lower-class wards ("Upper Class?" = "No," "Middle Class?" = "Yes"); and that progressive candidates would enjoy support from upper- and middle-class wards ("Upper Class?" not significant, "Middle Class?" = "Yes"). Fourteen of the twenty coefficients that are significant at the .05 level are in the hypothesized direction; at the .01 level, eleven of fourteen coefficients are in the right direction. Upper-class support for traditional reform and middle-class support for municipal populism are more evident in Table 12-2 than any common patterns of support for progressive candidates. Even where the differences between wards of one social class and wards of another are significant, they generally translate into differences in electoral support of only a few percentage points. The effects of class, as it is operationalized here, are thus smaller than the effects of ethnicity. This does not necessarily mean that class was more important than ethnicity in the electoral politics of the Progressive Era. The greater impact of ethnic variables in these estimates may instead reflect their more accurate measurement, since illiteracy levels are crude proxies for class, and the census data, based on self-reporting rather than actual testing, are themselves imperfect measures of true illiteracy.[10]

TABLE 12-2
Patterns of Reform Support, by Social Class

Type of Coalition	City	Reform Candidate	Year	Upper Class?	Middle Class?
Traditional Reform	New York	Bannard	1909	Yes[b]	
	Cleveland	Goulder	1903	Yes[b]	Yes[b]
	Cleveland	Burton	1907	Yes[b]	Yes[a]
	Chicago	Harlan	1905	Yes[a]	
	Chicago	Merriam	1911		No[b]
Municipal Populist	New York	Hearst	1909		Yes[b]
	Cleveland	Johnson	1903	Yes[b]	Yes[b]
	Cleveland	Johnson	1905		Yes[b]
	Cleveland	Johnson	1907		Yes[b]
	Cleveland	Johnson	1909		Yes[b]
	Cleveland	Witt	1915	Yes[a]	
	Chicago	Dunne	1905	No[b]	
	Chicago	Dunne	1907	No[a]	Yes[b]
Progressive	New York	Mitchel	1913	No[a]	No[b]
	Cleveland	Baker	1911		Yes[a]
	Cleveland	Baker	1913		

Note: Coefficients not significant at .05 level omitted.
[a]Coefficient significant at .05 level.
[b]Coefficient significant at .01 level.

PROGRESSIVISM AND SUBURBANIZATION

One approach to the study of cities has always been to emphasize the effects of an inexorable process of urbanization, which in twentieth-century America became a process of suburbanization. Richard Wade's suburban interpretation of reform, discussed in Chapter 2, applies this perspective to the Progressive Era.[11] This way of thinking about reform tends to treat city politics as a product of demographic factors that are impersonal, and hence apolitical. Michael McCarthy's imaginative distinction between "working-class spread" and "middle-class spread" cities pushes this tendency even further: in his approach, Lake Michigan plays a more important part in the political development of Chicago than Carter Harrison, Charles Merriam, Anton Cermak, or Richard J. Daley.[12]

Voting patterns, as shown in ward data or electoral maps, have always been the main evidence for the suburban interpretation of reform. Such evidence, however, does not allow us to distinguish the effects of suburban location per se from the association between reform support and membership in a particular class or ethnic group that might also have been more likely to live in the outer districts of a city. To test the hypothesis that suburban location was associated with reform support, I included the variable of suburban location, as measured by census data on the ratio of dwellings per family in each ward or AD, in the series of ecological regression equations for which estimates are reported in Chapters 3 to 11.

The results of these tests of the suburbanization hypothesis are summarized in Table 12-3. Each election in New York, Cleveland, or Chicago involving at least one reform candidate is classified according to whether it shows an association between suburbanization and reform support. If the coefficient for the suburbanization variable (dwellings per family) is greater for the reform candidate than for nonreform opponents, that election is listed in the "Yes" column. If the suburbanization coefficient is lower for the reform candidate, that election is listed in the "No" category. Four elections are listed as "Ambiguous." In the Cleveland elections of 1903 and 1907 and the Chicago election of 1905, both leading candidates were reformers. In the four-way Cleveland election of 1915, the suburbanization coefficient for Witt, the only reformer, was greater than that for Harry Davis, his major opponent, but less than that for the two other

TABLE 12-3
Was Suburbanization Positively Associated
with Reform Support?

	Yes	No	Ambiguous[a]
New York		1901	
		1903	
		1905	
		1909	
		1913	
		1917	
Cleveland	1905	1901	1903
	1909	1911	1907
		1913	1915
Chicago	1897	1911	1905
	1899		
	1907		
Total	5	10	4

Note: Elections with no reform candidate are omitted: Chicago$_{1901}$, Chicago$_{1903}$.
[a]Classification of elections as ambiguous explained in text.

organizational candidates. The three-way New York election of 1909 is categorized as a "No," since the suburbanization coefficient for William Gaynor, the nonreform candidate, is greater than that for either Bannard, the traditional reformer, or Hearst, the municipal populist.

The estimates summarized in Table 12-3 do not support the hypothesis that reform candidates were backed by suburban voters. Combining results from the three cities, five elections show an association between suburban location and reform support, but ten elections show an association between suburban location and support for the nonreform candidate(s). Four elections, again, are classified as ambiguous. The patterns for each city suggest that any association between suburbanization and reform support was due to the salience of transportation issues. The relationship is weakest in New York, where the traction issue, as it became politicized, had the least connection with the fares and conditions of daily commuting. The relationship is strongest in Chicago, where franchises, safety, consolidation of downtown lines, and subway construction were issues throughout the Progressive Era. For Cleveland, suburbanization is associated with reform support for the elections during Tom Johnson's war with the ConCon street railway, which focused on fares and transfers, but not for the elections after the Tayler settlement of 1910 defused the transit issue. To the extent that suburban voters supported reform, they did so to obtain lower fares and better service. Arthur Bentley was even able to explain the behavior of small electoral districts by their proximity to particular traction lines and the service they received.[13] Suburban voters were not showing any general preferences for centralization over decentralization or cosmopolitanism over localism. They were simply voting to lower their commuting costs.

PROGRESSIVISM AND EXPERTISE

If, as I have argued above, patterns of city politics in the Progressive Era were influenced, but not determined, by conflicts based on ethnicity, class, and spatial location, then multiple outcomes and multiple electoral coalitions were possible. Acting in conjunction with politicians, experts in some cities could affect which coalitions formed and which outcomes prevailed.

The urban political experts of the Progressive Era could potentially solve two persistent problems of reform politics: how to make temporary electoral coalitions enduring, and how to bring two contradictory sources of reform support together. Reformers, Tammany ward leader George Washington Plunkitt said in 1905, "were mornin' glories—looked lovely in the mornin' and withered up in a short time, while the regular machines went on flourishin' forever, like fine old oaks."[14] Plunkitt's observation was accurate as long as reformers, like those he had observed in New York, tried to mobilize as movements. The material benefits and social attachments that kept the regular party organizations together endured; the purposes that motivated both traditional reformers and municipal populists to join committees or form independent parties became less compelling with the resolution of the latest crisis. Even after reform victories, therefore, reformers ceased political activity and organizational politicians regained control.

With the incorporation of experts into city politics, this dynamic could be overcome. While reform activists were motivated by crises, experts were motivated by research problems, and there was always more research to be done. Experts could play this political role if and only if three conditions were met. Experts had to exist; they had to be relatively independent from business control; and they had to be linked with electoral actors. The organization of professional education and professional associations during the late nineteenth and early twentieth centuries fulfilled the first condition. Whether the second and third conditions were also met was determined by local patterns of political development. As long as experts' positions in city government were protected by sympathetic administrations or civil service laws, or as long as their autonomous institutes received funding from business or the federal government, experts engaged in continuous research. The nature of the training received by experts like William H. Allen, Henry Bruère, Frederic Howe, and Edward Bemis led them to focus their research upon practical problems like education, employment, transportation, and sanitation. The policy solutions they proposed could make city government an ongoing source of services capable of long-term competition with party organizations. Nineteenth-century New York reform administrations could not win reelection. Neither could New York's Seth Low or Chicago's Edward Dunne during the Progressive Era. But by developing ties to experts, Tom Johnson and Newton Baker won six of seven Cleveland elections between 1901 and 1913. And during the New Deal, Fiorello La Guardia won reelection twice to serve twelve years as mayor of New York.

An enduring reform coalition held together by experts' policy proposals was likely to contain a majority of the urban electorate, for the incorporation of expertise allowed reform candidates to mobilize two sets of potentially supportive voters at once. Elites and workers, native-stock voters and immigrants, all had grievances against the party organizations. But foreign-stock workers would support the organizations against traditional reformers who wanted economy and cultural conformity, and native-stock elites would support the organizations against municipal populists who seemed, to them, to threaten class and ethnic upheaval. Experts such as

Bruère and Mayo Fesler helped politicians such as Mitchel and Baker develop new appeals that could simultaneously appeal to both reform constituencies. Whether or not this occurred, and how long it continued, depended upon the city-specific relationships of experts, politicians, and business owners. The transformation of reform in New York lasted for only the election of 1913. Baker was able to maintain his Cleveland coalition through two mayoral elections. In Chicago, traditional reform and municipal populist voters could not be brought together at all.

Traditional reform and municipal populist electoral constituencies were mobilized throughout the nineteenth century. But the Progressive Era was a special window of opportunity for coalitions that linked the two. Since such coalitions depended upon expertise, they could not be formed until the 1890s, when the first generation with the appropriate training and orientation entered political life. These coalitions became more difficult to form with the coming of World War I, which exacerbated and nationalized ethnic antagonisms. In New York, the war pitted native-stock voters against Jews and Germans, splitting the traditional reform and municipal populist components of the Mitchel coalition. In Chicago and Cleveland, the war created conflict between Eastern Europeans seeking independence for their homelands and Germans or Austrians sympathetic to the Central Powers. These groups had previously been capable of uniting in support of municipal populist candidates.[15]

Like the Progressive Era, the New Deal and the racial upheaval that began in the 1960s were periods of crisis for urban political regimes, in which it became possible to change the ways people were divided. The New Deal created new urban coalitions reflecting the rise of organized labor and the increased numbers of blacks, Italians, and Eastern Europeans in northeastern cities. The War on Poverty and, in some cities, federal enforcement of the Voting Rights Act, again created new electoral coalitions, in which blacks and Hispanics played important roles. In each of the three periods, change came from outside, through diffusion from other cities. (Under the New Deal and the Great Society, change came from direct federal intervention as well.) And in each of the critical periods, experts shaped the proposals that made electoral change possible.

The outcome of each challenge to existing regimes was shaped by earlier reform outcomes. The collapse of the Mitchel administration in New York allowed Tammany Hall to regain its former dominance over New York politics, but Fiorello La Guardia and John Lindsay were able to put together their own versions of Mitchel's progressive coalition. In Cleveland, Dennis Kucinich evoked a municipal populist heritage that stretched back to Tom Johnson and Peter Witt. The inability of Edward Dunne or Charles Merriam to construct progressive coalitions in Chicago contributed to the consolidation of the machine that Mayor Daley ruled, and against which Harold Washington led a temporarily successful revolt. The sequence of reform outcomes in New York, Cleveland, and Chicago thus illustrates the partial determination of the present by the past that political scientists have described by borrowing from economists the concept of path dependence.[16] Karl Marx made a similar point when he said, "Men make their own history, but they do not make it just as they please; they do not make it under circumstances chosen by themselves, but under circumstances directly encountered, given and transmitted from the past."[17]

PROGRESSIVISM AND PUBLIC POLICY

Ethnic patterns of support for traditional reform and municipal populist candidates, experts' influence in fusing a progressive coalition, and the association between suburbanization and reform when transportation issues were salient all suggest linkages between electoral behavior and public policy. These linkages are contrary to the model of electoral politics developed by ethnocultural historians, in which voters form stable identifications with parties according to their symbolic, cultural "character." As Richard L. McCormick points out, the ethnocultural model posits a complete separation between the electoral process and the policy process, for if voters act on the basis of cultural images, they do not act on the basis of policy positions.[18] The approach taken in this book is closer to V. O. Key's maxim that, taken collectively, "voters are not fools." The urban electorate of the Progressive Era was less loyal to party than we have sometimes believed: voters were quite willing to support independent candidates or even cross over to the other side when it made sense to do so. These shifts were discernible and, in the aggregate, logical. The urban electorate of the Progressive Era was not always rational, as that term is used in rational choice approaches to political science, since voting behavior reflected ideas and identities as well as individual self-interest. Nor was it always responsible, since then as now voters wanted government to do more for less money. But the urban electorate was responsive, and what it responded to included the policy proposals of reform politicians and the policy records of reform administrations.[19]

This does not mean that the average voter read all the pamphlets, heard all the speeches, or carefully considered all the issues. But candidates' proposals did affect the coverage of the ethnic and popular press, which could in turn reach the average voter. The most politically salient policy questions, moreover, involved citizens' daily contact with government. Voters might not have well-defined views on municipal ownership, but they had opinions about whether the streetcars were cheap and safe enough. They might not be able to evaluate competing approaches to public health, but they knew when their children died of diphtheria or tuberculosis. They also knew whether new schools and parks had been built. During the Progressive Era, moreover, experts found new ways to educate voters about public policy, and thus facilitated informed decision making. The urban experts of the Progressive Era sought to share their knowledge with the average citizen through innovative experiments like the New York budget exhibits and the Cleveland Tax School. Critics who see experts as elitists seeking to create a passive and deferential mass public miss the democratic quality of this emphasis on civic education.[20]

The policies to which the urban electorate responded, and about which it was to become educated, reflected the influence of experts. Since professionalization occurred along disciplinary lines, this influence varied among policy areas. Public health, for example, was treated as a professional responsibility by the end of the nineteenth century; professionalization of police forces took until the 1930s.[21] The influence of experts was purer under reformers than under organizational politicians: reformers did not use public policy to enrich themselves and give material rewards to supporters. For traditional reformers, however, the claims of expertise were denied when they came into conflict with beliefs in Anglo-Saxon Protestant superiority or businesslike government. For municipal populists, similarly, the claims of expertise were denied when they came into conflict with the ideologies of municipal ownership or the Single Tax. The influence of expertise on policy was thus purest under administrations elected by progressive coalitions.

Expert influence also varied among cities. Because of reformers' electoral failures, experts had the least influence on policy in Chicago. In New York, experts' policy proposals were distorted by business's preference for economy. Experts had the most influence on public policy in Cleveland, but that influence waned after Johnson and Baker were replaced by organizational Republicans and Democrats sympathetic to business interests. Though experts still need to ally with local politicians to gain local power, since the New Deal they have often had federal resources to help them finance their research and implement their proposals. But competition among cities in the national market economy continues to constrain any city that might enact policies that produce a bad "business climate."[22]

Several other aspects of the influence of experts on public policy are illustrated by the Group Plan for Cleveland public buildings implemented under Johnson and Baker, discussed in Chapter 7.[23] First, the influence of experts led to the diffusion of policy ideas through networks that crossed city, state, and national lines, and through these experts' own travels. The two men who first proposed that Cleveland group its public buildings, Frederic Howe and Morris Black, had lived in Germany and wanted to construct a civic center like those of European capitals. The plan was carried out by three nationally prominent architects, Daniel H. Burnham, John M. Carrère, and Arnold W. Brunner. Burnham had already worked on the "White City" of the 1893 World's Columbian Exposition in Chicago and would later prepare the plan for Chicago's redevelopment.

Second, experts believed that there was such a thing as the civic good, upon which all could agree, and which reduced all remaining issues to questions of technique. The whole design of the Group Plan embodied this belief. Public buildings, not businesses or residences, were to be at the symbolic center of the city. Pedestrians would see the City Hall at the end of one major street and the County Courthouse at the end of another. A mall would allow the public to gather.

Third, what the experts of the Progressive Era saw as ideal was not necessarily correct, and in some fields became anathema to another generation of experts. The Group Plan's concentration of public buildings in downtown Cleveland has produced segregated use: people go downtown only to work. Jane Jacobs, however, argues for city planning based on diversity, in which downtowns have recreational and residential uses. The absence of the latter activities from downtown Cleveland creates squalor and at least the perception of danger.[24] That experts, in certain contexts, could operate with a significant degree of autonomy from business thus does not mean that their ideas were valid. Some of the policies proposed by experts during the Progressive Era seem in retrospect to have been appropriate. Others seem foolish or disastrous. Theories about the reversal of criminal tendencies by exposure to light may be laughable, but misguided attempts to cure diseases and racist assumptions about the capacities of people of non-Anglo-Saxon stock are not.

Fourth, experts' proposals were distorted to fit business demands. A city plan developed by experts was more completely implemented in Cleveland than in Chicago or Los Angeles, but the proposed railroad terminal was never constructed. During the 1930s, the Van Sweringen brothers, private developers, built a railroad terminal in a form that conflicted with the Group Plan. The terminal was placed in the Public Square, away from the Group Plan buildings, and the Terminal Tower, a commercial office building, was constructed above it. The Terminal Tower, until 1967 the tallest building outside New York, replaced the public buildings as the visual and symbolic focus of downtown Cleveland. Peter Witt and the members of the Soviet Table unsuccessfully opposed the project in favor of the lakefront terminal of the Group Plan. The design of the Terminal Tower copied that of the New York Municipal Building, completed in 1916.[25] The intercity diffusion of ideas that was so fundamental to the experts of the Progressive Era operated in this case against their original conception. The New York Municipal Building expressed the primacy of the public sphere vertically, through its tremendous height. The same form, imported for the private Terminal Tower, disrupted the horizontal design of the Group Plan, meant to embody the primacy of the public in Cleveland.

The conflicts between the Van Sweringens and Cleveland reformers, or the unhappiness of New York capitalists at the program of the Bureau of Municipal Research, show that experts were not always controlled by business. Rather, they tried to enlist business support for their own policy agendas. These agendas were always within the bounds of capitalism and sometimes corresponded to the long-run interests of capitalists. But these agendas might also bring reformers into real conflicts with business preferences, and when they did, business often won.

New York, Cleveland, and Chicago are all river cities, and the engineer is one important type of expert, so it may be appropriate to conclude by shifting our attention from the Terminal Tower and the Municipal Building to the bridges located nearby. Bridges join portions of cities that are physically divided: Manhattan and Brooklyn, the East and West Sides of Cleveland, the North and South Sides of Chicago. Bridges reflect their time: what was modern when constructed may look old-fashioned today. Ferries and tunnels are other ways of spanning the same divisions, with different consequences for their city's physical development. Without planning, bridges cannot be constructed. Without subsequent maintenance, bridges will not withstand the effects of time and unpredictable disasters. Both planning and maintenance require the joint participation of engineering experts and elected politicians.

Bridges can serve as a metaphor for the kind of electoral coalitions that some experts and politicians worked to build during the Progressive Era. In this period, New York, Cleveland, and Chicago were divided less by the East, Cuyahoga, and Chicago Rivers than by ethnicity, social class, and party. Policy proposals were connecting structures to link constituencies that would otherwise remain apart. Like literal bridges, these electoral bridges may seem quaint to us, and these bridges too required the collaboration of experts and politicians. Some of the bridges envisioned by political experts were never built; some of the bridges built were not properly maintained. We might prefer, with hindsight, to have built with other materials or in other locations. But we never have such choices, because the present-day city has been constructed upon the political infrastructure of the past.

WITH A FEW INTERESTING but unsystematic exceptions, we do not have individual-level data, such as that provided by surveys, relating voting behavior and demographic characteristics during the Progressive Era. We do have aggregate data on voting and on demographic traits, grouped by ward or Assembly District, for New York, Cleveland, and Chicago. In research on this period, we thus face the problem of cross-level inference: how to use aggregate data to estimate relationships at the level of the individual.

The simplest approach is to examine the districts that are most homogeneous with regard to the independent variable of interest, for example percentage belonging to a particular ethnic group. We then assume that the level of the dependent variable (say, vote for a particular candidate) in this district is also valid for the group as a whole, regardless of residential location.[1] While this approach can be a useful first step in identifying relationships, it has several drawbacks. First, few electoral units approach 100 percent membership in any group, so the data will be contaminated by the behavior of nonmembers. Second, voters in the homogeneous districts selected may be unrepresentative of the group with respect to other significant variables, such as class, education, or distance from the city center. Third, contextual effects may exist; that is, the homogeneity of the district may itself be a significant independent variable.[2]

Maps showing levels of variables by district can effectively convey information about an entire city.[3] However, the organization of this information on the basis of geography should not be taken to imply geographic causation. Spatial patterns may be spurious, reflecting the influence of other variables that are not illustrated in the maps. It is possible to incorporate additional variables into maps that combine, say, class and ethnic data with location, but as this is done the appealing simplicity of the map disappears.

Ecological correlation generates a single summary statistic that indicates the strength of a hypothesized relationship.[4] Various correlation coefficients are used, according to the level of data and other conditions; the known distributions of these statistics allow significance testing. We can eliminate spurious associations by controlling for other variables besides those in which we are most interested. However, the correlation coefficient does not yield direct estimates of transfer rates such as percentage Irish voting for Mitchel or percentage $Johnson_{1909}$ voting for $Baker_{1911}$, and these are often substantively necessary. Another problem is that the correlation coefficient typically becomes inflated as larger units are analyzed.[5]

Ecological regression, first proposed by Leo Goodman, is an alternative to ecological correlation that does yield estimates of transfer rates.[6] One estimates the coefficients of a linear regression model:

$$\overline{Y}_t = \beta_0 + \beta_1\overline{X}_t + \beta_2\overline{X}_t + \ldots + \beta_i\overline{X}_{it} + \overline{\epsilon}_t$$

where $\overline{Y}_t$ is the group mean of the dependent variable (here, vote percentage by ward or Assembly District), $\overline{X}_{it}$ are the group means for the independent variables (here percentage in an ethnic group or voting for a particular candidate in the earlier election), and $\overline{\epsilon}_t$ is an error term. Like ecological correlation and examination of homogeneous districts, ecological regression assumes there are no contextual effects. Another problem of ecological regression is the frequency of "inadmissible" estimates suggesting that the proportion of group *a* supporting candidate *b* was less than zero, or greater than 100 percent.

Another approach to ecological inference, proposed by Otis Dudley Duncan and Beverly Davis, is the method of bounds, in which inference is based on analysis of the limits to individual-level combinations of values (the cells) set by the aggregate totals for each value of each variable (the marginals). This approach requires less heroic assumptions than ecological regression and avoids inadmissible estimates. W. Phillips Shively has championed the method of bounds, and William Claggett and John Van Wingen show that it is an extension of the well-known techniques of linear programming.[7] Shively and Claggett and Van Wingen have applied the method of bounds/linear programming to U.S. voting behavior in the New Deal, to U.S. and British voting behavior in the 1930s and the 1970s, and to German support for the Social Democratic party in 1912. They demonstrate that with some reasonable assumptions based on external evidence such as national surveys or previous studies, the approach generates substantively important and impressively precise estimates that hold up well when tested against panel data. Unfortunately, for American cities of the Progressive Era, we lack even the limited external evidence upon which they rely in order to narrow the range of their estimates. Moreover, Shively notes that the estimates will be more precise in "hyperstructured electorates," where we can assume little cross-party switching, than in "relatively unstructured electorates" where we cannot make this assumption.[8] The independent candidacies, interparty alliances, and factional knifing discussed throughout this book suggest that the municipal electorate of the Progressive Era was relatively unstructured.

The approach I took for this study was to combine linear programming and ecological regression techniques to estimate transfer rates. Shively shows that if we assume the true parameter "is unlikely to fall near either tail of the bounds" and is unimodally distributed, the best estimate is the midpoint of the bounds.[9] However, when the ecological regression estimates are outside the bounds, the appropriate boundary point may be a better estimate. Thus, when the regression estimate was below the lower boundary for the parameter, I present the lower boundary as my estimate. Similarly, when the regression estimate was above the upper boundary, I present the upper boundary as my estimate. When the regression estimate falls within the bounds, I present a range, from the midpoint of the bounds to the regression estimate or vice versa. When the midpoint of the bounds and the regression estimate were equal (within 1 percent), that figure is reported as a single estimate. While it would probably not be wise to build a bridge or send a rocket to the moon using these estimates, for purposes of social science generalization they are probably adequate, particularly when compared with the alternatives discussed above.

For the regression estimates to be unbiased, error variance must be constant. In this context, however, error variance will vary with N (the number of potential voters in each district, generally not exactly equal). To fulfill the assumption of homoscedasticity, weighted least squares (WLS) can be used to estimate the model. The computed standard errors will be incorrect. The true standard errors can be obtained by dividing the computer-produced statistic by the standard error of the regression.[10]

Estimates of transition probabilities, the proportion of voters for candidate a at election t-1 who supported candidate b at election t, represent a special case of ecological regression.[11] This procedure assumes that the population is identical at t-1 and t, or, slightly less restrictively, that all individuals who leave the potential electorate through death or migration are replaced by others with identical characteristics for the variables included in the equation. The greater the difference in time between t and t-1, the more serious the violation of this assumption becomes. It is also assumed that transition rates are stable across districts; otherwise, the model will be misspecified. Again, WLS must be used to estimate the model.

To estimate the behavior of Republican and Democratic identifiers in the New York mayoral elections of 1901 and 1903, data from the presidential elections of the period were used. Rather than use any one election in a transition model, which might lead to bias due to the circumstances of that election, I used two stage least squares (2SLS).[12] I used ordinary least squares (OLS) to regress the 1904 vote on the 1900 vote. The mayoral election Assembly District (AD) totals were then regressed on the OLS-predicted 1904 values, rather than on the actual 1904 vote.

To estimate transition rates between elections when a city had been reapportioned in the interim, it was necessary to remap data for one election onto the wards (in New York, ADs) by which it was aggregated in the other election. This was a tedious operation that required the collection of voting data at the election district (ED) level and the assignment of EDs to pre-apportionment wards or ADs. To estimate transition rates between the New York elections of 1913 (or 1909) and 1917, for example, I used the 1917 vote by ED, available in the *City Record*, with a list of boundaries published in the *City Record*, October 8, 1917, and Assembly District maps available at the New York Public Library. Where 1917 EDs overlapped 1906–16 Assembly Districts, votes were assigned equally to each AD. I followed similar procedures for Cleveland to estimate transition rates between the elections of 1901 and 1903, and between the elections of 1909 and 1911.

Notes

Chapter 1

1. Huntington, *American Politics*; Shefter, "Party, Bureaucracy, and Political Change"; and Walters, *American Reformers*, preface and afterword.

2. This definition follows Wolfinger, *Politics of Progress*, 99–100.

3. Shefter, "Emergence of the Political Machine"; McCarthy, "New Metropolis," 49.

4. Bernard and Rice, "Political Environment and the Adoption of Progressive Municipal Reform," uses a cross-sectional approach to explain the adoption of council-manager government. Knoke, "Spread of Municipal Reform," takes an event history approach to the adoption and abandonment of the council-manager and commission systems. Brown and Halaby, "Bosses, Reform, and the Socioeconomic Bases of Urban Expenditure," pools cross-sectional and time series data, with machine, reform, and demographic measures as independent variables and expenditure levels as the dependent variable.

5. The statistical problems that can follow from this small N include untrustworthy significance tests and a strong likelihood that some independent variables of theoretical interest will have to be dropped because there are too few degrees of freedom to incorporate them all into the models being tested.

6. "In the smaller cities," Samuel P. Hays suggests, "business, professional, and elite groups could easily exercise a dominant influence. Their close ties readily enabled them to shape informal political power which they could transform into formal political power." But, "in the larger, more heterogeneous cities, whose subcommunities were more dispersed, such community-wide action was extremely difficult." As a result, "reformers in large cities often had to rest content with their Municipal Research Bureaus through which they could exert political influence from outside the municipal government." Hays, "Politics of Reform," 165. Hays's point is echoed by Schiesl, *Politics of Efficiency*, 133. Cf. Skocpol, *States and Social Revolutions*, 33–37.

7. Hofstadter, *Age of Reform*. See also Cornwell, "Bosses, Machines, and Ethnic Groups," 27–39; Banfield and Wilson, *City Politics*; and Glazer and Moynihan, *Beyond the Melting Pot*, 217–29.

8. Hays, "Politics of Reform." See also Weinstein, *Corporate Ideal*.

9. Hays, *Response to Industrialism*, 5–8.

10. Heclo, *Modern Social Politics*, 306.

11. "The diffusion of the Progressive program was so rapid and widespread because the reformers established a network of organizations, such as the National Municipal League, and publications, such as the *National Municipal Review*, for this very purpose, and they were linked to others (namely, professional associations and national magazines) in whose interest it was to advance the cause." Shefter, "Party, Bureaucracy, and Political Change," 231.

12. Fox, *Better City Government*, xviii, 63–89.

13. Wiebe, *Search for Order*, 112–21; Larson, *Rise of Professionalism*, 145–58; and Teaford, "Finis for Tweed and Steffens,"139.

14. Wiebe, *Search for Order*, 128.

15. Stewart, *Half Century of Reform*, 11–15.

16. Ibid., 15–27, 44–45, 146–72; Fox, *Better City Government*, 51–62. Schiesl, *Politics of Efficiency*, 31–36, critically examines the National Civil Service League. Childs, *Civic Victories*, chap. 9, recounts the author's experiences as secretary of the National Short Ballot Association.

17. "Taking advantage of a system of communication which now physically integrated the country," Magali Sarfatti Larson concludes, university-educated members of the professional and managerial middle class "sought links in other cities and regions with peers of like mind." "Journalists and editors," she points out, "played an important role in spreading and unifying their views." Larson, *Rise of Professionalism*, 154.

18. The positive side of Progressive Era magazine journalism, which is of more interest here, has received less attention than the concern for exposure that led Theodore Roosevelt to popularize the term "muckraking" in criticizing writers who were allegedly concerned only with the filth below them. See for example Filler, *Crusaders for American Liberalism*; Regier, *Era of the Muckrakers*; Hofstadter, *Age of Reform*, 186–98; and McCormick, "Discovery," 259–60, 265, 272.

19. Sarasohn, "Power without Glory," 474, 476.

20. Johnson, *My Story*, 52–54, 56.

21. Holmgren, "Bemis and Municipal Reform," 104–16, 204–45, 255–56.

22. Johnson, *My Story*, 54–55.

23. Rice, *Progressive Cities*, chap. 4.

24. Ibid., chaps. 6–7; Childs, *Civic Victories*, 136–38, 141–47, 157–63; Knoke, "Spread of Municipal Reform," 1315; and Schiesl, *Politics of Efficiency*, chap. 9. Among the weaknesses of the commission system addressed by the council-manager plan were the lack of leadership, the absence of administrative expertise, and the possibilities for conflict between commissioners.

25. Gill, *Municipal Research Bureaus*, 17–18; Dahlberg, *New York Bureau of Municipal Research*, 23.

26. Dahlberg, *New York Bureau of Municipal Research*, 164–67; Kahn, "Re-Presenting Government," 91–101; Schiesl, *Politics of Efficiency*, 116, 155–56; and Miller, *Boss Cox's Cincinnati*, 215–16.

27. Griffith, *Progressive Years*, 202.

28. Ibid., 226–29.

29. Fogelson, *Big-City Police*, preface and chap. 3.

30. Duffy, *History of Public Health in New York City*, 125; Johnson, "Shall the Street Railroads Control the People or Shall the People Control the Street Railroads" (pamphlet); and Johnson, *My Story*, 123.

31. Relevant works by these authors include Bridges, *City in the Republic*; idem, "Boss Tweed and V. O. Key in Texas"; idem, "Politics and Growth in Sunbelt Cities"; idem, "Winning the West to Municipal Reform"; Elkin, *City and Regime*; Erie, *Rainbow's End*; idem, "How the Urban West Was Won"; Fuchs, *Mayors and Money*; Judd, *Politics of American Cities*; Kantor, *Dependent City*; Katznelson, *Black Men, White Cities*; idem, *City Trenches*; Mollenkopf, *Contested City*; idem,

Phoenix in the Ashes; Shefter, *Political Crisis/Fiscal Crisis*; Stone, *Regime Politics*; Swanstrom, *Crisis of Growth Politics*; and idem, "Semisovereign Cities: The Politics of Urban Development." The selections and introductory comments in *Enduring Tensions*, a reader edited by Judd and Kantor, provide a good introduction to the urban political economy literature.

32. Peterson, *City Limits*. Elkin (*City and Regime*, 2–4); Erie (*Rainbow's End*, 254–58); Fuchs (*Mayors and Money*, 32); Judd and Kantor (*Enduring Tensions*, 2–3); Kantor (*Dependent City*, 7–8); Mollenkopf (*Phoenix in the Ashes*, 9, 32–37); Stone (*Regime Politics*, xi–xii, 164); and Swanstrom (*Crisis of Growth Politics*, 15–17, and "Semisovereign Cities," 83–84, 106–7) all frame their own analyses with critical comments on Peterson.

33. See Bridges, "Winning the West"; idem, "Boss Tweed and V. O. Key in Texas"; idem, "Politics and Growth in Sunbelt Cities"; and Erie, "How the Urban West Was Won."

34. Elkin, *City and Regime*, chaps. 1, 6; Stone, *Regime Politics*, chap. 1; and Swanstrom, "Semisovereign Cities," 106–10.

35. Bryce, *American Commonwealth*, vol. 2; Ostrogorski, *Democracy and the Organization of Political Parties*, vol. 2; Steffens, *Shame of the Cities*; and Myers, *History of Tammany Hall*. Allswang, *Bosses, Machines, and Urban Voters*, chap. 1, reviews the evolution of intellectual opinion about machine politics.

36. Merton, *Social Theory and Social Structure*, 51, 70–78.

37. Ibid., 192–94; O'Connor, *Last Hurrah*, esp. 374–76.

38. Hays, "Politics of Reform." McDonald, *Parameters of Urban Fiscal Policy*, 3, 277–78, suggests the connection between Merton and Hays. In "Burdens of Urban History," 3–29, McDonald makes compelling arguments against Merton's functionalist view of the machine and against the historians and political scientists he sees as influenced by it. As the paragraphs below should make clear, I think McDonald is very much mistaken in placing Bridges, Katznelson, Shefter, and Skocpol in the latter category. See also Katznelson, "'Burdens of Urban History': Comment"; and McDonald, "Reply to Professor Katznelson."

39. In addition to Hays, "Politics of Reform," see White, "City Affairs Are Not Political," in Judd and Kantor, *Enduring Tensions*; Wilson, "Character of Democracy in the United States," 577–88; and Hawley, *Nonpartisan Elections*.

40. Holli, *Reform in Detroit*, chap. 8.

41. Shefter, "Electoral Foundations of the Political Machine," 292–96; Elkin, *City and Regime*, 22–23; Wolfinger, *Politics of Progress*, 99–101; Green, "Chicago Democratic Party"; Fox, *Better City Government*, 12–16; Lotchin, "Power and Policy," 9–10; Teaford, "Finis for Tweed and Steffens," 136; Brown and Halaby, "Machine Politics in America," 587–612; idem, "Bosses, Reform, and the Socioeconomic Bases of Urban Expenditure," 73–77; and Brown and Warner, "Immigrants, Urban Politics, and Policing," 296, 299–303.

42. DiGaetano, "Rise and Development of Urban Political Machines," 252–63. See also idem, "Urban Political Reform."

43. Erie, *Rainbow's End*, 4–7, 13–14, 69–72, 91–106, 244–46; Katznelson, *Black Men, White Cities*, chaps. 5–7; Pinderhughes, *Race and Ethnicity in Chicago Politics*, chaps. 3–4; Grimshaw, *Bitter Fruit*, chaps. 4–6; and Allswang, *Bosses, Machines, and Urban Voters*, 166.

44. Erie, *Rainbow's End*, 57–66, 85–91, 241–44.

45. Levi, "Predatory Theory of Rule," 438. Cf. Zink, *City Bosses in the United States*, 36–37: "With the possible exception of [four of the bosses in his study] the twenty city barons kept the quest for gold fairly well to the fore in their lives. . . . Of the eighteen barons who have completed their political careers ten amassed fortunes of at least a million dollars." Zink qualifies his assessment by noting that most of the bosses had been as honest as their business counterparts, and that popular opinion tended to overstate their wealth.

46. Dorsett, *Roosevelt and the City Bosses*; idem, *Pendergast Machine*, chap. 8; idem, "Kansas City and the New Deal," 407–19; Stave, *New Deal and the Last Hurrah*; idem, "Pittsburgh and the New Deal," 376–406; Boulay and DiGaetano, "Why Did Political Machines Disappear?," 32–33; Katznelson, *City Trenches*, 125–29; and Erie, *Rainbow's End*, 16–17, 118–39. Mayhew, *Placing Parties*, 323–24, is less emphatic in its rejection of the "Last Hurrah" thesis.

47. See Wolfinger, *Politics of Progress*, chap. 4.

48. See for example Lowi, "Foreword to the Second Edition: Gosnell's Chicago Revisited."

49. Mollenkopf, *Phoenix in the Ashes*, 18–19, 76–80, 121–24, 187–88; Shefter, *Political Crisis/Fiscal Crisis*, xi–xx ("Introduction to the Paperback Edition"), 176–78; and Mayhew, *Placing Parties*, 32–38. Nearly four-fifths of New Yorkers live in the "outer boroughs," although one would not suspect this from reading either the *New York Times* or the *Village Voice*.

50. See for example Judd, *Politics of American Cities*, chap. 3; Kantor, *Dependent City*, chaps. 7–8; and Elkin, *City and Regime*, 22–24. Judd and Kantor, *Enduring Tensions*, includes selections from Bridges, Katznelson, DiGaetano, Shefter, and Erie.

51. See for example Judd, *Politics of American Cities*, chap. 4; Kantor, *Dependent City*, chap. 8; and Elkin, *City and Regime*, 25–30. Judd and Kantor, *Enduring Tensions*, includes selections from Hays, Holli, and, as an example of reform thought, Andrew Dickson White.

52. On progressivism, see Filene, "Obituary for 'The Progressive Movement'"; idem, "Narrating Progressivism"; and Rodgers, "In Search of Progressivism." On machine and reform, see Dorsett, "City Boss and the Reformer"; Thelen, "Urban Politics: Beyond Bosses and Reformers"; Allswang, *Bosses, Machines, and Urban Voters*, xi, 166–67; McDonald, "Burdens of Urban History," 28–29; and Teaford, "Finis for Tweed and Steffens." For arguments in favor of retaining the machine/reform dichotomy, see Brown and Halaby, "Machine Politics in America," 587–88, 612; and Ethington, "Urban Constituencies," 286–91, 295.

53. Mayhew, *Placing Parties*, 5–6, 19–21, 32–38, 69–70, 73–75, 209–10, 213, 219; Ostrogorski, *Democracy and the Organization of Political Parties*, 2:422.

Chapter 2

1. Cf. Ethington, "Urban Constituencies," 281–84.

2. Bridges, *City in the Republic*, 33–38 and chap. 7.

3. Hammack, *Power and Society*, 132, 147–51.

4. Weinstein, *Corporate Ideal*, chap. 4.

5. Ibid., 110.

6. Hays, "Politics of Reform," 163, 165.

7. Ibid., 162. Weinstein, *Corporate Ideal*, 109–10, also discusses the impact of citywide elections on the composition of governmental bodies.

8. Hays, "Politics of Reform," 159.

9. Hofstadter, *Age of Reform*, 173–84.

10. Banfield and Wilson, *City Politics*, 38–43, 329–46.

11. Larson, *Rise of Professionalism*, chap. 9. In discussing Progressive Era reform as a national movement, Hofstadter focuses on the role of ministers, lawyers, and academics. The status of these groups, he argues, was threatened by the rise of the great industrial capitalists. Yet Hofstadter also observes that the status of some reform-oriented professionals, such as architects, was actually improving during this period. See Hofstadter, *Age of Reform*, chap. 4, esp. 153 n. 8.

12. Ehrenreich and Ehrenreich, "Professional-Managerial Class."

13. Some group-based interpretations of reform do draw on electoral evidence. See for example Banfield and Wilson, *City Politics*, 234–40; Hays, "Politics of Reform," 160.

14. Chandler, "Origins of Progressive Leadership," 8:1462–65; Mowry, *California Progressives*, chap. 4.

15. Hays, "Politics of Reform," 160. Bonnie R. Fox, "Philadelphia Progressives," presents similar results for Philadelphia, but her sample is biased because it includes only reformers listed in social directories and biographical reference books, sources that are more likely to include members of the upper class than individuals of lower status.

16. See for example Thelen, "Social Tensions," 330–34. Jerome M. Clubb and Howard W. Allen have criticized both the studies supporting Hofstadter and those that refute him for their methodological and conceptual limitations. "It can easily be argued," they conclude, "that in all of these studies, neither the dependent variable (progressive behavior and attitudes), the independent variable (social and economic status and change), nor the theoretical rationale (the status revolution formulation) are well enough specified or viewed in sufficiently complex terms to permit either confirmation or refutation of the status revolution thesis." Clubb and Allen, "Collective Biography and the Progressive Movement," 524. The footnotes to this article provide an excellent bibliography of works on the social origins of reform leaders.

17. Ehrenreich and Ehrenreich, "Professional-Managerial Class," 24.

18. Wade, "Urbanization."

19. Miller, *Boss Cox's Cincinnati*; McCarthy, "New Metropolis"; idem, "'Suburban Power'"; idem, "Prelude to Armageddon"; and idem, "Bosses, Reformers, and Urban Growth."

20. Wade, "Urbanization," 198. Miller, *Boss Cox's Cincinnati*, and McCarthy, "New Metropolis," 51, follow Wade's suggestion for Cincinnati and Chicago, respectively.

21. This interpretation follows that of Arthur Bentley in his manuscript, "Municipal Ownership Interest Groups in Chicago." The manuscript is undated, but Bentley's acknowledgments suggest that it was written in 1908 or 1909; he thanks Isaac N. Powell, chief clerk of the Board of Election Commission from 1895 to 1909, and George E. Hooker, secretary of the City Club, whose service began in

1908. A photocopy, unfortunately without the finely detailed shaded maps that apparently accompanied it, is available at the Newberry Library, Chicago.

22. Bridges, *City in the Republic*, chap. 6.

23. Shefter, "Electoral Foundations of the Political Machine," 286–91.

24. Walter Lippmann, "On Municipal Socialism, 1913," in Stave, ed., *Socialism and the Cities*, 194. In the same volume, see Miller, "Milwaukee"; Hendrickson, "Tribune of the People"; and Stave, "Great Depression"; also, Judd, *Socialist Cities*; Critchlow, ed., *Socialism in the Heartland*; and Booth, "Municipal Socialism and City Government Reform."

25. Hendrickson, "Tribune of the People," 90; Weinbaum, "New York County Republican Politics, 1897–1922," 89; Shannon, *Socialist Party of America*, 124–25; Johnpoll, *Impossible Dream*, 306–8, 313; Judd, *Socialist Cities*, 21, 26, 106–12, 164–70; Walker, "Dayton Socialists and World War I," 117–32.

26. Wyman, "Middle Class Voters and Progressive Reform."

27. Rogin and Shover, *Political Change in California*, chaps. 2–3.

28. Shefter, "Regional Receptivity to Reform." Shefter explains the contrast by noting that working class voters in New York, but not in California, had earlier been mobilized by party organizations allied with economic elites.

29. Huthmacher, "Urban Liberalism and the Age of Reform," 234–35.

30. Buenker, *Urban Liberalism and Progressive Reform*.

31. Holli, *Reform in Detroit*, chap. 8. In a second article, Holli introduces the variable of fiscal crisis to explain the rise of structural reform in some cities toward the end of the Progressive Era. Holli, "Urban Reform in the Progressive Era," 150–51.

32. Kurland, *Seth Low*. See also Schiesl, *Politics of Efficiency*, 80, on Low, and 156, on Mayor Hunt of Cincinnati. Neither mayor, Schiesl suggests, fits either of Holli's categories.

33. Kusmer, *A Ghetto Takes Shape*, 246. Gerber, *Black Ohio*, 340, notes that Johnson was a personal friend of George Myers, a central figure among black Republicans, and that Johnson hired blacks as skilled workers on the streetcar lines he owned. These, however, were Johnson's actions as a private citizen rather than as a public official. Gerber (399) reports that the *Cleveland Journal*, a pro-business black newspaper, rejected Johnson as a demagogue and a socialist.

34. Quoted in Schiesl, *Politics of Efficiency*, 95–96.

35. De Witt, *Progressive Movement*, pt. IV.

36. This was true for an earlier period as well. See Bridges's comments on ethnocultural interpretations of antebellum urban politics in *City in the Republic*, 4–5, 13.

37. Baritz, *Servants of Power*.

38. Domhoff, "Where Do Government Experts Come From?"; idem, "Class, Power, and Parties in the New Deal."

39. See the critiques of this approach, as pursued by Domhoff and other scholars, in Finegold, "Between All and Nothing"; Skocpol, *Protecting Soldiers and Mothers*, 28–29; and Critchlow, *Brookings Institution*, 6–8, 12–13.

40. Smith, *Idea Brokers*, 106–8, 277–78.

41. Nadel, *Politics of Consumer Protection*, 176–91; Bartley, "Business and the New Class," 59–62. The ties between Nader's "public interest" movement and the

Carter administration were an exception to the usual political status of these organizations.

42. Critchlow, *Brookings Institution*, 5, 13, 165–71; Smith, *Idea Brokers*, 130–34. Smith (131) describes Brookings before its transformation as "none too secure financially . . . and with a reputation as a cranky opponent of New Deal and Fair Deal policies in the 1930s and 1940s." In the terms used here, the experts of the Brookings Institution became political experts rather than gadflies.

43. Finegold, "From Agrarianism to Adjustment"; Skocpol and Finegold, "State Capacity and Economic Intervention"; and Finegold and Skocpol, *State, Party, and Policy*.

44. Kirkendall, *Social Scientists and Farm Politics*, 257.

45. Howe, *Confessions of a Reformer*, 1.

46. Gossett, *Race*, 292–93, 307; Wilson, "Character of Democracy in the United States," 582–83, 585.

47. Godkin, *Problems of Modern Democracy*, 126–34.

48. Howe, *The City*, 2–3; idem, "City as a Socializing Agency," 590, 595; and idem, *Modern City and Its Problems*, vi.

The key racial distinction in this period was not between black and white, but between Anglo-Saxon and non-Anglo-Saxon. Many of the stereotypes used against blacks or Hispanics today were applied to ethnic groups such as Jews and Italians in the early 1900s, and these immigrant groups were commonly described as "races." This conception of race was particularly salient within northeastern cities, where the nonwhite populations were small until the Great Migration, which accelerated during World War I. In 1910, for example, the percentage of potential voters (males of voting age) who were black was 2.5 percent in New York; 2.0 percent in Chicago; and 1.9 percent in Cleveland. See Mink, "Lady and the Tramp," 114 n. 1; Gossett, *Race*, 287–309; *Thirteenth Census of the United States*, 2:505, 3:241, 419; and Katznelson, *Black Men, White Cities*, 31–32. Black-white relations thus played a secondary role in urban political conflicts of the Progressive Era. It is worth noting, however, that developments in race relations during this period could still have crucial impacts on future patterns of politics and policy, as illustrated in Katznelson, *Black Men, White Cities*, and in Philpott, *Slum and the Ghetto*.

49. Roosevelt, "Practical Work in Politics," 298.

50. Bruère, *New City Government*, 5; Allen, *Efficient Democracy*, 228–29.

51. Bruère, *New City Government*, 87.

52. Wilcox, "Inadequacy of Present City Government," 35. See also Fitzpatrick, "Preface," vii.

53. Allen, *Efficient Democracy*, 228–29, 284–85.

54. Allen, "Interpreting Expert Government to the Citizenship," 175. See also Woodruff, "Wide Scope of Municipal Improvement," 7–15; and idem, "New View of Municipal Government," 64–66, 68. Kahn, "Re-Presenting Government," properly emphasizes the adoption of advertising practices by Allen and the Bureau of Municipal Research. However, Kahn's depiction of these activities as elitist methods for one-way communication with a public composed of passive consumers ignores the role of community centers as intermediaries between experts and the public, and ignores as well the conception of civic education as a necessary

condition of public control over experts whose specialized skills had become indispensable. I discuss both these points below.

55. Collier, "Citizen Coöperation with Government through the Community Center," 151–67. Kahn, "Re-Presenting Government," 100–101, says, "Unmediated dialogue among citizens on issues of public concern was superfluous. . . . Government usurped the entire field of public action. Citizens did not develop a political discourse among themselves." The Wingate Center's study courses, and the extent to which they built upon preexisting class and ethnic identities, challenge this assertion.

56. Allen, "Interpreting Expert Government," 169.

57. Beard, "Control of the Expert," 339–40.

58. Morone, *Democratic Wish*, 98.

59. Howe, *The City*, 114. Americans' desire for a consensus founded upon the common good is a theme of Morone, *Democratic Wish*; see esp. 6–7, 113–15, 118–19, 123, and 126–27.

60. Burns, *Leadership*, esp. 4, 19–20, 425–26. See also Hargrove, "Two Conceptions of Institutional Leadership," 57–83.

61. Hays, "Politics of Reform," 169.

62. Griffith, *Progressive Years*, 17, 10; see also 10–33, 144–46.

63. Flanagan, *Charter Reform in Chicago*, 8.

64. Thelen, "Social Tensions," 341, 337–38, 339.

65. McCormick, "Discovery." See also idem, *From Realignment to Reform*, chap. 7 and 266–72.

66. De Witt, *Progressive Movement*, 14 (emphasis in original).

67. Ibid., 4–5.

68. Wiebe, *Search for Order*, 166; see esp. chap. 7.

69. Cerillo, "Impact of Reform Ideology"; idem, "Reform of Municipal Government."

70. Cf. McCormick, "Discovery," 248–49, 274; idem, *From Realignment to Reform*, 267–68, 271–72.

71. Shefter, "Electoral Foundations of the Political Machine," 292–96; Elkin, *City and Regime*, 22–23; Wolfinger, *Politics of Progress*, 99–101; Green, "Chicago Democratic Party"; Fox, *Better City Government*, 12–16; Lotchin, "Power and Policy," 9–10; Teaford, "Finis for Tweed and Steffens," 136; Brown and Halaby, "Machine Politics in America, 1870–1945," 587–612; idem, "Bosses, Reform, and the Socioeconomic Bases of Urban Expenditure," 73–77; and Brown and Warner, "Immigrants, Urban Politics, and Policing," 296, 299–303.

72. George McClellan, Sr., commanded the Army of the Potomac in the early years of the Civil War, in which capacity he passed up several chances to destroy Robert E. Lee's Confederate army. McClellan nonetheless went on to become the Democratic presidential nominee in 1864 and to serve a term as governor of New Jersey. Carter Harrison I was elected to five terms as mayor of Chicago; his tenure ended with his assassination in 1893.

73. This analysis is suggested by the discussion of Chicago's fragmentation in Merriam, *Chicago*, 98–99.

74. Ibid., 90–92.

75. Warner, *Progressivism in Ohio*, 16, 440–42; Richardson, "Political Reform in Cleveland," 158; and Howe, *Modern City*, 99–102. Authority was less centralized under the Nash code, which was imposed on Cleveland and other Ohio municipalities by a hostile legislature in 1902. See Warner, *Progressivism in Ohio*, 110–15.

76. Howe, *Modern City*, 103–4; Sayre and Kaufman, *Governing New York City*, 16–17; Mollenkopf, *Phoenix in the Ashes*, 77; and Arian et al., *Changing New York City Politics*, 9, 136.

77. Allen, *Efficient Democracy*, 255; Howe, *The City*, 51, 166.

78. Cerillo, "Reform of Municipal Government," 67–68; Lewinson, *John Purroy Mitchel*, 67–71, 82–83, 86.

79. Most of Low's appointees were gentlemen active in social organizations but without any professional training. Lowi, *At the Pleasure of the Mayor*, 30–31, 46–47, 57, 61–62, 203–4.

80. Howe, *Confessions of a Reformer*, 85–86.

81. Cramer, *Newton D. Baker*, 53.

82. Somit and Tannenhaus, *Development of American Political Science*, is the standard history. More recent works include Seidelman and Harpham, *Disenchanted Realists*; Ricci, *Tragedy of Political Science*; and Farr and Seidelman, eds., *Discipline and History*.

83. Mayhew, *Placing Parties*, 327–29, discusses the impact of the New Deal coalition on the political science of the 1940s and 1950s. Lowi, "State in Political Science," 4–5, suggests connections between the electoral success of the Republicans in the Reagan era and the rise of rational choice within political science during the same period.

Chapter 3

1. Hammack, *Power and Society*, 84. Cf. Mollenkopf, *Phoenix in the Ashes*, 59–60, on the ethnic class hierarchy of New York in the 1980s and 1990s.

2. Hammack, *Power and Society*, 65–69, 88–89; Henderson, *Tammany Hall and the New Immigrants*, 29–33, 50–52, 54, 63, 83; Erie, *Rainbow's End*, 50; and McNickle, *To Be Mayor*, 24–25.

3. Hammack, *Power and Society*, 119–29, 159–72; Bridges, *City in the Republic*, 101, 119–21, 140–42, 147; Shefter, "Emergence of the Political Machine," 15–17, 21–38; and idem, "Electoral Foundations of the Political Machine," 263–66.

4. Wesser, *Response to Progressivism*, 26; Kaplan, "Metropolitics, Administrative Reform, and Political Theory," 165, 176–78, 187–88; and Lanahan, "Brooklyn's Political Life," 294, 315–22.

5. Bridges, *City in the Republic*, 99–101, 148; Erie, *Rainbow's End*, 28, 31–35, 51–53; and Shefter, "Electoral Foundations of the Political Machine," 272–77, 281–83, 285–87.

6. *Thirteenth Census of the United States*, 3:253; Rosenwaike, *Population History of New York City*, 109–11, 122–23.

7. Henderson, *Tammany Hall and the New Immigrants*, esp. chap. 6; Erie,

Rainbow's End, 22, 69, 71–72, 91–106; Katznelson, *Black Men, White Cities*, 62–85; and Hertz, "Politics: New York," 265–66.

8. Cerillo, "Reform in New York City," 7–14; Bridges, *City in the Republic*, 117–20, 137–43, 150–52; Hammack, *Power and Society*, 134, 140–51; Shefter, "Emergence of the Political Machine," 31–32; idem, "New York City's Fiscal Crisis," 101–4; and Jaher, *Urban Establishment*, 259–63.

9. Hammack, *Power and Society*, 31–51, 69–79; Jaher, *Urban Establishment*, 251–59, 263–81.

10. Bridges, *City in the Republic*, 15, 19, 22–25, 78 (Walsh quotation), 90, 103–13, 152; Shefter, "Emergence of the Political Machine," 26; idem, "Electoral Foundations," 286–90; and Hammack, *Power and Society*, 112–13, 172–80.

11. Shefter, "Emergence of the Political Machine," 25–33; idem, "Electoral Foundations of the Political Machine," 290–96; and Hammack, *Power and Society*, 161–66.

12. Kurland, *Seth Low*, 104; Hammack, *Power and Society*, 178–80; and Cerillo, "Reform in New York City," 14–20.

13. Kurland, *Seth Low*, 113, 124–36.

14. Hammack, *Power and Society*, 134, 146–47, 170; Myers, *History of Tammany Hall*, 281–82.

15. Complete demographic and transition estimates for the Low elections of 1901 and 1903 are presented in Finegold, "Progressivism, Electoral Change, and Public Policy," 64–65, 67, 72–73.

16. Hertz, "Politics: New York," 257.

17. Wade, "Urbanization"; Miller, *Boss Cox's Cincinnati*; McCarthy, "Bosses, Reformers, and Urban Growth"; idem, "New Metropolis"; idem, "'Suburban Power'"; and idem, "Prelude to Armageddon."

18. Holli, *Reform in Detroit*, 164–67; Cerillo, "Reform of Municipal Government in New York City," 51–57.

19. This supports arguments that in some of its phases, machine politics was fiscally conservative. See Shefter, *Political Crisis/Fiscal Crisis*, 17–19, 26–28, 45–57; Brown and Halaby, "Bosses, Reform, and the Socioeconomic Bases of Urban Expenditure," 71–72, 83, 89–91; McDonald, *Parameters of Urban Fiscal Policy*, 85–115; and Erie, *Rainbow's End*, 45–57, 79–85, 111–18.

20. Schiesl, *Politics of Efficiency*, 77–81; Kurland, *Seth Low*, chap. 7, 200; Swett, "Test of a Reformer," 20–31; Cerillo, "Impact of Reform Ideology," 70–75; and Williams, "New York City's Public Baths," 50–52, 68–70.

21. Kurland, *Seth Low*, 151–57; Swett, "Test of a Reformer," 28–30.

22. Hammack, *Power and Society*, 156; Swett, "Test of a Reformer," 18, 28; Rischin, *Promised City*, 90, 228; Gilfoyle, *City of Eros*, 215–17, 257–58, 302; and McNickle, *To Be Mayor*, 18–19.

23. Lowi, *At the Pleasure of the Mayor*, 30–31, 46–47, 57, 61–62, 203–4.

24. Quotation from Kurland, *Seth Low*, 145–46. Low's rejection of Veiller is also discussed in Holli, *Reform in Detroit*, 166, and in Cerillo, "Impact of Reform Ideology," 70–72.

25. Swett, "Test of a Reformer," 32–39; Kurland, *Seth Low*, chaps. 8–9.

26. This paragraph draws on Swett, "Test of a Reformer," 32; and Kurland, *Seth Low*, 170–71, 177–78, 185–86, 197–98.

Chapter 4

1. My descriptions of the 1905 campaign draw on Yellowitz, *Labor and the Progressive Movement*, 188–202; Myatt, "William Randolph Hearst," chap. 4; Syrett, ed., *Gentleman and the Tiger*, 224; Swanberg, *Citizen Hearst*, 230–38; and Littlefield, *William Randolph Hearst*, 177–98.

2. Mitgang, *Man Who Rode the Tiger*, 28–36, 62–64, 80–85.

3. Myatt, "William Randolph Hearst," 203–16.

4. Wesser, *Response to Progressivism*, 27.

5. Myatt, "William Randolph Hearst," 71–75; Yellowitz, *Labor and the Progressive Movement*, 197–98; and Syrett, ed., *Gentleman and the Tiger*, 227–30. The electoral data used in computing the estimates presented here is from the *City Record*, Supplement, February 1906. These totals give McClellan 228,397 votes, Hearst 224,788, and Ivins 137,193.

6. Complete transition and demographic estimates for the Hearst elections of 1905 and 1909 can be found in Finegold, "Progressivism, Electoral Change, and Public Policy," 80–81, 84–85, 89–90, 93.

7. Ibid., 81, presents two-stage least squares (2SLS) estimates of the relationship between the 1905 mayoral vote and prior partisanship, as shown in the 1900 and 1904 presidential elections. These estimates also suggest an extreme association between support for Hearst and earlier support for Socialists. The unacceptable range of the estimates for the behavior of 1903 Socialists reflects the dangers of extrapolation: the transition rates represent the predicted behavior of a hypothetical district that voted 100 percent Social Democratic in 1903, while the actual citywide Social Democratic vote was only 2.7 percent of the total registration. See Kousser, "Making Separate Equal," 457–58.

8. Yellowitz, *Labor and the Progressive Movement*, 195–96.

9. Ibid., 199–200; Henderson, *Tammany Hall and the New Immigrants*, 107–8.

10. A charter revision before the 1905 election restored the mayoral term to four years. Hence, the next election was held in 1909.

11. Myatt, "William Randolph Hearst," 135–39; Littlefield, *William Randolph Hearst*, 192, 263–71; Swanberg, *Citizen Hearst*, 266–68; Mitgang, *Man Who Rode the Tiger*, 105; Yellowitz, *Labor and the Progressive Movement*, 225–26; Smith, *William Jay Gaynor*, chap. 4; and Lewinson, *John Purroy Mitchel*, 52.

12. These dummies divide the sixty-three ADs into three groups of twenty-one: high illiteracy = lower class ($Ill_1 = Ill_2 = 1$), intermediate illiteracy = intermediate class ($Ill_1 = 1$, $Ill_2 = 0$), and low illiteracy = upper class ($Ill_1 = Ill_2 = 0$). The dummy variables are awkward, but attempts to use separate terms for illiteracy and illiteracy squared to model the hypothesized curvilinear relationship between class and the 1909 Hearst vote resulted in multicollinearity due to the high correlation (.956) between the two terms. The log and log squared of illiteracy could not be used for the same reason ($r = -.989$).

13. See Henderson, *Tammany Hall and the New Immigrants*, 108–14 and chap. 6. These estimates do not support Henderson's judgment, based on an analysis of ethnically homogeneous Manhattan neighborhoods, that in 1909 Hearst maintained his popularity only among Jews.

14. Syrett, ed., *Gentleman and the Tiger*, 226.

15. McCormick, *From Realignment to Reform*, 207.

16. Lowi, *At the Pleasure of the Mayor*, 65, 88–90, 204; Syrett, ed., *Gentleman and the Tiger*, 26, 221–22, 230–43; and Littlefield, *William Randolph Hearst*, 98.

17. The next two paragraphs are based on Allen, *Reminiscences*, 88–112; Bruère, *Reminiscences*, 19–43; Dahlberg, *New York Bureau of Municipal Research*, chaps. 1, 8; Cerillo, "Reform of Municipal Government," 60–62; and Gulick, *National Institute of Public Administration*, 13–17.

18. Bruère, *Reminiscences*, 26.

19. Lowi, *At the Pleasure of the Mayor*, 65, 90–91, 204. See also Smith, *William Jay Gaynor*, 81–83, 141–55; Cerillo, "Reform of Municipal Government," 66; and Wesser, *Response to Progressivism*, 30.

20. Bruère, *Reminiscences*, 46–57, 86; Allen, *Reminiscences*, 112–15; Dahlberg, *New York Bureau of Municipal Research*, 20; Gulick, *National Institute of Public Administration*, 17–19; and Rodgers, *Robert Moses*, 17–18.

21. Bruère, "Efficiency in City Government," 5. The next three paragraphs draw on this article; Hopkins, "New York Bureau of Municipal Research"; Gulick, *National Institute of Public Administration*, 52–65; Dahlberg, *New York Bureau of Municipal Research*, chaps. 2 and 7, 164–67; Allen, *Reminiscences*, 96–98, 197–209; Rodgers, *Robert Moses*, 16–20; Caro, *Power Broker*, chaps. 4–5; and Kahn, "Re-Presenting Government," 84–101.

22. Holli, *Reform in Detroit*, 163–69.

23. Bruère, "Efficiency in City Government," 6.

24. Ibid., 20.

25. Yellowitz, *Labor and the Progressive Movement*, 202.

26. Syrett, ed., *Gentleman and the Tiger*, 285, 301; Smith, *William Jay Gaynor*, 177–81.

Chapter 5

1. Whitman then sought reelection as a Fusion candidate, while McAneny was slated for president of the Board of Aldermen. Both were successful.

2. Lewinson, *John Purroy Mitchel*, 67–71, and chaps. 5–6; Henderson, *Tammany Hall and the New Immigrants*, 120–23. The story of Becker, who was eventually convicted and executed, is told in Logan, *Against the Evidence*.

3. Wesser, *Response to Progressivism*, 129–30; Lewinson, *John Purroy Mitchel*, 89–95.

4. Bruère, *Reminiscences*, 87.

5. Cerillo, "Reform of Municipal Government in New York City," 67–68.

6. "Speech of the Hon. John Purroy Mitchel Accepting the Fusion Nomination for Mayor of New York City Delivered at Cooper Union on September 29th, 1913," in Circulars, Newspaper Articles, and Placards Relating to the New York City Election, 1913, New York Public Library. See also, in the same collection, "John Purroy Mitchel, Efficiency, Economy, Integrity, Who He Is, What He's Done, What He Advocates, What He'll Do."

7. "Do You Want 'Experts' Imported from Other Cities to Fix the Pay of New

York's Employees?" and "An Appeal to the People of New York for Fair Play; Some Things That Will Open the People's Eyes," ibid.

8. "The Invisible Government, A Speech Delivered by Charles Edward Russell, Socialist Candidate for Mayor at the Hippodrome in New York City," October 13, 1913, ibid.

9. Complete transition and demographic estimates for the Mitchel elections of 1913 and 1917 are given in Finegold, "Progressivism, Electoral Change, and Public Policy," 106, 108–10, 121, 123–25.

10. Lowi, *At the Pleasure of the Mayor*, 62, 65, 91, 204; Lewinson, *John Purroy Mitchel*, 104–8; and Cerillo, "Reform of Municipal Government," 69.

11. Bruère, *Reminiscences*, 87.

12. Cerillo, "Reform of Municipal Government," 70; Bruère, *Reminiscences*, 87–104.

13. Ravitch, *Great School Wars*, 196–97.

14. Ritchie, "Gary Committee"; Lewinson, *John Purroy Mitchel*, 137–43.

15. My discussion of the Gary Plan draws on Cohen and Mohl, *Paradox of Progressive Education*, chap. 2; Ravitch, *Great School Wars*, chaps. 17–20; Lewinson, *John Purroy Mitchel*, chap. 9; and Amberg and Allen, *Civic Lessons*, 15–20.

16. Quoted in Cohen and Mohl, *Paradox of Progressive Education*, 46.

17. Quoted in ibid., 51.

18. Lewinson, *John Purroy Mitchel*, chap. 10; Amberg and Allen, *Civic Lessons*, 24–26; and Bruère, *Reminiscences*, 111–13.

19. Fitzpatrick, *Endless Crusade*, 114–20. Upon leaving the Mitchel administration, Davis became full-time general secretary of the Rockefeller-financed Bureau of Social Hygiene. Her interest in female crime, particularly prostitution, led her to controversial studies of female sexuality. These studies resulted in her dismissal by Rockefeller in 1927. See Fitzpatrick, *Endless Crusade*, 120–29, 202–5.

20. Duffy, *History of Public Health in New York City*, 266–76.

21. Makielski, *Politics of Zoning*, 7–40, 119, 137–38, 166–69; Revell, "Regulating the Landscape," 19–45; and Weiss, "Density and Intervention," 46–63.

22. Lewinson, *John Purroy Mitchel*, 143–49; Amberg and Allen, *Civic Lessons*, 20–23.

23. Holli, *Reform in Detroit*, 167–68, emphasizes Mitchel's conservatism; Lewinson, *John Purroy Mitchel*, his insensitivity.

24. Lewinson, *John Purroy Mitchel*, 102, 125–27, 246–47. The pay-as-you-go policy was repealed in 1918.

25. Allen and Amberg, *Civic Lessons*, 64; Allen, *Reminiscences*, 236–41, 250–81; and idem, "Reasons Why Mr. Allen Believes That Mr. Rockefeller's Conditional Offer of Support to the New York Bureau of Municipal Research Should Not Be Accepted," speech to the Bureau of Municipal Research trustees, May 13, 1914.

26. Ritchie, "Gary Committee," 341–42.

27. Lewinson, *John Purroy Mitchel*, chap. 11; Amberg and Allen, *Civic Lessons*, 26–29; Henderson, *Tammany Hall and the New Immigrants*, 203–9, 215, 218–19; and Chern, "Politics of Patriotism," 293–94, 300–302, 305–6. After leav-

202 NOTES TO PAGES 62-73

ing the mayoralty, Mitchel joined the Army Air Corps and died falling out of an airplane during a training flight.

28. The next paragraph draws upon Lewinson, *John Purroy Mitchel*, 84–86 and chaps. 12–13; Henderson, *Tammany Hall and the New Immigrants*, 194–213; Chern, "Politics of Patriotism"; Wesser, *Response to Progressivism*, 196–97; Littlefield, *William Randolph Hearst*, 324–26; and Hylan, *Autobiography*, 61–63.

29. The method of remapping the electoral data is explained in the Appendix.

30. Examination of returns from ethnically homogeneous districts provide the basis for discussion of voting patterns in the 1917 election in Henderson, *Tammany Hall and the New Immigrants*, 213–19; Chern, "Politics of Patriotism"; Wesser, *Response to Progressivism*, 197–98; and Szajowski, "The Jews and New York City's Mayoralty Election of 1917."

31. Lowi, "Gosnell's Chicago Revisited via Lindsay's New York," x–xi.

32. Hylan was reelected in 1921, but in 1925, Hearst was unable to win renomination for Hylan against Governor Al Smith's efforts to replace him with Walker. Hylan was a product of the Brooklyn Democratic organization, while Walker was one of Tammany's own. See Swanberg, *Citizen Hearst*, 379–80; Sayre and Kaufman, *Governing New York City*, 688–89.

33. "Hirshfield in Job Tammany Wanted," *New York Times*, January 13, 1918, 5.

34. Revell, "Regulating the Landscape," 41.

35. Dahlberg, *New York Bureau of Municipal Research*, 133; Gulick, *National Institute of Public Administration*, 24–25, 69–106.

36. Leuchtenburg, preface to Lewinson, *John Purroy Mitchel*, 13.

37. Shefter, "Economic Crises, Social Coalitions, and Political Institutions"; idem, "Organizing for Armageddon"; Makielski, *Politics of Zoning*, 125–26; Caro, *Power Broker*, chaps. 19–20, 22–25, 27–28; Rodgers, *Robert Moses*, 18; Dorsett, *Roosevelt and the City Bosses*, chap. 4; Kessner, *La Guardia and the Making of Modern New York*, chap. 9; and idem, "LaGuardia and the Challenge of Democratic Planning," 315–29.

38. Greenstone and Peterson, *Race and Authority in Urban Politics*, 39–43, 208–9, 215, 244, 268–69, 274–75.

39. Shefter, *Political Crisis/Fiscal Crisis*, 49–56, 90–91, 109–24, 151–53, 163–66, 184–93; idem, "New York's Fiscal Crisis," 105–27.

40. Mollenkopf, *Phoenix in the Ashes*, 44–68, 204–7; Roberts, "Tide Turns on Voter Turnout." The *Times* exit polls suggest that the bimodal distribution of the Dinkins vote was even more pronounced in his 1993 rematch with Rudolph Giuliani than in 1989. In losing the 1993 election, Dinkins actually did better than he had in 1989 among blacks and among whites with postgraduate education. Whites at all lower educational levels, in contrast, gave Dinkins less support in 1993. Income data also show a bimodal pattern: Dinkins gained among the lowest and highest income groups, while losing votes at each level in between.

Chapter 6

1. Whipple, "Cleveland in Conflict," 7, 14–16, 30–63, 71–75, 86–110, 169–89; Randall, "Meaning of Progressivism," esp. 2–4, 58; Rose, *Cleveland*, 542; Weiner

and Beal, "Sixth City," 29–32, 39–43; and Miller and Wheeler, *Cleveland*, 79–82, 87–89.

2. Percentages for ethnic groups represent the total of foreign-born and native-born with both parents for that country. Thus, ethnic percentages combine first- and second-generation totals. Data is from *Thirteenth Census of the United States*, 3:418.

3. Holden, "Ethnic Accommodation," 169–72; Derthick, "Stability in City Politics," 19.

4. Miggins and Morgenthaler, "Ethnic Mosaic," 104–40; Miller and Wheeler, *Cleveland*, 82–87; and Gartner, *History of the Jews of Cleveland*, 109.

5. Fordyce, "Nationality Groups," 109–12, 123–24; Callahan and Hickey, *Irish Americans*, 94; Coulter, *Italians of Cleveland*, 42; Kusmer, *Ghetto Takes Shape*, 121–22, 138, 145–46, 153–54; Campbell, "Mounting Crisis and Reform," 303–4; and Gartner, *History of the Jews of Cleveland*, 98, 111–12.

6. Callahan and Hickey, *Irish Americans*, 122–23, 191–98.

7. Whipple, "Municipal Government," 7–8; Wilcox, "Municipal Government in Michigan and Ohio," 131–46.

8. Whipple, "Municipal Government," 4–5; Fordyce, "Nationality Groups," 110–12.

9. Campbell, "Background for Progressivism," 7; Holden, "Ethnic Accommodation," 176. Callahan and Hickey, *Irish Americans*, 122–23, discuss Farley's ethnic identification and note that he was elected in 1883 with little Irish support. Holden's judgment, that "Farley's election in 1883 . . . was of particular significance for it signified the advent of the Irish in power," thus seems misleading.

10. Beer, *Hanna*, 183.

11. Fordyce, "Nationality Groups," 111; Campbell, "Background for Progressivism," 12.

12. Croly, *Marcus Alonzo Hanna*, 81; Johnson, *My Story*, 22–24; and Whipple, "Municipal Government," 32–33.

13. Whipple, "Municipal Government," 8–9 (author's footnotes omitted).

14. Shefter, "New York City's Fiscal Crisis," 103–5; idem, "Electoral Foundations of the Political Machine," 263–66, 293–96.

15. Rose, *Cleveland*, 526–27, summarizes the new charter. For more detail on the Federal Plan and its origins, see Wilcox, "Municipal Government in Michigan and Ohio," 146–52; H[odge], *Reminiscences*, 1:177–80.

16. Campbell, "Background for Progressivism," 12–13.

17. Ibid., 92. In this sense, he was closer to Richard Daley than to his New York contemporary, George Washington Plunkitt. Cf. Riordan, *Plunkitt of Tammany Hall*, 3–6; and Rakove, *Don't Make No Waves*, 48–50.

18. Whipple, "Municipal Government," 16–17; Campbell, "Background for Progressivism," 16–18; idem, "Mounting Crisis and Reform," 301; and Warner, *Progressivism in Ohio*, 16–18.

19. Alan DiGaetano appropriately cites Cleveland under McKisson as one of the examples supporting his argument that governmental centralization facilitates rather than hinders machine building, as Robert K. Merton's functionalist analysis would suggest. See DiGaetano, "Rise and Development of Urban Political Machines," 260.

20. The remainder of this paragraph draws upon Campbell, "Background for Progressivism," 18–24, 71–72, 75, 78; idem, "Mounting Crisis and Reform," 301–2.

21. Campbell, "Background for Progressivism," 14, 38–39, 87; idem, "Mounting Crisis and Reform," 303–4.

22. Campbell, "Background for Progressivism," 5, 94–95.

23. Ibid., 44.

24. Ibid., 40–43.

25. Johnson, *My Story*, 189.

26. Campbell, "Background for Progressivism," 46–54; Croly, *Marcus Alonzo Hanna*, 250–59; and Beer, *Hanna*, 183–87. Hanna was endorsed by most Republican legislators and won the vote of the Assembly, but McKisson won the vote of the Senate by combining the support of a few Republicans with that of Democrats. McKisson told the Democrats he supported the Democratic platform of 1896 even though he had run as a Republican "before the people." A joint session of the legislature elected Hanna by a three-vote margin.

27. Campbell, "Background for Progressivism," 60–64, 72, 88–89; Howe, *Confessions of a Reformer*, 85–86.

28. Whipple, "Municipal Government," 13–15; idem, "Cleveland in Conflict," 201, 205–6; and Wittke, "Peter Witt," 363–64.

29. Witt, quoted in Whipple, "Cleveland in Conflict," 169; idem, "Municipal Government," 20.

30. Campbell, "Background for Progressivism," 74, 85.

31. Whipple, "Cleveland in Conflict," 205–6, 370; Warner, *Progressivism in Ohio*, 40–41.

32. Comer, *Harry Garfield's First Forty Years*, 218; Bourne, "My Best Course in Political Science," Bourne Papers, 1.

33. Municipal Association minutes, meetings of November 14, 1896 and December 5, 1896, available in the offices of the Citizens League of Cleveland. The formation of the Municipal Association is discussed in Citizens League, *75 Years of Doing Good*, 1–3; and in Campbell, "Mounting Crisis and Reform," 302–3.

34. "Appendix A, Charter Members of the Citizens League, December 5, 1896," in Citizens League, *75 Years of Doing Good*, 39–40. Some efforts were made to bring labor into the Association, but they do not seem to have accomplished much. See Comer, *Harry Garfield's First Forty Years*, 224–25; Campbell, "Background for Progressivism," 58.

35. Bourne, "My Best Course in Political Science," 2.

36. Howe, *Confessions of a Reformer*, 1–8, 22–39, 86–87.

37. See the entries for Bourne in *Book of Clevelanders*, 35, and in Van Tassel and Grabowski, eds., *Encyclopedia of Cleveland History*, 114–15; and the entry for Wilcox in Malone, ed., *Dictionary of American Biography*, 20:202–3.

38. Bourne, "My Best Course in Political Science," 4–10; Campbell, "Background for Progressivism," 56.

39. Howe, *Confessions of a Reformer*, 86–87; Citizens League, *75 Years of Doing Good*, 7; Bourne, "My Best Course in Political Science," 3; and Campbell, "Background for Progressivism," 57. Wilcox went on to become a major force in the National Municipal League and the author of texts on utility regulation and other municipal problems.

40. Citizens League, 75 *Years of Doing Good*, 3–4; Campbell, "Mounting Crisis and Reform," 303–5.

41. *Bulletin of the Municipal Association*, No. 5, February 21, 1899.

42. Campbell, "Background for Progressivism," 84.

43. The low corrected R^2 of .19 for the unconstrained regression estimates of the McKisson vote also suggests that his support departed from conventional partisan patterns. The corrected R^2 for the Farley vote is higher, .41. See Finegold, "Progressivism, Electoral Change, and Public Policy," 155.

44. Howe, *Confessions of a Reformer*, 86.

45. Campbell, "Background for Progressivism," 91; *Bulletin of the Municipal Association*, April 1, 1901, November 7, 1905, and September 7, 1909. Miner G. Norton, another McKisson ally, finished third in the 1915 mayoral election.

46. Howe, *Confessions of a Reformer*, 85; Whipple, "Municipal Government," 24; and Comer, *Harry Garfield's First Forty Years*, 231.

47. Campbell describes McKisson's challenge to Hanna's Senate nomination in 1897, when Hanna's power was at its peak, as an exception to McKisson's usual political astuteness. Campbell, "Background for Progressivism," 90.

Chapter 7

1. Steffens, *Struggle for Self-Government*, 183.

2. The Republican riposte was that under the Democrats, Cleveland was "a city built on a bluff." Both labels are mentioned in Wilcox, "Inadequacy of Present City Government," 26.

3. Briggs, "Progressive Era in Cleveland," 117.

4. Johnson, *My Story*, 59–81. Johnson dedicated his autobiography to George's memory. When Johnson died in April 1911, he was buried next to George's grave in Greenwood Cemetery, Brooklyn. Ibid., v, 313.

5. "Tom Johnson's Past Utterances on Present Issues: Three Cent Fares and Other Municipal Questions," 1901, in Johnson Pamphlets; Briggs, "Progressive Era in Cleveland," 17.

6. *Bulletin of the Municipal Association*, April 1, 1901.

7. Johnson, *My Story*, 9–33, 89–107.

8. Witt, *Cleveland before St. Peter*, 46–48.

9. Murdock, "Elected Mayor," 33–36. For Salen's role in the 1901 campaign, see ibid., 34 n. 17; Lorenz, *Tom L. Johnson*, 27–28; and Howe, *Confessions of a Reformer*, 98. Murdock, "The Cabinet," 378, summarizes Salen's political background.

10. Johnson, *My Story*, 115; "Tom Johnson's Public Utterances on Present Issues: Three Cent Fares and other Municipal Questions," 1901, in Johnson Pamphlets, 7.

11. Murdock, "Elected Mayor," 36.

12. Corrected R^2s for the 1901 equations (.66 for Akers vote, .70 for Johnson vote) are much higher than those for 1899 (.19 for McKisson vote, .41 for Farley vote). This also suggests a stronger correspondence to national partisan cleavages. See Finegold, "Progressivism, Electoral Change, and Public Policy," 155, 162.

13. Murdock, "The Cabinet," 398; Lorenz, *Tom L. Johnson*, 52–53; and Johnson, *My Story*, 179.

14. Lorenz, *Tom L. Johnson*, 118–20; untitled editorial, *Public*, July 21, 1911, 674; and Warner, *Progressivism in Ohio*, 119, 128, 148–49, 180.

15. The ability of the Chamber of Commerce to shape educational policy under Johnson is the theme of Randall, "Meaning of Progressivism," stated most explicitly on 231. Ibid., 6, suggests Johnson had little interest in education, but a 1902 Johnson pamphlet strongly supported Starr Cadwallader for school director. "The Issues This Spring: Mayor Johnson's Open Letter to the Voters of Cleveland," Johnson Pamphlets. The mayor had no authority over the independently elected director and school board. Wilcox, "Municipal Government in Michigan and Ohio," 152, 156–57.

16. Randall, "Meaning of Progressivism," 55, 62; Howe, "Cleveland's Education through Its Chamber of Commerce," 747–48.

17. Holmgren, "Edward Webster Bemis," 18, 23, 103–16, 147, 184, 186, 204–6; Johnson, *My Story*, chap. 14; Warner, *Progressivism in Ohio*, 87–101; Murdock, "The Cabinet," 386–87; and Bremner, "Tax Equalization in Cleveland," 302–4.

18. Holmgren, "Edward Webster Bemis," 207–11, 244–46; Johnson, *My Story*, 180–81; Lorenz, *Tom L. Johnson*, 51–52; Warner, *Progressivism in Ohio*, 74, 84 n. 12; Murdock, "The Cabinet," 387–88; and Murdock, "First Term," 42–44.

19. Howe, *Confessions of a Reformer*, 80–82; Huff, "Frederic C. Howe, Progressive," 27, 38–39; Bremner, "Humanizing Cleveland and Toledo," 187–90; Hines, "Paradox of 'Progressive' Architecture," 426–44; and Rarick, *Progressive Vision*, 14–34. On Los Angeles, see Fogelson, *Fragmented Metropolis*, 264–71.

20. *Book of Clevelanders*, 101.

21. Flower, "How Cleveland Stamped Out Smallpox," 426–28; Rose, *Cleveland*, 629; and Murdock, "The Cabinet," 389. Surprisingly, Murdock accepts Flower's judgment that Friedrich had wiped out the disease, and fails to mention the epidemic that followed. He does point out that Johnson, before Friedrich's appointment, had also demonstrated his aversion to vaccination, telling the health officers, "Don't go shooting people full of poison against their will." On the advice of local medical authorities, however, he had reversed his decision the following day. "The Cabinet," 389 n. 33.

22. Johnson, *My Story*, 173–79; Warner, *Progressivism in Ohio*, 64–65, 77–78; Lorenz, *Tom L. Johnson*, 54–57; Murdock, "The Cabinet," 378–79; and Bremner, "Harris R. Cooley and Cooley Farms," 71–74.

23. "The Record of the Past Is the Promise of the Future," 1905, in Johnson Pamphlets. See also, in the same collection, an untitled 1909 pamphlet by the Democratic Executive Committee. The Municipal Association criticized Cooley as lacking the business management skills needed to run his projects. *Bulletin of the Municipal Association*, November 5, 1907 and November 2, 1909.

24. The next two paragraphs are based on Johnson, *My Story*, 122–23, 181–83; Warner, *Progressivism in Ohio*, 76–77; Murdock, "The Cabinet," 381–84; Howard, "I, Fred Kohler"; Bremner, "Police, Penal and Parole Policies in Cleveland and Toledo," 387–88; "A Reply by Tom L. Johnson, Mayor of Cleveland to a Communication from a Committee of the Ministers' Union of Cleveland" [1906], in Johnson Pamphlets; Kohler, "Golden Rule Policy," 254–56; Fogelson, *Big-City*

Police, 48; and Campbell, "Mounting Crisis and Reform," 305–7. For a contemporary critique, see Norton, "Chief Kohler of Cleveland and His Golden Rule Policy," 537–42.

25. Howe, *Confessions of a Reformer*, 73; Cramer, *Newton D. Baker*, 29–30.

26. Howe, *Confessions of a Reformer*, 142–44.

27. In 1902, the Ohio Supreme Court struck down the Federal Plan charter, along with the Toledo Police Board Act, on the grounds that the classification system allowing the legislation to pass laws applying to specific localities violated the state constitution's ban on special legislation. The Nash Code, passed over the opposition of Johnson and most other Democrats, applied to all Ohio cities. It provided for the election of cabinet officers and for the appointment of the Board of Public Safety by the governor if the mayor's nominees were not endorsed by two-thirds of the council. The code also abolished the right of the mayor and his cabinet to participate in council proceedings, although this was circumvented in Cleveland. Warner, *Progressivism in Ohio*, chap. 5; Johnson, *My Story*, 163–64, 185–87.

28. Howe, *Confessions of a Reformer*, chap. 13; Holmgren, "Edward Webster Bemis," 248; and Bemis, "Significance of Mayor Johnson's Election," 582–83.

29. Johnson, *My Story*, 94–95; Holli, *Reform in Detroit*, 104–20.

30. This account of the streetcar wars is based on Johnson, *My Story*, chaps. 16, 18, 20–23, 25; Briggs, "Progressive Era in Cleveland," 11–35; Lorenz, *Tom L. Johnson*, chaps. 9–10; Bremner, "Street Railway Controversy in Cleveland," 185–204; Haworth, "Mayor Johnson of Cleveland," 471–74; Shaw, *Plain Dealer*, 294; and Richardson, "Political Reform in Cleveland," 160.

31. *The People's Side*, June 11, 19, 1909, and July 17, 31, 1909, in Johnson Pamphlets.

32. Bremner, "Political Techniques of the Progressives," 193–94; McCarthy, "'Suburban Power,'" 24; Lorenz, *Tom L. Johnson*, 101–2; Johnson, *My Story*, 82–84; Briggs, "Progressive Era in Cleveland," 106–7; and Campbell, "Mounting Crisis and Reform," 308–9.

33. Warner, *Progressivism in Ohio*, 125; Bremner, "Political Techniques," 192.

34. Bremner, "Political Techniques," 191; Johnson, *My Story*, 125–31; and Richardson, "Political Reform in Cleveland," 160. The Tax School operated for twenty months, ceasing operations after W. J. Crawford, a Republican politician and property owner, won an injunction against use of city funds for this purpose.

35. Wittke, "Peter Witt," 368.

36. Johnson's support for Dunne was the only time he responded to requests to personally participate in streetcar battles in other cities. The *Chicago Journal* warned Dunne against the advice of Johnson, "THE FAT CASUIST OF CLEVELAND." Johnson, *My Story*, 243–46; Briggs, "Progressive Era in Cleveland," 25. On July 21, 1911, *The Public* put out a special Johnson memorial issue.

37. *Bulletin of the Municipal Association*, April 6, 1903, November 7, 1905, November 5, 1907, and November 2, 1909. Harry A. Garfield, by then a professor of politics at Princeton, criticized Johnson's ties to the Forest City Railway in Garfield, "Private Rights in Street Railways," 256–58.

38. *Public* 6 (April 1, 1903): 2.

39. Johnson, *My Story*, 170.

40. Briggs, "Progressive Era in Cleveland," 165.

41. Otis, *Here I Am*, 108–9.

42. Lorenz, *Tom L. Johnson*, 48. Lorenz provides no evidence or examples.

43. Quoted in Briggs, "Progressive Era in Cleveland," 179. Similarly, see Steffens, *Struggle for Self-Government*, 192.

44. Briggs, "Progressive Era in Cleveland," 47–48, 125–27, 149 (quotation), 197.

45. Ibid., 127; Johnson, *My Story*, 150–52, 202–3.

46. The Central Labor Union's Socialism is discussed in Whipple, "Cleveland in Conflict," 207, and in Briggs, "Progressive Era in Cleveland," 139, 214.

47. Briggs, "Progressive Era in Cleveland," 124–41; Bemis, "Significance of Mayor Johnson's Election," 582–85; Johnson, *My Story*, 171–72; *Bulletin of the Municipal Association*, April 6, 1903; and "Shall the Street Railroads Control the People or Shall the People Control the Street Railroads?" 1903, Johnson Pamphlets.

48. Since data by ward was available only for the foreign-born, and not for second-generation immigrants, the ethnic categories understate group proportions. Dummy variables for class were derived from the illiterate proportion of the population ten years or older. These dummies divide the twenty-six wards into three groups: low illiteracy = upper class ($Ill_1 = Ill_2 = 0$), intermediate class ($Ill_1 = 1$, $Ill_2 = 0$), and high illiteracy = lower class ($Ill_1 = Ill_2 = 1$). As with the 1900 data, suburbanization was measured as dwellings per family.

49. "Typewritten Manuscript of Johnson-Boyd Debates, 1905," in Cleveland Public Library (quotations from first and fifth debates); *Bulletin of the Municipal Association*, November 5, 1905; and Briggs, "Progressive Era in Cleveland," 151–52, 157.

50. "Typewritten Manuscript of Johnson-Boyd Debates, 1905," first, fourth, and sixth debates (quotation from first debate).

51. "The Record of the Past is the Promise of the Future," 1905, in Johnson Pamphlets.

52. "Typewritten Manuscript of Johnson-Boyd Debates, 1905," first debate.

53. Briggs, "Progressive Era in Cleveland," 160–61, points out that Johnson carried the predominantly ethnic West Side in 1905, as he had done in 1903, while also carrying the more native-stock East Side, which he lost to Goulder in the earlier election.

54. This paragraph draws on Johnson, *My Story*, chap. 24; Briggs, "Progressive Era in Cleveland," 163–86; Crissey, *Theodore Burton*, chap. 14; and Murdock, "The Burton Campaign," 413–23.

55. Quotation from "Johnson Says Win! Burton Says Quit!," 1907, in Johnson Pamphlets.

56. Johnson, *My Story*, 273–74.

57. "Seldom," the *Bulletin of the Municipal Association* proclaimed (November 5, 1907), "has any American city had the opportunity to hire for its mayor a man of such marked ability and unimpeachable integrity."

58. Finegold, "Progressivism, Electoral Change, and Public Policy," 200, 205. Alternatively, this shift might reflect the closer correspondence between the 1910 census data and the real, unmeasured variable for 1907. This latter explanation

would not, however, tell us why the differential would be greater for 1903 than for 1905, or why the differential for 1909 would be less than for any of the three previous elections.

59. Maschke, "Memoirs," August 1–11, 1934; Briggs, "Progressive Era in Cleveland," 189–90, 194–95, 197–98; Howard, "I, Fred Kohler"; and "Herman C. Baehr Rites Tomorrow," *Plain Dealer*, February 5, 1942.

60. Briggs, "Progressive Era in Cleveland," 190–93; untitled pamphlet, Democratic Executive Committee, 1909, Johnson Pamphlets; and Johnson, *My Story*, 289.

61. Whitlock, *Forty Years of It*, 174.

62. The Municipal Association noted its disapproval of Maschke but accepted Baehr's assurances he would be an independent mayor. *Bulletin of the Municipal Association*, November 2, 1909.

63. The unconstrained estimates for the 1909 election are given in Finegold, "Progressivism, Electoral Change, and Public Policy," 211.

64. McCarthy, "'Suburban Power,'" 23–25. McCarthy's analysis of support for Johnson, based on raw ward data, conflates class, ethnicity, and suburban location. The data presented here suggests that with the impact of suburbanization held constant, native-stock, upper-class voters gave Johnson little support in any of his campaigns except 1905, when he was still outpolled by Boyd among this group.

65. Howe, *Confessions of a Reformer*, chap. 22; Bremner, "Tax Equalization in Cleveland," 311–12; and Warner, *Progressivism in Ohio*, 227–31. Though Howe had written a study of the federal tax system, the Municipal Association would not recommend him, citing his lack of technical and practical knowledge of local real estate. *Bulletin of the Municipal Association*, November 2, 1909. Purdy later played an active role in the formulation of New York's pioneering zoning ordinance, discussed in Chapter 5.

66. *Bulletin of the Municipal Association*, April 6, 1903, November 7, 1905, November 5, 1907, and November 2, 1909. Unconstrained regression estimates for the vote in the 1909 Solicitor's race suggest that Baker won more native-stock support than Johnson received in the mayoral race. See Finegold, "Progressivism, Electoral Change, and Public Policy," 216–17.

Chapter 8

1. Briggs, "Progressive Era in Cleveland," 203.

2. Waite, *Warm Friend for the Spirit*, 117–18.

3. Howard, "I, Fred Kohler," February 21–25, 1934.

4. Young, *Twentieth-Century Experience in Urban Transit*, 12–13; Malin, "Government," 2:936. Frank B. Hogen, the Republican mayoral candidate in 1911, found it necessary to say he would not reappoint Dahl. Campbell, *Daniel E. Morgan*, 41.

5. Otis, *Here I Am*, 110.

6. Newton D. Baker to Frank B. Hogen, October 31, 1911, Baker to Joseph W. Falk, November 9, 1911, Baker to Ben T. Cable, November 9, 1911, Baker to W. C. Sharp, November 9, 1911, Baker to Henry George, Jr., November 9, 1911, Baker to Rev. Charles D. William, November 9, 1911, Baker Papers; *Plain*

Dealer, November 6–8, 1911; *Bulletin of the Municipal Association*, May 1911; Cramer, *Newton D. Baker*, 46–49; Briggs, "Progressive Era in Cleveland," 264–66.

7. Variables for the Irish and native populations of the wards, and for illiteracy and suburbanization, are defined as in Chapter 7.

8. Unconstrained regression coefficients for the Irish vote for Hogen and the Irish vote for Baker both yield inadmissible estimates of greater than 100 percent support. The higher coefficient of Irish support for Baker (4.188 versus 1.161) suggests that he won more Irish votes than Hogen. See Finegold, "Progressivism, Electoral Change, and Public Policy," 223.

9. Waite, *Warm Friend*, 117–18.

10. The woman's husband found her in a kimono, while Kohler was fully dressed but without a tie, collar, or socks. Kohler denied any wrongdoing, but the American Civic Reform Union pressed Baker to remove him. Kohler's later political comeback culminated in 1921, when he was elected mayor after an independent, door-to-door campaign. He proceeded to erect billboards stating, "I Alone Am Your Mayor," and to paint all public buildings orange and black. The *New York Tribune* said, "Mayor Kohler's administration appears to have been largely actuated by the theory that the course to follow is to find out what makes people mad—and then go do a lot of it." On the scandal, see Howard, "I, Fred Kohler," February 26, 1934; Dolger, "His Honor?" On Kohler's election and mayoralty, see Rarick, *Progressive Vision*, 48; Maxey, "Cleveland Election and the New Charter," 84–86; Porter, *Cleveland*, 19–21; Saltzer, "Colorful Kohler Rebounds from Disgrace"; and Condon, *Cleveland*, 208–14.

11. Rex, "Municipal Dance Halls," 416–17; Hopwood, "Newton D. Baker's Administration," 464.

12. "From Mayor to Moulder," 1915 Witt campaign pamphlet, Witt Papers.

13. Baker, "Municipal Ownership and Control," 232.

14. Johnson, *My Story*, 26.

15. Wittke, "Peter Witt," 369–70; Young, *Twentieth-Century Experience in Urban Transit*, 14–17; Hopwood, "Newton D. Baker's Administration," 452; and "For Mayor Peter Witt," 1915 campaign pamphlet, Witt Papers.

16. This summary draws upon Cramer, *Newton D. Baker*, 51; Baker, "Municipal Ownership and Control," 232; and Arbuthnot, "Mayor Baker's Administration," 238–39.

17. Baker to Albert Ihlenfield, October 30, 1913, Baker Papers. Baker's reference to Johnson was misleading since Johnson had engaged the city in an all-out war with the ConCon.

18. Cramer, *Newton D. Baker*, 41.

19. Ibid., 49. See also Arbuthnot, "Mayor Baker's Administration," 240; Moulton, "Speaking Effectiveness of Newton D. Baker," 86.

20. Cramer, *Newton D. Baker*, 53; Rose, *Cleveland*, 730. Arbuthnot, "Mayor Baker's Administration," 232, criticizes the orchestra as premature.

21. Gerber, *Black Ohio*, 340; Gossett, *Race*, 280–86.

22. Miggins, "Businessmen, Pedagogues, and Progressive Reform," vi, 57–76.

23. The next two paragraphs draw on ibid., 96, 99–108; and Feder, *Unemployment Relief in Periods of Depression*, 226–27, 238, 245. The Cleveland Labor

Exchange was a free employment agency created by the home rule charter of 1912. Campbell, *Daniel E. Morgan*, 56.

24. *Municipal Bulletin*, May 5, 1910, October 1910, May 1911, September 1911 (quotation), and October 1915; Minutes, Municipal Association/Civic League Board of Trustees, May 22, 1911, April 10, 1912, November 21, 1912, January 11, 1913, September 10, 1913, and June 1, 1915 (available in offices of the Citizens League of Cleveland); Hilpert, "Function of the Citizens League," 8–18; Citizens League, *75 Years of Doing Good*, 12; and Pangrace, *Citizens League of Cleveland*, 7–11, 16. Brief biographical sketches of Fesler are given in *Book of Clevelanders*, 94; Campbell, *Freedom's Forum*, 95–96; and Van Tassel and Grabowski, eds., *Encyclopedia of Cleveland History*, 397–98. James F. Richardson, "Political Reform in Cleveland," 161, says that Fesler was "a man with a strong belief in his own righteousness and rightness. This characteristic did not always increase his or his organization's political effectiveness."

25. *Municipal Bulletin*, December 1914. The fiscal crisis is also described in Cramer, *Newton D. Baker*, 56; Arbuthnot, "Mayor Baker's Administration," 226–31; and Ardussi, "Newton D. Baker," 89–100.

26. Ardussi, "Newton D. Baker," 19–28; Hilpert, "Function of the Citizens League," 18; Citizens League, *75 Years of Doing Good*, 12; Minutes, Municipal Association Board of Trustees, August 1, 1912; and Warner, *Progressivism in Ohio*, 330–32. Hatton had studied for a Ph.D. under Charles Merriam at the University of Chicago. Campbell, *Freedom's Forum*, 104–5, has a biographical sketch.

27. Campbell, "Mounting Crisis and Reform," 310–11; idem, *Daniel E. Morgan*, 47–53; and Ardussi, "Newton D. Baker," 29–39. The Non-partisan and Progressive Constitution League statements are included in *Documents of the First Charter Commission*, 1–4, 4a-4b. *Municipal Bulletin* (February 1913), 4–5, contains brief biographical listings for both slates.

28. *Journals of the First Charter Commission*, February 10, 1913; *Documents*, 18, 21, 25–34, 68–69, 71–72, 116–20.

29. Fesler, "Home Rule Charter," 6–18, 26; Cramer, *Newton D. Baker*, 61; *Journals*, March 14, 1913; Campbell, "Mounting Crisis and Reform," 312.

30. Fesler, "Home Rule Charter," 9; *Journals*, March 6, 7, and 18, 1913; *Documents*, 35–41, 43–58, 60–65, 133–35; and Campbell, *Daniel E. Morgan*, 58–61; Ardussi, "Newton D. Baker," 41–43, 61; Richardson, "Political Reform in Cleveland," 158; and Campbell, "Mounting Crisis and Reform," 312–14. Westenhaver was originally included on the Non-partisan slate but replaced; he is discussed briefly in Cramer, *Newton D. Baker*, 29.

31. Campbell, *Daniel E. Morgan*, 62; *Journals*, February 20, February 21, and May 9, 1913; and Ardussi, "Newton D. Baker," 45–50. The Socialist statement is in *Documents*, 14–17. Johnson, "Best Form of Preferential Vote," 751–52, explains the preferential system.

32. Sources for this paragraph are Minutes, Civic League Board of Trustees, June 27, 1913; *Municipal Bulletin*, July 1914; Campbell, *Daniel E. Morgan*, 64–65; Ardussi, "Newton D. Baker," 50; and Warner, *Progressivism in Ohio*, 50.

33. Campbell, *Freedom's Forum*, 21–28, 31–32, 34, 63–73, 78.

34. My discussion of the 1913 election draws on Baker to Thomas Howells,

November 5, 1913, Baker to Waechter and Anzeiger, November 5, 1913, Baker to Svet Publishing, November 5, 1913, Baker to Ernest M. Pappas, November 5, 1913, Baker to Atlee Pomerene, November 5, 1913, Baker to John Zangerle, November 5, 1913, Baker to William G. Votteler, November 5, 1913, Baker to Miles Gallagher, November 5, 1913, Baker to N. Feigenbaum, November 5, 1913, Baker to Rev. Gilbert P. Jennings, November 5, 1913, Baker Papers; *Plain Dealer*, November 3–6, 1913; Cramer, *Newton D. Baker*, 56–58; and Ardussi, "Newton D. Baker," 82–83.

35. As in 1911, the unconstrained coefficients for Irish voting yield inadmissible estimates of greater than 100 percent support for each candidate, but the estimate for Baker (2.229) is greater than the estimate for Davis (1.674). See Finegold, "Progressivism, Electoral Change, and Public Policy," 247.

36. Barone, "Social Basis of Urban Progressivism," 66–68, groups wards according to the percentage of the total 1913 vote going to Baker and presents the average for several census categories within each group. Barone's data suggest that wards voting strongly for Baker had higher percentages of German, Austrian/Czech, Hungarian/Yugoslav, and Polish voters, and fewer native-born, Italian, or Negro voters. He notes, however, that Baker received more support from native-born voters than James M. Cox, the Democratic gubernatorial candidate in 1912 and 1914. Barone found only a slight relationship between the Baker vote and variables for illiteracy and the proportion of children attending school, suggesting that Baker's support spanned class divisions.

37. After leaving the mayoralty, Baker became President Wilson's Secretary of War; throughout the 1920s, he was a leading exponent of Wilsonian internationalism. Walter Lippmann endorsed him for president in 1932 and he might well have won the Democratic nomination if the anti-Roosevelt forces had succeeded in denying Roosevelt the necessary two-thirds vote. See Cramer, *Newton D. Baker*, chaps. 5–9, 12–13; Rosen, *Hoover, Roosevelt, and the Brains Trust*, 96–102, 235–42, 256–65.

38. Louis Post, notes for intended biography of Witt, 1937, Witt Papers; Maschke, "Memoirs," *Plain Dealer*, August 15, 1934; *Plain Dealer*, October 6, 1915; and Wittke, "Peter Witt," 370–71. After the Socialists split over the Bolshevik Revolution, Ruthenberg became a leader of the new Communist party. He and John Reed are the only Americans whose remains were buried in the Kremlin Wall. See Van Tassel and Grabowski, eds., *Encyclopedia of Cleveland History*, 849.

39. "1912–1915 The Record in a Nutshell," "For Mayor Peter Witt," "What Tractioner Witt Has Done," 1915 campaign pamphlets, Witt Papers; opening and closing speeches, debates with Miner G. Norton, October 11, 20, 1915, debate with Davis, October 23, 1915, Witt Papers.

40. Witt statement on municipal ownership, October 21, 1915, Witt to George E. Edwards, September 22, 1915, Charles Hockenbrouch to Witt, October 27, 1915, Witt to Hockenbrouch, October 28, 1915, Witt Papers; opening speech, debate with Norton, October 20, 1915; *Plain Dealer*, October 17, 20 (ed.), 1915; and Wittke, "Peter Witt," 371.

41. Herman E. Eisler to Witt, February 11, 1915, Witt to Eisler, February 15, 1915, John McF. Howie to Witt, February 16, 1915, Witt Papers.

42. Post notes, Witt Papers; Witt to Edgar Brass, October 26, 1915, Witt Papers; "From Moulder to Mayor," 1915 campaign pamphlet, Witt Papers; *Plain Dealer*, October 25, 1915; Young, *Twentieth-Century Experience in Urban Transit*, 14; and Wittke, "Peter Witt," 370. Evidence that some union members supported Witt may be found in Robert W. Hobbs to Witt, December 14, 1915, Molders Union to Witt, December 14, 1914, and Witt to James S. Kennedy, October 1, 1915, Witt Papers.

43. Saul Feigenbaum to Witt, February 10, 1915, H. Katznel to Witt, October 17, 1915, Witt to Katznel, October 21, 1915, Witt Papers; Wittke, "Peter Witt," 372–73; Fordyce, "Nationality Groups," 117; and Saltzer, "The People's Choice."

44. Witt to Olive Maguire, September 22, 1915, Witt to Denny O'Neill, October 4, 1915, Witt to W. A. Stinchcomb, October 20, 1915, Witt to Daniel Young, October 26, 1915, H. H. Timby to Witt, November 1, 1915, F. H. Goff to Witt, November 2, 1915, and F. T. Peitch to Witt, November 2, 1915, Witt Papers. Election day odds were 6–10 on Witt and 10–5 on Davis. *Plain Dealer*, November 2, 1915.

45. *Plain Dealer*, November 3, 1915; Wittke, "Peter Witt," 373.

46. Witt to H. C. DeRan, quoted in Wittke, "Peter Witt," 374. See also Witt to F. T. Peitch, November 9, 1915, Witt to W. A. Greenlund, November 10, 1915, Witt to John McF. Howie, November 9, 1915, Witt to A. W. McIntyre, November 11, 1915, Witt to Charles R. Eckert, November 11, 1915, Witt to W. E. White, November 11, 1915, and Witt to S. A. Stockwell, November 11, 1915, Witt Papers.

47. Baker to Woodrow Wilson, November 4, 1915, Baker to Henry D. Lindsley, November 9, 1915, Baker Papers.

48. Witt to John F. McKay, October 20, 1915, Witt Papers.

49. Wittke, "Peter Witt," 375–76; Graham, *Encore for Reform*, 70, 110, 124, 167; and Cramer, *Newton D. Baker*, 259–71.

50. Raper, *Soviet Table*, 31, 9; Campbell, *Freedom's Forum*, 36, 45–48, 96, 112–13; idem, *Daniel E. Morgan*, 102–4, 127–29; Childs, *Civic Victories*, 159–63; Porter, *Cleveland*, 38–46; and Richardson, "Political Reform," 164.

51. "A Report to the People of Cleveland: One Year of Public Service" (1916), "How the Present City Government Has Made Good" (1917), "Re-Elect Him! Harry L. Davis, Mayor of Cleveland" (1919), all in Subject File, Mayors, Cleveland Municipal Library; Porter, *Cleveland*, 17, 48–49; and Saltzer, "People's Choice."

52. Campbell, *Daniel E. Morgan*, 98–99; idem, *Freedom's Forum*, 34–35, 118; Richardson, "Political Reform in Cleveland," 161–64; Childs, *Civic Victories*, 157–58; Maxey, "Cleveland Election and the New Charter," 83–84; idem, "Analysis of Cleveland's New Charter," 29–35; and Van Tassel and Grabowski, eds., *Encyclopedia of Cleveland History*, 185–86.

53. Campbell, "Mounting Crisis and Reform," 321; idem, *Daniel E. Morgan*, 100, 129 n. 72; Porter, *Cleveland*, 34–37; Richardson, "Political Reform," 161–64; Saltzer, "People's Choice"; and Raper, *Soviet Table*, 41–44.

54. Derthick, "Stability in City Politics," 1–2, 6; Porter, *Cleveland*, 88, 94–95, 109–11, 123–25, 133–34, 177–80, 211. The law director, appointed by the mayor, represents Cleveland in both criminal and civil matters and thus combines the

responsibilities of a prosecutor with those of a city solicitor. The law director be-comes acting mayor in the mayor's absence and is first in line of succession when the mayor's office is vacated. See Kollar, "Cleveland City Government," 220.

55. Swanstrom, *Crisis of Growth Politics*, 100–118; Porter, *Cleveland*, 224–33, 237–57, 262–72, 277–79, 297–98; and Ardey and Nelson, "Maturation of Black Political Power."

56. My discussion of the Kucinich administration draws on Swanstrom, *Crisis of Growth Politics*, chaps. 5–10; Van Tassel and Grabowski, "Epilogue," 178–79; Wagner, "Corsi Acts the Bad Guy"; Miller, "Waxman Cultivates a Tough-Guy Stance"; Carlson, "Legal Eagle"; Wagner, "Barrett's Aim"; Wagner, "Hey, Joe Teg-reene"; McGunagle, "Commissioner Jack Nicholl"; Daniels, "Weissman"; Bean, "Chief Fox Is Confident He Can Run Department"; Marschall, ed., *Battle of Cleveland*; and Judis, "Decline and Fall," 36–39.

57. Swanstrom relates that as a political science graduate student interested in the Kucinich administration as a dissertation topic, he wrote the mayor asking for a job. Bob Weissman, Kucinich's top aide, soon called to offer one. Swanstrom, *Crisis of Growth Politics*, xiv.

58. *Thirteenth Census of the U.S.: Population*, 3:418 (1910); Bureau of the Census, *Census of Population and Housing: 1970 Census Tracts, Final Report PHC(1)-45, Cleveland, Ohio SMSA*, P-1.

Introduction to Part IV

1. "Why Municipal Reform Succeeds in Chicago and Fails in New York," *Independent*, 929–35; Steffens, *Autobiography*, 2:422–29.

Chapter 9

1. Kantowicz, "Carter H. Harrison II," 16–17.

2. Merriam, *Chicago*, 98–99; Green, "Chicago Democratic Party," 89–95, 182; McCarthy, "Businessmen and Professionals," 44–51; Schmidt, *"Mayor Who Cleaned Up Chicago,"* 17–18; and Pinderhughes, *Race and Ethnicity in Chicago Politics*, 40–42.

3. Green, "Chicago Democratic Party," 338; Wendt and Kogan, *Lords of the Levee*, 64, 86–88.

4. Green, "Chicago Democratic Party," 33–34, 44, 52. The elder Harrison was shot by an office seeker in 1893.

5. Harrison, *Stormy Years*, 75–76, 188, 210–11; Green, "Chicago Democratic Party," 100 n. 1; Schmidt, *"Mayor Who Cleaned Up Chicago,"* 18–19.

6. Tarr, *Boss Politics*, 175–78, 285–86; Schmidt, *"Mayor Who Cleaned Up Chicago,"* 19.

7. Roberts, "Businessmen in Revolt," 141–46; Wendt and Kogan, *Lords of the Levee*, 39, 111–13, 117–21; and Stead, *If Christ Came to Chicago*, chap. 9.

8. Einhorn, *Property Rules*, 239–41; Roberts, "Businessmen in Revolt," 3–27; Jaher, *Urban Establishment*, 505; and Pierce, *History of Chicago*, 3:308.

9. Roberts, "Businessmen in Revolt," 39–46; Grant, *Fight for a City*, 29–47, 67–79.

10. Stead, *If Christ Came to Chicago*, 386 (quote), chaps. 9, 10, 13, 23; Roberts, "Businessmen in Revolt," 115–33; Wendt and Kogan, *Lords of the Levee*, 91–95; Jaher, *Urban Establishment*, 506; and McCarthy, "Businessmen and Professionals," 49.

11. Miller, "Politics of Municipal Reform," 15–20; Roberts, "Businessmen in Revolt," 152–81; and McCarthy, "Businessmen and Professionals," 27–32. Two aldermen represented each of thirty-four wards, coming up for election in alternate years. The annexation of Austin in 1899 increased the size of the council to seventy aldermen representing thirty-five wards.

12. McCarthy, "Businessmen and Professionals," 38–40; Harrison, *Stormy Years* culled material, Harrison Papers; Wendt and Kogan, *Lords of the Levee*, 93; Grant, *Fight for a City*, 78, 99, 143; Jaher, *Urban Establishment*, 502; and Roberts, "Businessmen in Revolt," 4.

13. McCarthy, "New Metropolis," 49; idem, "Businessmen and Professionals," 25–27; King, *Citizen Cole*, 20; Taylor, *Pioneering*, 67; and Jaher, *Urban Establishment*, 483, 502.

14. Taylor, *Pioneering*, 65–66; Diner, *City and Its Universities*, 156; and Davis, *Spearheads for Reform*, 151–69.

15. Davis, *Spearheads for Reform*, 151–69; Nelli, *Italians in Chicago*, 97–100; Taylor, *Pioneering*, 72–74; McCarthy, "Businessmen and Professionals," 30–31; Miller, "Politics of Municipal Reform," 32–36; Schmidt, *"Mayor Who Cleaned Up Chicago,"* 23–28, 31–32; and Flanagan, *Charter Reform in Chicago*, 131.

16. According to the 1910 Federal Census (*Thirteenth Census of the United States*, 1:512), 23.0 percent of Chicago's population was native-stock (native-born with native parents, English, and Scottish). First- or second-generation Germans were the largest ethnic group, 19.5 percent of the population. First- or second-generation Austrians, including Poles and Bohemians, were 9.9 percent. First- or second-generation Russians, including many Jews, made up 8.2 percent. First- or second-generation Scandinavian (Danish, Norwegian, and Swedish) were 7.7 percent, while 7.5 percent were first- or second-generation Irish. First- or second-generation Italians were 3.3 percent of the population. The black population was 2.0 percent. The Chicago school census of 1908, which categorized respondents by their preferred classification, listed 6.7 percent as Poles and 4.5 percent as Bohemians. Chicago Board of Education, *School Census Report*, 1908.

17. Kantowicz, *Polish-American Politics*, 64–69; Tarr, *Boss Politics*, 13–14; Nelli, *Italians in Chicago*, 95–96; and Harrison, *Stormy Years*, 85–86.

18. Nelli, *Italians in Chicago*, 96.

19. Ibid., 98–99; Hofmeister, *Germans of Chicago*, 94, 96; and Green, "Chicago Democratic Party," 10, 16, 27, 125.

20. Zoline, "Politics: Chicago," 277–79; Tierney, *Darrow*, 172–76.

21. Becker, "Edward Dunne," 9–12; Green, "Irish Chicago," 227–28. On New York, see Shefter, "Electoral Foundations of the Political Machine," 290–96. Green, "Irish Chicago," 221, points out that Chicago did not have a consolidated Irish machine until the New Deal.

22. Wendt and Kogan, *Lords of the Levee*, 136–37, 161, 166–74, 182–99, 232–34, 240; Harrison, *Stormy Years*, 86, 156–59, 190, 229.

23. Harrison, *Stormy Years*, 67–68, 75–76, 79–80, 86–87; Green, "Chicago Democratic Party," 79–80, 102–3.

24. Harrison, *Stormy Years*, 101–2, 175–82; Kantowicz, "Carter H. Harrison II," 23.

25. Manuscript beginning, "My resentment. . . ," and statement on Municipal Voters' League, Harrison Papers; Harrison, *Stormy Years*, 218, 301.

26. Roberts, "Businessmen in Revolt," 183–217; Jaher, *Urban Establishment*, 48; Tarr, *Boss Politics*, 80–83; Harrison, *Stormy Years*, 136–75; and Kantowicz, "Carter Harrison II," 23–28. McDonald, *Insull*, 84–88, defends Yerkes, arguing he was the victim rather than the perpetrator of political corruption. McDonald does not document his conclusion (85) that Yerkes made Chicago's transit system "more extensive, more comfortable, faster and cheaper than any then existing in any large American city." This judgment was not shared by contemporary observers: see the sources cited in Barrett, *Automobile and Urban Transit*, 221 n. 3, and in Bentley, "Municipal Ownership Interest Groups," chap. 1, 10.

27. Harrison, *Stormy Years* culled material, Harrison Papers.

28. Green, "Chicago Democratic Party," 89.

29. Tingley, "From Carter Harrison II to Fred Busse," 28, 31–33; Tarr, *Boss Politics*, 83–84; Ickes, *Autobiography of a Curmudgeon*, 82–88; Harrison, *Stormy Years*, 52–53, 100–104, 115–16; Komons, "Chicago, 1893–1907," 181–94; and Green, "Chicago Democratic Party," 50, 77.

30. The methods used are explained in the Appendix.

31. Tarr, *Boss Politics*, 85, notes a positive rank-order correlation between wards' vote for Harlan and percentage Protestant, and between wards' vote for Harrison and percentage Catholic. He suggests Harlan did well among native, upper-class Protestants and among Scandinavians. In the heavily Swedish Twenty-third Ward, Harlan received 3,389 votes to 1,824 for Harrison. This was better than Harlan's share of the citywide vote, but short of the plurality he received in three other wards.

32. The unconstrained estimates for Sears and Hesing have very low corrected R^2s, and should be treated as less reliable than the estimates for Harrison and Harlan. These estimates are presented in Finegold, "Progressivism, Electoral Change, and Public Policy," 280.

33. The methods used to derive these estimates are explained in the Appendix.

34. Tarr, *Boss Politics*, 85, reports a correlation between the Harlan and McKinley votes.

35. Harrison, *Stormy Years*, 124–26, 129–35; Tompkins, "John Peter Altgeld," 656–61; Cooling, *Chicago Democracy*, 25–30, 34–55, 95–96; Tingley, "From Carter Harrison II to Fred Busse," 53, 62; Green, "Chicago Democratic Party," 87; Komons, "Chicago, 1893–1907," 227–31; and Tarr, *Boss Politics*, 24.

36. Cooling, *Chicago Democracy*, 70, 72–89; Tompkins, "John Peter Altgeld," 671–72; Tingley, "From Carter Harrison II to Fred Busse," 66, 70; Komons, "Chicago, 1893–1907," 231–32; *Chicago's Champion* (pro-Harrison newspaper), March 2, 1899, Harrison Papers; Harrison, *Stormy Years*, 188–91, 193–94; Wendt and Kogan, *Lords of the Levee*, 120; and Barnard, *Eagle Forgotten*, 406–11.

37. Tompkins, "John Peter Altgeld," 675; Komons, "Chicago, 1893–1907," 225–26; Cooling, *Chicago Democracy*, 58; Ickes, *Autobiography of a Cur-*

mudgeon, 89; and Flanagan, *Charter Reform,* 44. Ickes's discussion of the 1899 election does not even mention Altgeld, though Ickes had supported him for governor.

38. Darrow, *Story of My Life,* 108–9; Komons, "Chicago, 1893–1907," 231; and Cooling, *Chicago Democracy,* 45.

39. Tompkins, "John Peter Altgeld," 673; Cooling, *Chicago Democracy,* 104.

40. Cooling, *Chicago Democracy,* 105; Tompkins, "John Peter Altgeld," 675–76.

41. Estimates for the Altgeld vote, however, have a negative (!) corrected R^2 and should be considered unreliable. The unconstrained regression estimates are presented in Finegold, "Progressivism, Electoral Change, and Public Policy," 291.

42. Tarr, *Boss Politics,* 94–96.

43. *Thirteenth Census of the United States,* 1:512. The 1900 census does not provide this breakdown.

44. Corrected R^2s for the Carter and Harrison estimates are low, which warns against making too much of this result. See Finegold, "Progressivism, Electoral Change, and Public Policy," 294.

45. Harrison, *Stormy Years,* 204–6; Harrison, *Stormy Years* culled material, Harrison Papers; and Tingley, "From Carter Harrison II to Fred Busse," 109–13.

46. Harrison, *Stormy Years,* 104.

47. This paragraph draws on Ickes, *Autobiography of a Curmudgeon,* 91–101; Harrison, *Stormy Years,* 222–26; Tarr, *Boss Politics,* 118–21; Collins, *Autobiography,* 113–17; Komons, "Chicago, 1893–1907," 298–305; and Darrow, *Story of My Life,* 117–18.

48. Ickes, *Autobiography of a Curmudgeon,* 100.

49. Harrison notes Hopkins-Sullivan defections in *Stormy Years,* 229, 266–67, and in the *Stormy Years* culled material, Harrison Papers.

50. Ickes, *Autobiography of a Curmudgeon,* 99–100.

51. Harrison, Address at Conference of Mayors, Philadelphia, Pennsylvania, November 13, 1914, 2, 6, Harrison Papers. For similar views about the "scientific study of politics," see Harrison, *Stormy Years,* 292.

52. Kantowicz, "Carter Harrison II," 24–25; *Chicago Tribune,* May 11, 1905, 6.

53. Harrison, "Some Phases of the Municipal Problem," Address Delivered before the Good Government Club of the University of Michigan, Ann Arbor, Michigan, February 27, 1903 and the Yale Law School Political Club, New Haven, Connecticut, March 9, 1905, 3–7, Harrison Papers; Harrison, Address at Conference of Mayors, 5–6; and Harrison, *Stormy Years,* 246–55. Barrett, *Automobile and Urban Transit,* 22, suggests Harrison was uninterested in the details of transportation policy.

54. Diner, *City and Its Universities,* 81–85; Smith, *Ella Flagg Young,* 54; Harrison, *Stormy Years* culled material, Harrison Papers; and Candeloro, "Chicago School Board Crisis," 397.

55. Harrison's presidential hopes are discussed in Wendt and Kogan, *Lords of the Levee,* 207, 216, 242; and Green, "Chicago Democratic Party," 85.

Chapter 10

1. Becker, "Edward Dunne," 1–16, 22; Green, "Irish Chicago," 227–28; Gottfried, *Boss Cermak*, 134; Morton, "Edward F. Dunne," 219–21; Schmidt, *"Mayor Who Cleaned Up Chicago,"* 27, 34–35; and Buenker, "Limits of Municipal Reform," 34.

2. The next two paragraphs draw on Becker, "Edward Dunne," 19–21, 30–40, 50–51; Tingley, "From Carter Harrison II to Fred Busse," 168, 171–72; Wendt and Kogan, *Lords of the Levee*, 242–46, 329; and Buenker, "Limits of Municipal Reform," 36–39.

3. Despite this, the Socialist party did run a mayoral candidate, John Collins. John D. Buenker suggests that if Collins had not run, most of his 23,034 votes would have gone to Dunne. Buenker, "Limits of Municipal Reform," 226 n. 17.

4. Tingley, "From Carter Harrison II to Fred Busse," 173, 177, 182; Komons, "Chicago, 1893–1907," 326–29, 337; Tarr, *Boss Politics*, 177; and Becker, "Edward Dunne," 42–44, 55–57.

5. Dunne's and Harlan's views on traction are discussed in Becker, "Edward Dunne," 24–29, 47–54, 56; Komons, "Chicago, 1893–1907," 307–25; and Barrett, *Automobile and Urban Transit*, 33–34.

6. Harrison, *Stormy Years*, 255.

7. Ibid.

8. Becker, "Edward Dunne," 59, 62. Becker himself argues that the immediate municipal ownership issue, because it could easily be grasped by the public, was responsible for Dunne's election. See also Tingley, "From Carter Harrison II to Fred Busse," 182–83.

9. Class and suburbanization estimates are based on unconstrained regression coefficients presented in Finegold, "Progressivism, Electoral Change, and Public Policy," 317.

10. Buenker, "Limits of Municipal Reform," 39–40, comes to the opposite conclusion on the basis of ward totals. Buenker reports a correlation greater than .90 between the Dunne vote and the pro-municipal ownership vote on the traction ordinances that were also on the ballot. This contradicts the conclusion of Arthur F. Bentley, who worked from precinct-level data, that there was no correspondence between the 1905 mayoral vote and the 1905 municipal ownership votes. Precincts with the lowest level of support for municipal ownership, Bentley noted, included some that were among the weakest for Dunne, and some that were among the strongest for him, such as Kenna and Coughlin's First Ward. Bentley, "Municipal Ownership Interest Groups," chap. 5, 1.

11. Becker, "Edward Dunne," 67, 73–74, 160–61, 164; Grosser, "Chicago"; Davis, *Spearheads for Reform*, 192; and Candeloro, "Chicago School Board Crisis," 397–98.

12. My discussion of the traction controversy draws on Becker, "Edward Dunne," 99–146; Barrett, *Automobile and Urban Transit*, 35–44; Komons, "Chicago, 1893–1907," 357–64, 370–77; Schmidt, *"Mayor Who Cleaned Up Chicago,"* 32–36; Buenker, "Limits of Municipal Reform," 41–46; and Gould, "Walter L. Fisher," 168–70.

13. Quoted in Becker, "Edward Dunne," 146.

14. Barrett, *Automobile and Urban Transit*, 43.

15. The implementation of the Gary Plan in New York is discussed in Chapter 5. On education in Cleveland, see Randall, "Meaning of Progressivism," 210–23; and Miggins, "Businessmen, Pedagogues, and Progressive Reform," 140–42.

16. My discussion of education under Dunne draws on Candeloro, "Chicago School Board Crisis," 397–401; Addams, *Twenty Years*, 327–39; Smith, *Ella Flagg Young*, 134–37; and Buenker, "Limits of Municipal Reform," 42, 48.

17. *Tribune* quotation in Candeloro, "Chicago School Board Crisis," 401. Butler's role as leader of traditional reformers in the New York City school conflicts of the 1890s is described in Ravitch, *Great School Wars*, chap. 14.

18. Addams, *Twenty Years*, 330–31, 333–34; Smith, *Ella Flagg Young*, 135–36, 138. The Federation saw Addams as an unreliable ally who could be manipulated by Cooley and who was willing to compromise on teachers' retirement benefits to gain playgrounds.

19. Becker, "Edward Dunne," 165–66, 169, 174, 177; Grosser, "Chicago"; Tingley, "From Carter Harrison II to Fred Busse," 197, 220; and Buenker, "Limits of Municipal Reform," 47–48. Police Chief Collins, a long-time member of the force, should be distinguished from the John Collins who ran for mayor as a Socialist in 1905. Patterson later joined his family at the *Tribune* and then founded the *New York Daily News*.

20. McCarthy, "Businessmen and Professionals," 44–56; Flanagan, *Charter Reform in Chicago*, chap. 2.

21. A complete list of delegates is given in the letterhead of a letter from M. L. McKinley to Charles E. Merriam, March 5, 1906, Merriam Papers, Box 72. See also Merriam, "Chicago Charter Convention," 2; Flanagan, *Charter Reform*, 59–63.

22. Hatton, *Digest of City Charters*; Merriam, "Chicago Charter Convention," 4; and Diner, *City and Its Universities*, 158. In 1905 and 1906, Merriam had done a comparative study of municipal finances for the City Club. Merriam, "Report of an Investigation of the Municipal Revenues of Chicago"; see also Karl, *Charles E. Merriam*, 51–52.

23. Chicago Charter Convention, *Proceedings*, 62–81. The original *Proceedings*, 65, had the delegates discussing the theories of "Oscar Gorsky," but this was later corrected.

24. Ibid., 97–130; Merriam, "Chicago Charter Convention," 9. Other evidence of Fisher's belief "in the importance of keeping national politics out of municipal elections" is discussed in Gould, "Walter L. Fisher," 162.

25. Chicago Charter Convention, *Proceedings*, 208–72, 929–46; Flanagan, *Charter Reform*, 65, 68–70, 90.

26. Chicago Charter Convention, *Proceedings*, 376–424, 1146–60.

27. Ibid., 561–716.

28. Ibid., 785–93; McCarthy, "Businessmen and Professionals," 65–67; Flanagan, *Charter Reform*, 71–73, 86–91.

29. Chicago Charter Convention, *Proceedings*, 785; Flanagan, *Charter Reform*, 83–86.

30. Chicago Charter Convention, *Proceedings*, 1192–95.

31. Merriam, "Chicago Charter Convention," 7–8, 13–14; McCarthy, "Busi-

nessmen and Professionals," 68–81; *Real Estate News*, "Proposed Charter for Chicago"; Flanagan, *Charter Reform*, chap. 5. Pamphlets for and against the charter are in the Merriam Papers, Box 72. Included in the collection are the "Proposed Charter" article in *Real Estate News* and "An Analysis and Discussion of the Proposed New Charter," by Raymond Robins. "Academic theorists and sycophant reformers," Robins wrote, "cooperating with a misguided press have united to stampede the independent voters and force this betrayal of the public interests upon the City of Chicago" (7). The article was published as part of *Public Policy League Bulletin* 1:1 (September 1907); Robins and Post were both listed as directors of the League.

32. Becker, "Edward Dunne," 187–94, 210; Tingley, "From Carter Harrison II to Fred Busse," 201; Green, "Chicago Democratic Party," 118–19; Komons, "Chicago," 398; Wendt and Kogan, *Lords of the Levee*, 250; Harrison, *Stormy Years* culled material, Harrison Papers; and Buenker, "Limits of Municipal Reform," 41, 44.

33. Flanagan, "Fred A. Busse," 50–56; idem, *Charter Reform*, 99–105; Becker, "Edward Dunne," 195–97; Komons, "Chicago," 386–87; and Buenker, "Limits of Municipal Reform," 45. Harold Ickes supported Dunne but did not take an active part in the campaign until the end. Ickes, *Autobiography of a Curmudgeon*, 109–10.

34. Becker, "Edward Dunne," 209.

35. Class and suburbanization estimates are based on unconstrained regression coefficients in Finegold, "Progressivism, Electoral Change, and Public Policy," 299, 304, 317, 339.

36. Wendt and Kogan, *Lords of the Levee*, 250; Harrison, *Stormy Years*, 256.

37. From his study of precinct data, Arthur Bentley concluded that the 1907 mayoral vote bore a close correspondence to the traction ordinance vote. Bentley, "Municipal Ownership Interest Groups," chap. 5, 1. Buenker, "Limits of Municipal Reform," 45, reports a .90 correlation at the ward level between votes for Dunne and votes against the Settlement Ordinances.

38. Johnson, *My Story*, 123, mentions that Johnson "took down the 'Keep Off the Grass' signs in the parks" and "commenced to institute people's amusements in the parks." See also Murdock, "First Term," 39.

39. Davis, *Spearheads for Reform*, 191–93; Becker, "Edward Dunne," 69–71. Taylor's commission collapsed when neither side would testify.

Chapter 11

1. On Busse, see Harrison, *Stormy Years*, 256–57, 282; McCarthy, "Businessmen and Professionals," 139–41; Flanagan, *Charter Reform*, 99–100; and idem, "Fred A. Busse," 50–52, 60. On Baehr, see Chapters 7 and 8.

2. An exception to this general assessment is Ickes, *Autobiography of a Curmudgeon*, 110, which accuses Busse of cynically giving the wealthy the services they wanted for their own neighborhoods while permitting vice and corruption to flourish elsewhere.

3. On McClellan and Gaynor, see Chapter 4.

4. Quoted in Flanagan, *Charter Reform*, 103.

5. Barrett, *Automobile and Urban Transit*, 40, chaps. 3–4; Merriam Commission–suggested questions, Merriam Papers, Box 80.

6. Addams, *Twenty Years*, 336; Candeloro, "Chicago School Board Crisis," 402–7; Smith, *Ella Flagg Young*, 137–39; and Flanagan, "Fred A. Busse," 57–58.

7. Smith, *Ella Flagg Young*, 139–57, 183–85; Candeloro, "Chicago School Board Crisis," 406.

8. This paragraph and the next draw on Hines, *Burnham of Chicago*, 312–45; Bach, "Reconsideration," 132–41; McCarthy, "Businessmen and Professionals," 106–38; Merriam, *Chicago*, 70–75; Barrett, *Automobile and Urban Transit*, 73–81; Mayer and Wade, *Chicago*, 274–81; and Charles Merriam, unpublished autobiographical fragment, Merriam Papers, Box 3.

9. Under the urban renewal program of the 1960s, a giant expressway exchange and the University of Illinois Chicago Circle campus were constructed on Burnham's proposed site. Mayer and Wade, *Chicago*, 441–42; Hines, *Burnham of Chicago*, 341.

10. Quoted in Bach, "Reconsideration," 134.

11. The Cleveland Group Plan is discussed in Chapter 7. On the shift in Burnham's architectural style, see Hines, "Paradox of 'Progressive' Architecture," 430–31; and idem, *Burnham of Chicago*, 71–72.

12. McCarthy, "Businessmen and Professionals," 141–43.

13. Merriam, *Chicago*, 271–72.

14. My discussion of the Merriam Commission draws on the following sources: memo on Merriam Commission and Merriam Commission suggested questions, Merriam Papers, Box 80; City Club (Chicago), "Work and Accomplishments of the Chicago Commission on City Expenditures," 195–208; Merriam, "Investigations," 281–303; idem, "Work of the Chicago Bureau of Public Efficiency," 63–66; idem, *Chicago*, 238–39; Karl, *Charles E. Merriam*, 62–63; and Tinzmann, "Education of Charles E. Merriam," 37–49.

15. Unpublished autobiographical fragment, Merriam Papers, Box 3.

16. Merriam, "Investigations," 294.

17. Merriam, *Chicago*, 239–40; Tinzmann, "Education of Charles E. Merriam," 49; and Chicago Bureau of Public Efficiency, "Waterworks System of the City of Chicago," 3.

18. Werner, *Julius Rosenwald*, 139–40; Gould, "Walter L. Fisher," 165–66; Merriam, "Investigations," 300–301; and idem, "Work of the Chicago Bureau of Public Efficiency," 66.

19. Chicago Bureau of Public Efficiency, "Methods of Preparing and Administering the Budget of Cook County, Illinois," January 1911.

20. Schiesl, *Politics of Efficiency*, 123–24.

21. Chicago Bureau of Public Efficiency reports: "Methods of Preparing and Administering the Budget of Cook County"; "Proposed Purchase of Voting Machines by the Board of Election Commissioners of the City of Chicago"; "Street Pavement Laid in the City of Chicago"; "Electrolysis of Water Pipes in the City of Chicago"; "Administration of the Office of Recorder of Cook County, Illinois"; "Plea for Publicity in the Office of County Treasurer"; "Preparing Asphalt Pavement"; "Municipal Court Acts"; "Waterworks System of the City of Chicago"; "Bureau of Streets, Civil Service Commission, and Special Assessment Accounting

System of the City of Chicago"; "Administration of the Office of Coroner of Cook County, Illinois"; "Administration of the Office of Sheriff of Cook County, Illinois"; "Park Governments of Chicago—General Summary and Conclusion"; and "Nineteen Local Governments in Chicago." The Bureau's early projects are also discussed in Merriam, "Investigations," 301–2, and idem, "Work of the Chicago Bureau of Public Efficiency," 66–68.

22. Ickes, *Autobiography of a Curmudgeon*, 119–31; Merriam, *Chicago*, 282; Merriam, "An Intimate View of Urban Politics," draft, Merriam Papers, Box 94; idem, unpublished autobiographical fragment, Merriam Papers, Box 3; "Merriam," "Thompson," and "Smulski," Merriam Papers, Box 74; Karl, *Charles E. Merriam*, 66–68; and McCarthy, "Prelude to Armageddon," 505–11.

23. Harrison, *Stormy Years*, 262–70, 315; Wendt and Kogan, *Lords of the Levee*, 290–91; and Merriam mass meeting proceedings, April 1, 1911, Merriam Papers, Box 74. Aided greatly by the Republican-Progressive split, Dunne was elected governor of Illinois in 1912. He supported social welfare and labor legislation, utility regulation, tax reform, direct election of Senators, women's suffrage, and campaign finance legislation. With the Republicans reunified, Frank Lowden defeated Dunne in 1916. Dunne remains the only mayor of Chicago to become governor of Illinois. See Buenker, "Edward F. Dunne," 3–21; Morton, "Illinois' Most Progressive Governor," 222–34; and Hutchinson, *Lowden of Illinois*, 1:267, 273, 278–79, 286–91.

24. Merriam mass meeting proceedings, April 1, 1911, Merriam Papers, Box 74. Similarly, see "Coats Off for Chicago! Into Her Fight for Honesty and Decency!" and "Who Got $40,000?," Merriam Papers, Box 74.

25. Merriam mass meeting proceedings, April 1, 1911, Merriam Papers, Box 74; "Merriam and the Hyde Park Protective Association" and "Professor Charles E. Merriam, Republican Candidate for Mayor," Merriam Papers, Box 74; "An Intimate View of Urban Politics," draft, chapter 3, Merriam Papers, Box 94; unpublished autobiographical fragment, Merriam Papers, Box 3; McCarthy, "Prelude to Armageddon," 515; Merriam, *Chicago*, 285; and Karl, *Charles E. Merriam*, 68–69.

26. "Union Men Vote AGAINST Prof. Merriam," Merriam Papers, Box 74.

27. Karl, *Charles E. Merriam*, 68; Merriam, *Chicago*, 235, 284; McCarthy, "Prelude to Armageddon," 512–13; Merriam, "An Intimate View of Urban Politics," draft, Merriam Papers, Box 94, chap. 3; and Flanagan, *Charter Reform*, 153 and 188 n. 10.

28. Karl, *Charles E. Merriam*, 68; Ickes, *Autobiography of a Curmudgeon*, 139; Harrison, *Growing Up with Chicago*, 301–3; and idem, *Stormy Years*, 272–75.

29. Merriam, *Chicago*, 283.

30. Ickes, *Autobiography of a Curmudgeon*, 130–36; Harrison, *Stormy Years*, 282–83; idem, *Growing Up with Chicago*, 299–300; and Merriam, "An Intimate View of Urban Politics," draft, chap. 3, Merriam Papers, Box 94.

31. Merriam mass meeting proceedings, Merriam Papers, Box 74; Merriam, "An Intimate View of Urban Politics," draft, chap. 3, Merriam Papers, Box 94; McCarthy, "Prelude to Armageddon," 513; Harrison, *Stormy Years*, 275, 277; and Merriam, *Chicago*, 286.

32. The corrected R² for the Merriam estimates, however, is only .01, suggesting unreliability. This may reflect organizational switching or fraud. The Harrison estimates, with corrected R² of .45, are more reliable. The unconstrained regression estimates are given in Finegold, "Progressivism, Electoral Change, and Public Policy," 360.

33. To calculate the independent variable, raw primary votes for each candidate were divided by the total of eligible voters in that ward. Minor candidates in either election are not shown. Again, corrected R² for the Merriam general election vote is an unreliable .01, but the corrected R² for the Harrison general election vote is a much stronger .82. The unconstrained estimates are given in Finegold, "Progressivism, Electoral Change, and Public Policy," 362.

34. Both Harrison and Merriam suggested that some of the Dunne vote went to the Socialist candidate, W. E. Rodriguez. The Socialist vote did increase from 13,429 in the 1907 mayoral election to 24,825 in 1911. As Barry Karl points out, however, this was also a period of national growth in Socialist support: in 1912, Eugene Debs received 49,401 Chicago votes as the Socialist candidate for president. Unfortunately, even in 1911, the Socialist vote was too low (6.8 percent of the three-way vote) for reliable regression estimates of its origins. See Karl, *Charles E. Merriam*, 71; and Harrison, *Stormy Years*, 292.

35. As with other estimates for the 1911 Merriam general election vote, those in Table 11-2 have an extremely low corrected R² (.01). The Harrison demographic estimates (corrected R² = .25) are less reliable than the transition rate estimates for 1911 given earlier. See Finegold, "Progressivism, Electoral Change, and Public Policy," 360, 362, 364–65.

36. Harrison, *Stormy Years*, 294.

37. Merriam mass meeting proceedings, April 1, 1911, Merriam Papers, Box 74.

38. Merriam, *Chicago*, 287.

39. Ibid., 235.

40. Merriam, "An Intimate View of Urban Politics," draft, Merriam Papers, Box 94, 20–21.

41. Quoted in McCarthy, "Prelude to Armageddon," 517.

42. Shefter, "Emergence of the Political Machine," 27, 33, 37–38.

43. Allswang, *House for All Peoples*, 52–53, 65–66, 104–5, 128, 134, 142–43, 145–50, 156–60; Schottenhamel, "How Big Bill Thompson Won Control," 31–40, 42–45; Gosnell, *Negro Politicians*, 40–62, 171, 176–77, 179–83, 198–201; idem, *Machine Politics*, 10–12; and Gottfried, *Boss Cermak*, 205–6. Thompson was originally associated with William Lorimer's West Side organization. He became a protégé of Frederick Lundin, the "Poor Swede," when Lundin took over the Lorimer organization. Thompson eventually cut his ties to both bosses, completing his transformation from organizational to personalistic (and idiosyncratic) politician. On Lundin, see Zink, *City Bosses in the United States*, 275–90; Lund, "Swedish-American Politics," 296–306; and Tarr, *Boss Politics*, 313–14.

44. Karl, *Charles E. Merriam*, 81–82, 97, and chaps. 12–13; "Win with Merriam," 1919 mayoral campaign pamphlet, Merriam Papers, Box 75; Dorsett, *Roosevelt and the City Bosses*, 87; and Diner, *A City and Its Universities*, chap. 8.

Many other Chicago experts and reformers participated in the New Deal's welfare, education, or planning activities. The most notable appointee was Harold Ickes, who became Roosevelt's Secretary of the Interior.

45. Karl, *Charles E. Merriam*, esp. chap. 7; Merriam, *New Aspects of Politics*, chap. 7 ("The Next Step in the Organization of Municipal Research").

46. Gunnell, "Continuity and Innovation," 133–42. See also Seidelman and Harpham, *Disenchanted Realists*, chaps. 4–5; Ross, *Origins of American Social Science*, 395–97, 448–67; Ricci, *Tragedy of Political Science*, 77–78, 87, 114–15; and Somit and Tannenhaus, *Development of American Political Science*, 110–13.

47. Karl, *Charles E. Merriam*, 128.

48. My discussion of Harrison's final administration draws on the following sources: manuscript beginning "My resentment" and *Stormy Years* culled material, both in Harrison Papers; Harrison, *Stormy Years*, chaps. 28–29, 31; Barrett, *Automobile and Urban Transit*, 94, 100; Wendt and Kogan, *Lords of the Levee*, chaps. 24–26; Green, "Chicago Democratic Party," 154–55, 197–204, 210–13, 232–39; and Kantowicz, "Carter Harrison II," 29–30.

49. In June 1913, state legislation gave women the right to vote in national and local elections. They could not vote in state elections without a constitutional amendment. Votes for each gender were recorded separately.

50. Green, "Chicago Democratic Party," 172–368 passim; Green, "Irish Chicago," 231–36; and Gottfried, *Boss Cermak*, 170.

51. Schmidt, "*Mayor Who Cleaned Up Chicago*," chaps. 4–10; Green, "Irish Chicago," 238–39; Allswang, *House for All Peoples*, 125–26, 134–35, 174–75; Ickes, *Autobiography of a Curmudgeon*, 247–48; Nelli, *Italians in Chicago*, 214, 217–18, 227–30; and Schottenhamel, "How Big Bill Thompson Won Control," 44.

52. Green, "Irish Chicago," 245–51, 255–57; Buenker, "Dynamics of Chicago Ethnic Politics," 199; Gottfried, *Boss Cermak*, chaps. 10–11; Gosnell, *Machine Politics*, 12–14; Wendt and Kogan, *Lords of the Levee*, 350–51; Schottenhamel, "How Big Bill Thompson Won Control," 45–49; and Allswang, *House for All Peoples*, 156–62.

53. Green, "Irish Chicago," 257–59; Gosnell, *Machine Politics*, 14–26. In February 1933, Cermak went to Florida to discuss patronage and federal aid with President-elect Franklin Roosevelt and was shot by Giuseppe Zangara; he died of complications three weeks later. Zangara's statements after his arrest indicated that the bullet was meant for Roosevelt, but the Chicago-centric view has always been that Cermak was the intended target. Gottfried, *Boss Cermak*, 316–31; Green, "Anton Cermak," 109–10.

54. Dorsett, *Roosevelt and the City Bosses*, 83–97; Wilson, *Amateur Democrat*, 69; and Greenstone and Peterson, *Race and Authority in Urban Politics*, 19–24, 242, 272–74.

55. Gosnell, *Machine Politics*, 221–38; Wilson, *Amateur Democrat*, 77–85; idem, "Introduction," in Gosnell, *Negro Politicians*, viii; Kantowicz, *Polish-American Politics*, 214–15, 222; and Rakove, *Don't Make No Waves*, 163–97. Also see Kemp and Lineberry, "Last of the Great Urban Machines"; Zikmund, "Mayoral Voting"; Grimshaw, "Daley Legacy"; and Rakove, "Jane Byrne," in Gove and Masotti, eds., *After Daley*.

56. Gill, *Municipal Research Bureaus*, 31, 121–22.

57. See Holli and Green, eds., *The Making of the Mayor*, for the following essays: Green, "1983 Chicago Democratic Mayoral Primary"; Preston, "Resurgence of Black Voting"; Rose, "How the 1983 Election Was Won"; Rakove, "Reflections on the Machine"; and especially Grimshaw, "Is Chicago Ready for Reform?" Also see Barker, "Political Mobilization of Black Chicago"; Preston, "Election of Harold Washington"; Peterson, "Washington's Election in Chicago"; Kleppner, *Chicago Divided*, chaps. 6–7; Pinderhughes, *Race and Ethnicity in Chicago Politics*, 1–5, 236–50; and Grimshaw, *Bitter Fruit*, 167–82.

58. Clavel and Wiewel, eds., *Washington and the Neighborhoods*, esp. 14–19, 281–83; Bennett, "Washington and the Black Urban Regime," 423–40; Grimshaw, *Bitter Fruit*, 182–96; and Pinderhughes, *Race and Ethnicity*, 250–53. In his first two years, Washington was opposed by the "Vrdolyak 29," an unbreakable bloc of twenty-nine of the city council's fifty members. The stalemate of the "council wars" was broken when the federal courts, acting under the Voting Rights Act, ordered new council elections in seven newly redistricted wards with predominantly minority populations. The special elections added four pro-Washington members to the council, producing a 25–25 tie with the mayor holding the tie-breaking vote.

59. Washington's council opponents, conceding the need to choose a black Acting Mayor to succeed him, picked Eugene Sawyer, a Daley organization loyalist, over Timothy Evans, who as the administration's floor leader on the council could more legitimately claim to represent continuity with the deceased mayor. Pitted against Richard M. Daley in the 1989 Democratic primary, Sawyer failed to mobilize either black voters, among whom he had been discredited by the manner of his selection, or any significant white reform support. Daley went on to defeat Evans, who ran as an independent, in the 1989 general election and to win easy reelection in 1991. See Grimshaw, *Bitter Fruit*, 195–220; and Green and Holli, eds., *Restoration 1989*.

60. Grimshaw, *Bitter Fruit*, 219.

Chapter 12

1. See the critical comments on ethnocultural history in Bridges, *City in the Republic*, 62–70, 81, 159–60; and in McCormick, *Party Period*, chap. 1.

2. Since Table 12-1 is based on point estimates from generalized least squares (GLS) ecological regressions, the characterization of some elections may differ from what is suggested by the ranges given in the tables of Chapters 3 through 11, which combine regression and linear programming estimates. My methodology is explained in the Appendix.

3. Ethington, "Urban Constituencies," 296–302, reaches similar conclusions on the basis of regression analysis of pooled data from New York, Chicago, Boston, and San Francisco.

4. Schottenhamel, "How Big Bill Thompson Won Control," 35, 38–39; Allswang, *House for All Peoples*, 48–49.

5. Katznelson, "Working-Class Formation: Constructing Cases and Comparisons," 5–6, 13–22; Ethington, "Recasting Urban Political History," 312–14, 326 n. 3; and idem, "Urban Constituencies," 277. Ethington's construction of individual-

level data from the public use samples of the 1900 and 1910 census manuscripts is the most promising effort to solve these problems for the Progressive Era. His methodology is explained in "Urban Constituencies," 279–80, 311–12.

6. Katznelson, *City Trenches*, esp. chap. 3.

7. Ibid., chap. 6; Oestreicher, "Urban Working-Class Political Behavior," 1267–68.

8. Bridges, *City in the Republic*, 70. See also Hammack, *Power and Society*, 82–87; and Zolberg, "How Many Exceptionalisms?," 427.

9. *Thirteenth Census of the United States*, 2:512–14. See also Kaestle, "Studying the History of Illiteracy," 25, 27; and Nelli, *Italians in Chicago*, 17, 72.

10. Kaestle, "Studying the History of Literacy," 24.

11. Wade, "Urbanization."

12. McCarthy, "Bosses, Reformers, and Urban Growth"; idem, "New Metropolis."

13. Bentley, "Municipal Ownership Interest Groups."

14. Riordan, *Plunkitt of Tammany Hall*, 17. See also Banfield and Wilson, *City Politics*, 116–21, 143–44.

15. Cf. Link, "What Happened to the Progressive Movement in the 1920's?," 838–40, 850. At the national level, Link argues, reform activity continued into the 1920s, but the war generated conflicts between workers and farmers that kept these two components of the 1916 Wilson coalition apart.

16. Arthur, "Competing Technologies, Increasing Returns, and Lock-In," 127; David, "Clio and the Economics of QWERTY," 332–37; Krasner, "Sovereignty," 83–85; and Karl, "Dilemmas of Democratization," 7–8.

17. Marx, *Eighteenth Brumaire*, 11:103.

18. McCormick, *Party Period*, 36–37, 55–63, 136–37. See also Bridges, *City in the Republic*, 77–81.

19. Key, *Responsible Electorate*, 7; idem, *Public Opinion and American Democracy*, 165–68; and Page and Shapiro, *Rational Public*.

20. Two examples of this criticism that are particularly relevant here are Kahn, "Re-Presenting Government," esp. 86–87, 100–101; and Larson, "Production of Expertise," esp. 39, 43–44, 51–52, 61–64, 67–68.

21. Lotchin, "Power and Policy," 26.

22. Peterson, *City Limits*; Mollenkopf, *Contested City*, 262–63; and Swanstrom, "Semisovereign Cities," 84–96.

23. This discussion of the Group Plan draws on Johannesen, *Cleveland Architecture*; Howe, *Confessions of a Reformer*, 80–82; Huff, "Frederic C. Howe," 27, 38–39; Bremner, "Humanizing Cleveland and Toledo," 187–90; Hines, "Paradox of 'Progressive' Architecture," 426–44; and Rarick, *Progressive Vision*, 14–34.

24. Jacobs, *Death and Life of Great American Cities*. Jacobs specifically criticizes Cleveland as an example of "the City Monumental" on 24. The segregation of uses is evident from Drexler, "Public Square," a diary of twenty-four hours downtown, or from a visit to downtown Cleveland at night or on the weekend.

25. Johannesen, *Cleveland Architecture*, 177–83; Rarick, *Progressive Vision*, 43–45, 55–60; Wittke, "Peter Witt," 376; Raper, *Soviet Table*, 22, 32; and Van Tassel and Grabowski, eds., *Encyclopedia of Cleveland History*, 279. On the Mu-

nicipal Building, designed by William Mitchell Kendall for the firm McKim, Mead & White, see Roth, *McKim, Mead & White*, 337–39.

Appendix

1. See for example Henderson, *Tammany Hall and the New Immigrants.*

2. Langbein and Lichtman, *Ecological Inference*, 39–42; Stokes, "Cross-Level Inference," 80–83; Shively, "Utilizing External Evidence," 68–69, 72 n. 3; and Firebaugh, "Rule for Inferring Individual-Level Relationships."

3. See for example Miller, *Boss Cox's Cincinnati*; and McCarthy, "New Metropolis."

4. See for example Allswang, *Bosses, Machines, and Urban Voters*; Tarr, *Boss Politics*; and Rogin and Shover, *Political Change in California.*

5. Langbein and Lichtman, *Ecological Inference*, 33–38; Hannan, *Aggregation and Disaggregation*, 35–38.

6. Goodman, "Ecological Regressions"; idem, "Some Alternatives to Ecological Correlation." For examples, see Wyman, "Middle Class Voters and Progressive Reform"; and Shefter, "Regional Receptivity to Reform."

7. Duncan and Davis, "Alternative to Ecological Correlation"; Shively, "General Extension of the Method of Bounds"; idem, "Utilizing External Evidence"; and Claggett and Van Wingen, "Application of Linear Programming to Ecological Inference."

8. Shively, "General Extension of the Method of Bounds," 83, 90.

9. Ibid., 83.

10. Hanushek and Jackson, *Statistical Methods for Social Scientists*, 193 n. 13.

11. See Iversen, "Group Data and Individual Behavior."

12. Johnston, *Econometric Methods*, 380–84.

Bibliography

Sources concerning more than one of the cities discussed in this book, on other cities, or of more general relevance to the study of reform in the Progressive Era are listed under the "General" heading. Works primarily about New York, Cleveland, or Chicago are listed under the heading for that city. Many of these, of course, have broader significance. A note on statistical sources follows.

General

Allen, William H. *Efficient Democracy.* New York: Dodd, Mead, 1907.

———. "Interpreting Expert Government to the Citizenship." In Edward A. Fitzpatrick, ed., *Experts in City Government.* New York: D. Appleton and Co., 1919.

Allswang, John M. *Bosses, Machines, and Urban Voters.* Rev. ed. Baltimore: Johns Hopkins University Press, 1986.

Arthur, W. Brian. "Competing Technologies, Increasing Returns, and Lock-In by Historical Events." *Economic Journal* 99:1 (March 1989).

Banfield, Edward C., and James Q. Wilson. *City Politics.* Cambridge: Harvard University Press, 1963.

Baritz, Loren. *The Servants of Power: A History of the Use of Social Science in American Industry.* Middletown, Conn.: Wesleyan University Press, 1960.

Bartley, Robert L. "Business and the New Class." In B. Bruce-Biggs, ed., *The New Class?* New Brunswick, N.J.: Transaction, 1979.

Beard, Charles A. "The Control of the Expert." In Edward A. Fitzpatrick, ed., *Experts in City Government.* New York: D. Appleton and Co., 1919.

Bernard, Richard M., and Bradley R. Rice. "Political Environment and the Adoption of Progressive Municipal Reform." *Journal of Urban History* 1:2 (February 1975).

Booth, Douglas E. "Municipal Socialism and City Government Reform: The Milwaukee Experience, 1910–1940." *Journal of Urban History* 12:1 (November 1985).

Boulay, Harvey, and Alan DiGaetano. "Why Did Political Machines Disappear?" *Journal of Urban History* 12:1 (November 1985).

Bridges, Amy. "Boss Tweed and V. O. Key in Texas." In Char Miller and Heywood T. Sanders, eds., *Urban Texas: Politics and Development.* College Station: Texas A&M Press, 1990.

———. "Politics and Growth in Sunbelt Cities." In Raymond A. Mohl, ed., *Searching for the Sunbelt: Historical Perspectives on a Region.* Knoxville: University of Tennessee Press, 1990.

———. "Winning the West to Municipal Reform." *Urban Affairs Quarterly* 27:4 (June 1992).

Brown, M. Craig, and Charles N. Halaby. "Bosses, Reform, and the Socioeconomic Bases of Urban Expenditure, 1890–1940." In Terrence J. McDonald and Sally K. Ward, eds., *The Politics of Urban Fiscal Policy*. Beverly Hills, Calif.: Sage Publications, 1984.

———. "Machine Politics in America, 1870–1945." *Journal of Interdisciplinary History* 17:3 (Winter 1987).

Brown, M. Craig, and Barbara D. Warner. "Immigrants, Urban Politics, and Policing in 1900." *American Sociological Review* 57:3 (June 1992).

Bruère, Henry. *The New City Government*. New York: D. Appleton and Co., 1912.

Bryce, James. *The American Commonwealth*. Rev. ed. New York: Macmillan, 1916.

Buenker, John D. *Urban Liberalism and Progressive Reform*. New York: Norton, 1973.

Burns, James MacGregor. *Leadership*. New York: Harper and Row, 1978.

Chandler, Alfred D., Jr. "The Origins of Progressive Leadership." In Elting Morrison, ed., *The Letters of Theodore Roosevelt*. Cambridge: Harvard University Press, 1954.

Childs, Richard S. *Civic Victories: The Story of an Unfinished Revolution*. New York: Harper and Brothers, 1952.

Claggett, William, and John Van Wingen. "An Application of Linear Programming to Ecological Inference: An Extension of an Old Procedure." *American Journal of Political Science* 37:2 (May 1993).

Clubb, Jerome M., and Howard W. Allen. "Collective Biography and the Progressive Movement: The 'Status Revolution' Revisited." *Social Science History* 1:4 (Summer 1977).

Collier, John. "Citizen Coöperation with Government through the Community Center." In Edward A. Fitzpatrick, ed., *Experts in City Government*. New York: D. Appleton and Co., 1919.

Cornwell, Elmer E., Jr. "Bosses, Machines, and Ethnic Groups." *Annals of the American Academy of Political and Social Science*, no. 353 (May 1964).

Critchlow, Donald T. *The Brookings Institution, 1916–1952: Expertise and the Public Interest in a Democratic Society*. DeKalb: Northern Illinois University Press, 1985.

———, ed. *Socialism in the Heartland: The Midwestern Experience, 1900–1925*. Notre Dame, Ind.: University of Notre Dame Press, 1986.

David, Paul A. "Clio and the Economics of QWERTY." *American Economic Review* 75:2 (May 1985).

Davis, Allen F. *Spearheads for Reform: The Social Settlements and the Progressive Movement, 1890–1914*. New York: Oxford University Press, 1967.

De Witt, Benjamin Park. *The Progressive Movement*. 1915. Reprint. Seattle: University of Washington Press, 1968.

DiGaetano, Alan. "The Rise and Development of Urban Political Machines: An Alternative to Merton's Functional Analysis." *Urban Affairs Quarterly* 24:2 (December 1988).

———. "Urban Political Reform: Did It Kill the Machine?" *Journal of Urban History* 18:1 (November 1991).

Domhoff, G. William. "Class, Power, and Parties in the New Deal: A Critique of

Skocpol's State Autonomy Theory." *Berkeley Journal of Sociology*, no. 36 (1991).

————. "Where Do Government Experts Come From? The CEA and the Policy-Planning Network." In G. William Domhoff and Thomas R. Dye, eds., *Power Elites and Organizations*. Newbury Park, Calif.: Sage Publications, 1987.

Dorsett, Lyle W. "The City Boss and the Reformer: A Reappraisal." *Pacific Northwest Quarterly* 63:4 (October 1972).

————. *Franklin D. Roosevelt and the City Bosses*. Port Washington, N.Y.: Kennikat, 1977.

————. "Kansas City and the New Deal." In John Braeman, Robert H. Bremner, and David Brody, eds., *The New Deal: The State and Local Levels*. Columbus: Ohio State University Press, 1975.

————. *The Pendergast Machine*. New York: Oxford University Press, 1968.

Duffy, John. *A History of Public Health in New York City, 1866–1966*. New York: Russell Sage, 1974.

Duncan, Otis Dudley, and Beverly Davis. "An Alternative to Ecological Correlation." *American Sociological Review* 18:6 (December 1953).

Ehrenreich, Barbara, and John Ehrenreich. "The Professional-Managerial Class." In Pat Walker, ed., *Between Labor and Capital*. Boston: South End Press, 1979.

Elkin, Stephen L. *City and Regime in the American Republic*. Chicago: University of Chicago Press, 1987.

Erie, Steven P. "How the Urban West Was Won: The Local State and Economic Growth in Los Angeles, 1880–1932." *Urban Affairs Quarterly* 27:4 (June 1992).

————. *Rainbow's End: Irish-Americans and the Dilemmas of Urban Machine Politics, 1840–1985*. Berkeley: University of California Press, 1988.

Ethington, Philip J. "Recasting Urban Political History: Gender, the Public, the Household, and Political Participation in Boston and San Francisco during the Progressive Era." *Social Science History* 16:2 (Summer 1992).

————. "Urban Constituencies, Regimes, and Policy Innovation in the Progressive Era: An Analysis of Boston, Chicago, New York, and San Francisco." *Studies in American Political Development* 7:2 (Fall 1993).

Farr, James, and Raymond Seidelman, eds. *Discipline and History: Political Science in the United States*. Ann Arbor: University of Michigan Press, 1993.

Feder, Leah Hannah. *Unemployment Relief in Periods of Depression: A Study of Measures Adopted in Certain American Cities, 1857 through 1922*. New York: Russell Sage, 1936.

Filene, Peter G. "Narrating Progressivism: Unitarians v. Pluralists v. Students." *Journal of American History* 79:4 (March 1993).

————. "An Obituary for 'The Progressive Movement.'" *American Quarterly* 22:1 (Spring 1970).

Filler, Louis. *Crusaders for American Liberalism*. 3rd ed. Yellow Springs, Ohio: Antioch Press, 1964.

Finegold, Kenneth. "Between All and Nothing: A Comment on G. William Domhoff's 'Class, Power, and Parties in the New Deal.'" *Berkeley Journal of Sociology*, no. 36 (1991).

———. "From Agrarianism to Adjustment: The Political Origins of New Deal Agricultural Policy." *Politics & Society* 11:1 (1982).

———. "Progressivism, Electoral Change, and Public Policy: Reform Outcomes in New York, Cleveland, and Chicago." Ph.D. diss., Harvard University, 1985.

Finegold, Kenneth, and Theda Skocpol. *State, Party, and Policy: Industry and Agriculture in America's New Deal.* Madison: University of Wisconsin Press, 1995.

Firebaugh, Glenn. "A Rule for Inferring Individual-Level Relationships from Aggregate Data." *American Sociological Review* 43:4 (August 1978).

Fitzpatrick, Edward A. "Preface." In Edward A. Fitzpatrick, ed., *Experts in City Government.* New York: D. Appleton and Co., 1919.

Fitzpatrick, Ellen. *Endless Crusade: Women Social Scientists and Progressive Reform.* New York: Oxford University Press, 1990.

Fogelson, Robert M. *Big-City Police.* Cambridge: Harvard University Press, 1977.

———. *The Fragmented Metropolis: Los Angeles, 1850–1930.* Cambridge: Harvard University Press, 1967.

Fox, Bonnie R. "The Philadelphia Progressives: A Test of the Hofstadter-Hays Thesis." *Pennsylvania History* 34:4 (October 1967).

Fox, Kenneth. *Better City Government: Innovation in American Urban Politics, 1850–1937.* Philadelphia: Temple University Press, 1977.

Fuchs, Ester R. *Mayors and Money: Fiscal Policy in New York and Chicago.* Chicago: University of Chicago Press, 1992.

Gill, Norman N. *Municipal Research Bureaus: A Study of the Nation's Leading Citizen-Supported Agencies.* Washington, D.C.: American Council on Public Affairs, 1944.

Glazer, Nathan, and Daniel P. Moynihan. *Beyond the Melting Pot: The Negroes, Puerto Ricans, Jews, Italians, and Irish of New York City.* 2nd ed. Cambridge: MIT Press, 1970.

Godkin, Edwin Lawrence. *Problems of Modern Democracy: Political and Economic Essays.* New York: Charles Scribner's Sons, 1896.

Goodman, Leo A. "Ecological Regressions and the Behavior of Individuals." *American Sociological Review* 18:6 (December 1953).

———. "Some Alternatives to Ecological Correlation." *American Journal of Sociology* 64:6 (May 1959).

Gossett, Thomas F. *Race: The History of an Idea in America.* Dallas: Southern Methodist University Press, 1963.

Graham, Otis L., Jr. *An Encore for Reform: The Old Progressives and the New Deal.* New York: Oxford University Press, 1967.

Greenstone, J. David, and Paul E. Peterson. *Race and Authority in Urban Politics: Community Participation and the War on Poverty.* Chicago: University of Chicago Press, 1973.

Griffith, Ernest S. *A History of American City Government: The Progressive Years and Their Aftermath, 1900–1920.* New York: Praeger, 1974.

Hannan, Michael T. *Aggregation and Disaggregation in Sociology.* Lexington, Mass.: Lexington Books, 1971.

Hanushek, Eric A., and John E. Jackson. *Statistical Methods for Social Scientists.* New York: Academic Press, 1977.

Hargrove, Erwin C. "Two Conceptions of Institutional Leadership." In Bryan D. Jones, ed., *Leadership and Politics: New Perspectives in Political Science.* Lawrence: University Press of Kansas, 1989.

Hawley, Willis D. *Nonpartisan Elections and the Case for Party Politics.* New York: Wiley, 1973.

Hays, Samuel P. "The Politics of Reform in Municipal Government in the Progressive Era." *Pacific Northwest Quarterly* 55:4 (October 1964).

————. *The Response to Industrialism, 1885–1914.* Chicago: University of Chicago Press, 1957.

Heclo, Hugh. *Modern Social Politics in Britain and Sweden.* New Haven, Conn.: Yale University Press, 1974.

Hendrickson, Kenneth E., Jr. "Tribune of the People: George R. Lunn and the Rise and Fall of Christian Socialism in Schenectady." In Bruce M. Stave, ed., *Socialism and the Cities.* Port Washington, N.Y.: Kennikat, 1975.

Hofstadter, Richard. *The Age of Reform: From Bryan to F.D.R.* New York: Knopf, 1955.

Holli, Melvin G. *Reform in Detroit: Hazen S. Pingree and Urban Politics.* New York: Oxford University Press, 1969.

————. "Urban Reform in the Progressive Era." In Lewis L. Gould, ed., *The Progressive Era.* Syracuse: Syracuse University Press, 1974.

Howe, Frederic C. *The City: Hope of Democracy.* 1905. Reprint. Seattle: University of Washington Press, 1967.

————. "The City as a Socializing Agency." *American Journal of Sociology* 17:5 (March 1912).

————. *The Modern City and Its Problems.* New York: Charles Scribner's Sons, 1915.

Huntington, Samuel P. *American Politics: The Promise of Disharmony.* Cambridge: Harvard University Press, 1981.

Huthmacher, J. Joseph. "Urban Liberalism and the Age of Reform." *Mississippi Valley Historical Review* 49:2 (September 1962).

Iversen, Gudmund I. "Group Data and Individual Behavior." In Jerome M. Clubb, William H. Flanagan, and Nancy H. Zingale, eds., *Analyzing Electoral History.* Beverly Hills, Calif.: Sage Publications, 1981.

Jacobs, Jane. *The Death and Life of Great American Cities.* New York: Vintage, 1961.

Jaher, Frederic Cople. *The Urban Establishment: Upper Strata in Boston, New York, Charleston, Chicago and Los Angeles.* Urbana: University of Illinois Press, 1982.

Johnpoll, Bernard K., with Lillian Johnpoll. *The Impossible Dream: The Rise and Demise of the American Left.* Westport, Conn.: Greenwood, 1981.

Johnston, J. *Econometric Methods.* 2nd ed. New York: McGraw-Hill, 1972.

Judd, Dennis. *The Politics of American Cities: Private Power and Public Policy.* 3rd ed. Glenview, Ill.: Scott, Foresman, 1988.

Judd, Dennis, and Paul Kantor, eds. *Enduring Tensions in Urban Politics.* New York: Macmillan, 1992.

Judd, Richard W. *Socialist Cities: Municipal Politics and the Grass Roots of American Socialism.* Albany: State University of New York Press, 1989.

Kaestle, Carl F. "Studying the History of Illiteracy." In Carl F. Kaestle et al., eds., *Literacy in the United States: Readers and Reading since 1880.* New Haven, Conn.: Yale University Press, 1991.

Kahn, Jonathan. "Re-Presenting Government and Representing the People: Budget Reform and Citizenship in New York City, 1908–1911." *Journal of Urban History* 19:3 (May 1993).

Kantor, Paul, with Stephen David. *The Dependent City: The Changing Political Economy of Urban America.* Glenview, Ill.: Scott, Foresman, 1988.

Karl, Terry Lynn. "Dilemmas of Democratization in Latin America." *Comparative Politics* 23:1 (October 1990).

Katznelson, Ira. *Black Men, White Cities: Race, Politics, and Migration in the United States, 1900–30, and Britain, 1948–68.* New York: Oxford University Press, 1973.

———. "'The Burdens of Urban History': Comment." *Studies in American Political Development,* no. 3 (1989).

———. *City Trenches: Urban Politics and the Patterning of Class in the United States.* New York: Pantheon, 1981.

———. "Working-Class Formation: Constructing Cases and Comparisons." In Ira Katznelson and Aristide R. Zolberg, eds., *Working-Class Formation: Nineteenth-Century Patterns in Western Europe and the United States.* Princeton: Princeton University Press, 1986.

Key, V. O., Jr. *Public Opinion and American Democracy.* New York: Knopf, 1961.

———. *The Responsible Electorate: Rationality in Presidential Voting, 1936–1960.* Cambridge: Harvard University Press, Belknap Press, 1966.

Kirkendall, Richard S. *Social Scientists and Farm Politics in the Age of Roosevelt.* Columbia: University of Missouri Press, 1966.

Knoke, David. "The Spread of Municipal Reform." *American Journal of Sociology* 87:6 (May 1982).

Kousser, J. Morgan. "Making Separate Equal: Integration of Black and White School Funds in Kentucky." *Journal of Interdisciplinary History* 10:3 (Winter 1980).

Krasner, Stephen D. "Sovereignty: An Institutional Perspective." *Comparative Political Studies* 21:1 (April 1988).

Langbein, Laura Irwin, and Allan J. Lichtman. *Ecological Inference.* Beverly Hills, Calif.: Sage Publications, 1978.

Larson, Magali Sarfatti. "The Production of Expertise and the Constitution of Expert Power." In Thomas L. Haskell, ed., *The Authority of Experts: Studies in History and Theory.* Bloomington: Indiana University Press, 1984.

———. *The Rise of Professionalism: A Sociological Analysis.* Berkeley: University of California Press, 1977.

Levi, Margaret. "The Predatory Theory of Rule." *Politics & Society* 10:4 (1981).

Link, Arthur S. "What Happened to the Progressive Movement in the 1920's?" *American Historical Review* 64:4 (July 1959).

Lippmann, Walter. "On Municipal Socialism, 1913: An Analysis of Problems and

Strategies." In Bruce M. Stave, ed., *Socialism and the Cities*. Port Washington, N.Y.: Kennikat, 1975.

Lotchin, Roger W. "Power and Policy: American City Politics between the Two World Wars." In Scott Greer, ed., *Ethnics, Machines, and the American Urban Future*. Cambridge: Schenkman, 1981.

Lowi, Theodore. "Foreword to the Second Edition: Gosnell's Chicago Revisited via Lindsay's New York." In Harold F. Gosnell, *Machine Politics: Chicago Model*, 2nd ed. Chicago: University of Chicago Press, 1968.

————. "The State in Political Science: How We Become What We Study." *American Political Science Review* 86:1 (March 1992).

Malone, Dumas, ed. *Dictionary of American Biography*. New York: Scribner's, 1936.

Marx, Karl. *The Eighteenth Brumaire of Louis Bonaparte*. In Karl Marx and Frederick Engels, *Collected Works*, vol. 11. New York: International Publishers, 1979.

Mayhew, David R. *Placing Parties in American Politics: Organization, Electoral Settings, and Government Activity in the Twentieth Century*. Princeton: Princeton University Press, 1986.

McCarthy, Michael P. "On Bosses, Reformers, and Urban Growth: Some Suggestions for a Political Typography of American Cities." *Journal of Urban History* 4:1 (November 1977).

McCormick, Richard L. "The Discovery That Business Corrupts Politics: A Reappraisal of the Origins of Progressivism." *American Historical Review* 86:2 (April 1981).

————. *The Party Period and Public Policy: American Politics from the Age of Jackson to the Progressive Era*. New York: Oxford University Press, 1986.

McDonald, Terrence J. "The Burdens of Urban History: The Theory of the State in Recent American Social History." *Studies in American Political Development*, no. 3 (1989).

————. *The Parameters of Urban Fiscal Policy: Socioeconomic Change and Political Culture in San Francisco, 1860–1906*. Berkeley: University of California Press, 1986.

————. "Reply to Professor Katznelson." *Studies in American Political Development*, no. 3 (1989).

Merton, Robert K. *Social Theory and Social Structure*. Rev. and enlarged ed. Glencoe, Ill.: Free Press, 1957.

Miller, Sally M. "Milwaukee: Of Ethnicity and Labor." In Bruce M. Stave, ed., *Socialism and the Cities*. Port Washington, N.Y.: Kennikat, 1975.

Miller, Zane L. *Boss Cox's Cincinnati: Urban Politics in the Progressive Era*. New York: Oxford University Press, 1968.

Mink, Gwendolyn. "The Lady and the Tramp: Gender, Race, and the Origins of the American Welfare State." In Linda Gordon, ed., *Women, the State, and Welfare*. Madison: University of Wisconsin Press, 1990.

Mollenkopf, John H. *The Contested City*. Princeton: Princeton University Press, 1983.

Morone, James A. *The Democratic Wish: Popular Participation and the Limits of American Government*. New York: Basic Books, 1990.

Mowry, George. *The California Progressives*. Berkeley: University of California Press, 1951.

Nadel, Mark V. *The Politics of Consumer Protection*. Indianapolis: Bobbs-Merrill, 1971.

O'Connor, Edwin. *The Last Hurrah*. Boston: Little, Brown, 1956.

Oestreicher, Richard. "Urban Working-Class Political Behavior and Theories of American Electoral Politics, 1870–1940." *Journal of American History* 74:4 (March 1988).

Ostrogorski, M. *Democracy and the Organization of Political Parties*. New York: Macmillan, 1902.

Page, Benjamin I., and Robert Y. Shapiro. *The Rational Public: Fifty Years of Trends in Americans' Policy Preferences*. Chicago: University of Chicago Press, 1992.

Peterson, Paul E. *City Limits*. Chicago: University of Chicago Press, 1981.

Regier, C. C. *The Era of the Muckrakers*. Chapel Hill: University of North Carolina Press, 1932.

Ricci, David M. *The Tragedy of Political Science: Politics, Scholarship, and Democracy*. New Haven, Conn.: Yale University Press, 1984.

Rice, Bradley Robert. *Progressive Cities: The Commission Government Movement in America, 1901–1920*. Austin: University of Texas Press, 1977.

Rodgers, Daniel T. "In Search of Progressivism." *Reviews in American History* 10:4 (December 1982).

Rogin, Michael Paul, and John L. Shover. *Political Change in California: Critical Elections and Social Movements, 1890–1966*. Westport, Conn.: Greenwood, 1970.

Roosevelt, Theodore. "Practical Work in Politics." In *Proceedings of the National Conference for Good City Government*, Philadelphia, January 25–26, 1894. Philadelphia: Municipal League, 1894.

Rosen, Elliot A. *Hoover, Roosevelt, and the Brains Trust: From Depression to New Deal*. New York: Columbia University Press, 1977.

Ross, Dorothy. *The Origins of American Social Science*. Cambridge: Cambridge University Press, 1991.

Roth, Leland M. *McKim, Mead & White, Architects*. New York: Harper and Row, 1983.

Schattschneider, E. E. *The Semisovereign People: A Realist's View of Democracy in America*. New York: Holt, Rinehart, and Winston, 1960.

Schiesl, Martin J. *The Politics of Efficiency: Municipal Administration and Reform in America, 1800–1920*. Berkeley: University of California Press, 1977.

Seidelman, Raymond, and Edward J. Harpham. *Disenchanted Realists: Political Science and the American Crisis, 1884–1984*. Albany: State University of New York Press, 1985.

Shannon, David A. *The Socialist Party of America: A History*. New York: Macmillan, 1955.

Shefter, Martin. "Party, Bureaucracy, and Political Change in the United States." In Louis Maisel and Joseph Cooper, eds., *Political Parties: Development and Decay*. Beverly Hills, Calif.: Sage Publications, 1978.

————. "Regional Receptivity to Reform: The Legacy of the Progressive Era." *Political Science Quarterly* 98:3 (Fall 1983).

Shively, W. Phillips. "A General Extension of the Method of Bounds, with Special Application to Studies of Electoral Transition." *Historical Methods* 24:2 (Spring 1991).

————. "Utilizing External Evidence in Cross-Level Inference." *Political Methodology* 1:4 (Fall 1974).

Skocpol, Theda. *Protecting Soldiers and Mothers: The Political Origins of Social Policy in the United States.* Cambridge: Harvard University Press, Belknap Press, 1992.

————. *States and Social Revolutions: A Comparative Analysis of France, Russia, and China.* New York: Cambridge University Press, 1979.

Skocpol, Theda, and Kenneth Finegold. "State Capacity and Economic Intervention in the Early New Deal." *Political Science Quarterly* 97:2 (Summer 1982).

Smith, James Allen. *The Idea Brokers: Think Tanks and the Rise of the New Policy Elite.* New York: Free Press, 1991.

Somit, Albert, and Joseph Tannenhaus. *The Development of American Political Science: From Burgess to Behavioralism.* Boston: Allyn and Bacon, 1967.

Stave, Bruce M. "The Great Depression and Urban Political Continuity: Bridgeport Chooses Socialism." In Bruce M. Stave, ed., *Socialism and the Cities.* Port Washington, N.Y.: Kennikat, 1975.

————. *The New Deal and the Last Hurrah: Pittsburgh Machine Politics.* Pittsburgh: University of Pittsburgh Press, 1970.

————. "Pittsburgh and the New Deal." In John Braeman, Robert H. Bremner, and David Brody, eds., *The New Deal: The State and Local Levels.* Columbus: Ohio State University Press, 1975.

————, ed. *Socialism and the Cities.* Port Washington, N.Y.: Kennikat, 1975.

Steffens, Lincoln. *The Autobiography of Lincoln Steffens.* New York: Harcourt, Brace and World, 1931.

————. *The Shame of the Cities.* 1904. Reprint. New York: Peter Smith, 1948.

————. *The Struggle for Self-Government.* New York: McClure, Phillips and Co., 1906.

Stewart, Frank Mann. *A Half Century of Reform: The History of the National Municipal League.* Berkeley: University of California Press, 1950.

Stokes, Donald E. "Cross-Level Inference as a Game against Nature." In Joseph L. Bernd, ed., *Mathematical Applications in Political Science IV.* Charlottesville: University Press of Virginia, 1969.

Stone, Clarence N. *Regime Politics: Governing Atlanta, 1946–1988.* Lawrence: University Press of Kansas, 1989.

Swanstrom, Todd. "Semisovereign Cities: The Politics of Urban Development." *Polity* 21:1 (Fall 1988).

Teaford, Jon C. "Finis for Tweed and Steffens: Rewriting the History of Urban Rule." *Reviews in American History* 10:4 (December 1982).

Thelen, David P. *The New Citizenship: Origins of Progressivism in Wisconsin, 1885–1900.* Columbia: University of Missouri Press, 1972.

――――. "Social Tensions and the Origins of Progressivism." *Journal of American History* 56:2 (September 1969).

――――. "Urban Politics: Beyond Bosses and Reformers." *Reviews in American History* 7:3 (September 1979).

Wade, Richard C. "Urbanization." In C. Vann Woodward, ed., *The Comparative Approach to American History*. New York: Basic Books, 1968.

Walker, John T. "The Dayton Socialists and World War I: Surviving the White Terror." In Donald T. Critchlow, ed., *Socialism in the Heartland: The Midwestern Experience, 1900–1925*. Notre Dame, Ind.: University of Notre Dame Press, 1986.

Walters, Ronald G. *American Reformers, 1815–1860*. New York: Hill and Wang, 1978.

Weinstein, James. *The Corporate Ideal in the Liberal State*. Boston: Beacon Press, 1968.

White, Andrew D. "City Affairs Are Not Political." 1890. Reprinted in Dennis Judd and Paul Kantor, eds., *Enduring Tensions in Urban Politics*. New York: Macmillan, 1992.

Wiebe, Robert H. *The Search for Order, 1877–1920*. New York: Hill and Wang, 1967.

Wilcox, Delos F. "The Inadequacy of Present City Government." In Edward A. Fitzpatrick, ed., *Experts in City Government*. New York: D. Appleton and Co., 1919.

Wilson, James Q. *The Amateur Democrat: Club Politics in Three Cities*. Chicago: University of Chicago Press, 1962.

Wilson, Woodrow. "Character of Democracy in the United States." *Atlantic Monthly* 64:385 (November 1889).

Wolfinger, Raymond. *The Politics of Progress*. Englewood Cliffs, N.J.: Prentice-Hall, 1974.

Woodruff, Clinton Rogers. "The New View of Municipal Government." In Edward A. Fitzpatrick, ed., *Experts in City Government*. New York: D. Appleton and Co., 1919.

――――. "The Wide Scope of Municipal Improvement." In Edward A. Fitzpatrick, ed., *Experts in City Government*. New York: D. Appleton and Co., 1919.

Wyman, Roger E. "Middle Class Voters and Progressive Reform: The Conflict of Class and Culture." *American Political Science Review* 68:2 (June 1974).

Zink, Harold. *City Bosses in the United States: A Study of Twenty Municipal Bosses*. Durham, N.C.: Duke University Press, 1930.

Zolberg, Aristide R. "How Many Exceptionalisms?" In Ira Katznelson and Aristide R. Zolberg, eds., *Working-Class Formation: Nineteenth-Century Patterns in Western Europe and the United States*. Princeton: Princeton University Press, 1986.

New York

Allen, William H. "Reasons Why Mr. Allen Believes That Mr. Rockefeller's Conditional Offer of Support to the New York Bureau of Municipal Research Should

Not Be Accepted." Speech to the Bureau of Municipal Research trustees, May 13, 1914.

———. *Reminiscences*. New York: Columbia University Oral History Project, 1950.

Amberg, Edna, and William H. Allen. *Civic Lessons from Mayor Mitchel's Defeat*. New York: Institute for Public Service, 1921.

Arian, Asher, Arthur S. Goldberg, John H. Mollenkopf, and Edward T. Rogowsky. *Changing New York City Politics*. New York: Routledge, 1991.

Bridges, Amy. *A City in the Republic: Antebellum New York and the Origins of Machine Politics*. New York: Cambridge University Press, 1984.

Bruère, Henry. "Efficiency in City Government." In *Efficiency in City Government. The Annals of the American Academy of Political and Social Science*, no. 41 (May 1912).

———. *Reminiscences*. New York: Columbia University Oral History Project, 1949.

Caro, Robert A. *The Power Broker: Robert Moses and the Fall of New York*. New York: Vintage, 1974.

Cerillo, Augustus, Jr. "The Impact of Reform Ideology: Early Twentieth Century Municipal Government in New York City." In Michael H. Ebner and Eugene M. Tobin, eds., *The Age of Urban Reform: New Perspectives on the Progressive Era*. Port Washington, N.Y.: Kennikat Press, 1977.

———. "The Reform of Municipal Government in New York City: From Seth Low to John Purroy Mitchel." *New-York Historical Society Quarterly* 57:1 (January 1973).

———. "Reform in New York City: A Study of Urban Progressivism." Ph.D. diss., Northwestern University, 1969.

Chern, Kenneth S. "The Politics of Patriotism: War, Ethnicity, and the New York Mayoral Campaign, 1917." *New-York Historical Society Quarterly* 63:4 (October 1979).

Cohen, Ronald D., and Raymond A. Mohl. *The Paradox of Progressive Education: The Gary Plan and Urban Schooling*. Port Washington, N.Y.: Kennikat Press, 1979.

Dahlberg, Jane S. *The New York Bureau of Municipal Research: Pioneer in Government Administration*. New York: New York University Press, 1966.

Duffy, John. *A History of Public Health in New York City, 1866–1966*. New York: Russell Sage, 1974.

Gilfoyle, Timothy J. *City of Eros: New York City, Prostitution, and the Commercialization of Sex, 1790–1920*. New York: Norton, 1992.

Gulick, Luther. *The National Institute of Public Administration: A Progress Report*. New York: National Institute of Public Administration, 1928.

Hammack, David C. *Power and Society: Greater New York at the Turn of the Century*. New York: Russell Sage, 1982.

Henderson, Thomas M. *Tammany Hall and the New Immigrants: The Progressive Years*. New York: Arno Press, 1976.

Hertz, Emanuel. "Politics: New York." In Charles S. Bernheimer, ed., *The Russian Jew in the United States*. Philadelphia: John C. Winston Co., 1905.

"Hirshfield in Job Tammany Wanted." *New York Times*, January 13, 1918, 5.

Hopkins, George B. "The New York Bureau of Municipal Research." In *Efficiency in City Government. The Annals of the American Academy of Political and Social Science*, no. 41 (May 1912).

Hylan, John Francis. *Autobiography of John Francis Hylan, Mayor of New York*. New York: Rotary Press, 1922.

Kahn, Jonathan. "Re-Presenting and Representing the People: Budget Reform and Citizenship in New York City, 1908–1911." *Journal of Urban History* 19:3 (May 1993).

Kaplan, Barry J. "Metropolitics, Administrative Reform, and Political Theory: The Greater New York City Charter of 1897." *Journal of Urban History* 9:2 (February 1983).

Kessner, Thomas. "Fiorello H. LaGuardia and the Challenge of Democratic Planning." In David Ward and Oliver Zunz, eds., *The Landscape of Modernity: Essays on New York City, 1900–1940*. New York: Russell Sage, 1992.

———. *Fiorello H. La Guardia and the Making of Modern New York*. New York: McGraw-Hill, 1989.

Kurland, Gerald. *Seth Low: The Reformer in an Urban Industrial Age*. New York: Twayne, 1971.

Lanahan, Anna Mary. "Brooklyn's Political Life, 1898–1916." Ph.D. diss., St. John's University, 1977.

Lewinson, Edwin R. *John Purroy Mitchel: The Boy Mayor of New York*. New York: Astra, 1965.

Littlefield, Roy Everett III. *William Randolph Hearst: His Role in American Progressivism*. Lanham, Md.: University Press of America, 1980.

Logan, Andy. *Against the Evidence: The Becker-Rosenthal Affair*. New York: McCall, 1970.

Lowi, Theodore. *At the Pleasure of the Mayor: Patronage and Power in New York City, 1898–1958*. New York: Free Press of Glencoe, 1964.

Makielski, S. J., Jr. *The Politics of Zoning: The New York Experience*. New York: Columbia University Press, 1966.

McCormick, Richard L. *From Realignment to Reform: Political Change in New York State, 1893–1910*. Ithaca, N.Y.: Cornell University Press, 1981.

McNickle, Chris. *To Be Mayor of New York: Ethnic Politics in the City*. New York: Columbia University Press, 1993.

Mitgang, Herbert. *The Man Who Rode the Tiger: The Life and Times of Judge Samuel Seabury*. Philadelphia: J. B. Lippincott, 1963.

Mollenkopf, John H. *A Phoenix in the Ashes: The Rise and Fall of the Koch Coalition in New York City Politics*. Princeton: Princeton University Press, 1992.

Moses, Robert. *Working for the People: Promise and Performance in Public Service*. New York: Harper and Brothers, 1956.

Myatt, James Allen. "William Randolph Hearst and the Progressive Era, 1900–1912." Ph.D. diss., University of Florida, 1960.

Myers, Gustavus. *The History of Tammany Hall*. 2nd ed. New York: Boni and Liveright, 1917.

Ravitch, Diane. *The Great School Wars: New York City, 1805–1973*. New York: Basic Books, 1974.

Revell, Keith D. "Regulating the Landscape: Real Estate Values, City Planning, and the 1916 Zoning Ordinance." In David Ward and Oliver Zunz, eds., *The Landscape of Modernity: Essays on New York City, 1900–1940*. New York: Russell Sage, 1992.

Riordan, William L. *Plunkitt of Tammany Hall*. 1905. Reprint. New York: Dutton, 1963.

Rischin, Moses. *The Promised City: New York's Jews, 1870–1914*. New York: Harper and Row, 1962.

Ritchie, Donald A. "The Gary Committee: Businessmen, Progressives and Unemployment in New York City, 1914–1915." *New-York Historical Society Quarterly* 57:4 (October 1973).

Roberts, Sam. "News Analysis: The Tide Turns on Voter Turnout." *New York Times*. November 4, 1993, B-6.

Rodgers, Cleveland. *Robert Moses: Builder for Democracy*. New York: Henry Holt, 1952.

Rosenwaike, Ira. *Population History of New York City*. Syracuse: Syracuse University Press, 1972.

Sarasohn, David. "Power without Glory: Hearst in the Progressive Era." *Journalism Quarterly* 53:3 (Autumn 1976).

Sayre, Wallace S., and Herbert Kaufman. *Governing New York City: Politics in the Metropolis*. New York: Norton, 1965.

Shefter, Martin. "Economic Crises, Social Coalitions, and Political Institutions: New York City's Little New Deal." Paper presented to the American Political Science Association annual meeting, September 1981.

———. "The Electoral Foundations of the Political Machine: New York City, 1884–1897." In Joel H. Silbey, Allan G. Bogue, and William H. Flanigan, eds., *The History of American Electoral Behavior*. Princeton: Princeton University Press, 1978.

———. "The Emergence of the Political Machine: An Alternative View." In Willis D. Hawley et al., *Theoretical Perspectives on Urban Politics*. Englewood Cliffs, N.J.: Prentice-Hall, 1976.

———. "New York City's Fiscal Crisis: The Politics of Inflation and Retrenchment." *Public Interest*, no. 48 (Summer 1977).

———. "Organizing for Armageddon: The Political Consequences of the New York City Fiscal Crisis." Paper presented to the American Political Science Association annual meeting, August 1980.

———. *Political Crisis/Fiscal Crisis: The Collapse and Revival of New York City*. New York: Basic Books, 1985.

Smith, Mortimer. *William Jay Gaynor: Mayor of New York*. Chicago: Regnery, 1951.

Swanberg, W. A. *Citizen Hearst*. New York: Scribner, 1961.

Swett, Steven C. "The Test of a Reformer: A Study of Seth Low, New York City Mayor, 1902–1903." *New-York Historical Society Quarterly* 44:1 (January 1960).

Syrett, Harold C., ed. *The Gentleman and the Tiger: The Autobiography of George B. McClellan, Jr.* Philadelphia: J. B. Lippincott, 1956.

Szajowski, Zosa. "The Jews and New York City's Mayoralty Election of 1917." *Jewish Social Studies* 32:4 (October 1970).

Weinbaum, Marvin G. "New York County Republican Politics, 1897–1922: The Quarter Century after Municipal Consolidation." *New-York Historical Society Quarterly* 50:1 (January 1966).

Weiss, Marc A. "Density and Intervention: New York's Planning Traditions." In David Ward and Oliver Zunz, eds., *The Landscape of Modernity: Essays on New York City, 1900–1940*. New York: Russell Sage, 1992.

Wesser, Robert J. *A Response to Progressivism: The Democratic Party and New York Politics, 1902–1918*. New York: New York University Press, 1986.

Williams, Marilyn Thornton. "New York City's Public Baths: A Case Study in Urban Progressive Reform." *Journal of Urban History* 7:1 (November 1980).

Yellowitz, Irwin. *Labor and the Progressive Movement in New York State, 1897–1916*. Ithaca, N.Y.: Cornell University Press, 1965.

Cleveland

Arbuthnot, C. C. "Mayor Baker's Administration in Cleveland." *National Municipal Review* 5:2 (April 1916).

Ardey, Saundra C., and William E. Nelson. "The Maturation of Black Political Power: The Case of Cleveland." *PS* 23:2 (June 1990).

Ardussi, Steve. "Newton D. Baker and Cleveland's Struggle for Home Rule." Senior thesis, Princeton University, 1965.

Baker, Newton D. Papers. Western Reserve Historical Society. Cleveland.

———. "What Has and Can Be Done by Municipal Ownership and Control." *Hearst's* 32:3 (September 1917).

"Baker and Hogen Alike Face Test Confidently." *Plain Dealer*, November 7, 1911.

"Baker Victor by Over 12,000; Carries Ticket with Him." *Plain Dealer*, November 8, 1911.

Barone, Michael. "The Social Basis of Urban Progressivism: Four Midwestern Cities, 1900–1912." Honors thesis, Harvard University, 1966.

Bean, Donald L. "Chief Fox Is Confident He Can Run Department." *Plain Dealer*, October 25, 1978.

Beer, Thomas. *Hanna*. New York: Knopf, 1929.

Bemis, Edward W. "The Significance of Mayor Johnson's Election." *Arena* 29:6 (June 1903).

The Book of Clevelanders. Cleveland: Burrow Brothers Company, 1914.

Bourne, Henry E. Papers. Western Reserve Historical Society. Cleveland.

Bremner, Robert H. "The Civic Revival in Ohio: Harris R. Cooley and Cooley Farms." *American Journal of Economics and Sociology* 14:1 (October 1954).

———. "The Civic Revival in Ohio: Humanizing Cleveland and Toledo." *American Journal of Economics and Sociology* 13:2 (January 1954).

———. "The Civic Revival in Ohio: Police, Penal and Parole Policies in Cleveland and Toledo." *American Journal of Economics and Sociology* 14:4 (July 1955).

———. "The Civic Revival in Ohio: The Political Techniques of the Progressives." *American Journal of Economics and Sociology* 12:2 (January 1953).

———. "The Civic Revival in Ohio: The Street Railway Controversy in Cleveland." *American Journal of Economics and Sociology* 10:2 (January 1951).

————. "The Civic Revival in Ohio: Tax Equalization in Cleveland." *American Journal of Economics and Sociology* 8:3 (April 1949).

Briggs, Robert L. "The Progressive Era in Cleveland: Tom L. Johnson's Administration, 1901–1909." Ph.D. diss., University of Chicago, 1962.

Bureau of the Census, *Census of Population and Housing: 1970 Census Tracts, Final Report PHC(1)-45, Cleveland, Ohio SMSA.* Washington, D.C.: U.S. Government Printing Office, 1972.

Callahan, Nelson J., and William F. Hickey. *Irish Americans and Their Communities of Cleveland.* Cleveland: Cleveland State University, 1978.

Campbell, Thomas Francis. "Background for Progressivism: Machine Politics in the Administration of Robert E. McKisson, Mayor of Cleveland, 1895–99." M.A. thesis, Western Reserve University, 1960.

————. *Daniel E. Morgan, 1877–1949: The Good Citizen in Politics.* Cleveland: Press of Western Reserve University, 1966.

————. *Freedom's Forum: The City Club, 1912–1962.* Cleveland: The City Club, 1963.

————. "Mounting Crisis and Reform: Cleveland's Political Development." In Thomas F. Campbell and Edward M. Miggins, eds., *The Birth of Modern Cleveland, 1865–1930.* Cleveland: Western Reserve Historical Society, 1988.

Carlson, William. "Legal Eagle: Schulman Is a Soft-Spoken Pro in a Nest of City Hall Neophytes." *Plain Dealer*, February 13, 1978.

Citizens League of Cleveland. *75 Years of Doing Good: The Story of the Citizens League.* Cleveland: Citizens League, 1971.

Comer, Lucretia Garfield. *Harry Garfield's First Forty Years: Man of Action in a Troubled World.* New York: Vantage, 1965.

Condon, George E. *Cleveland: The Best Kept Secret.* Garden City, N.Y.: Doubleday, 1967.

Coulter, Charles W. *The Italians of Cleveland.* Cleveland: Cleveland Americanization Committee, 1919.

Cramer, C. H. *Newton D. Baker: A Biography.* Cleveland: World, 1961.

Crissey, Forest. *Theodore Burton: American Statesman.* Cleveland: World, 1956.

Croly, Herbert. *Marcus Alonzo Hanna: His Life and Work.* New York: Macmillan, 1912.

Daniels, Robert. "Weissman: Controversy Is His Middle Name. Admired or Hated, He's Never Ignored." *Plain Dealer*, August 10, 1978.

Davis, Harry L. Pamphlets. Cleveland Municipal Library.

Derthick, Martha. "Stability in City Politics: The Case of Cleveland." Unpublished ms., c.1963.

Dolger, Robert. "His Honor? Fred Kohler's Career Here Controversial, But Never Dull." *Plain Dealer*, June 27, 1976.

Drexler, Madeline. "Public Square." *Plain Dealer*, July 17, 1983.

"Election's In Your Hands, Voters." *Plain Dealer*, November 2, 1915.

Fesler, Mayo. "A Home Rule Charter for Cleveland." Address before the Council of Sociology, Cleveland, Ohio, October 14, 1912.

First Charter Commission. *Documents.* Cleveland. 1913.

————. *Journals.* Cleveland: 1913.

Flower, B. O. "Topics of the Times: How Cleveland Stamped Out Smallpox." *Arena* 27:4 (April 1902).

Fordyce, Wellington G. "Nationality Groups in Cleveland Politics." *Ohio State Archaeological and Historical Quarterly* 46:1 (January 1937).

Garfield, Harry A. "Private Rights in Street Railways." *Outlook* 85 (February 2, 1907).

Gartner, Lloyd P. *History of the Jews of Cleveland.* Cleveland: Western Reserve Historical Society, 1978.

Gerber, David A. *Black Ohio and the Color Line.* Urbana: University of Illinois Press, 1976.

Haworth, Paul Leland. "Mayor Johnson of Cleveland: A Study of Mismanaged Political Reform." *Outlook* 93 (October 23, 1909).

"Hear Socialists Plead for Street Railway Purchase." *Plain Dealer*, October 17, 1915.

"Herman C. Baehr Rites Tomorrow." *Plain Dealer*, February 5, 1942.

Hilpert, Elmer Ernest. "The Function of the Citizens League in the Government of the City of Cleveland and Cuyahoga County." M.A. thesis, University of Minnesota, 1931.

Hines, Thomas S. "The Paradox of 'Progressive' Architecture: Urban Planning and Public Building in Tom Johnson's Cleveland." *American Quarterly* 25:4 (October 1973).

H[odge], O[rlando] J. *Reminiscences.* Cleveland: Imperial Press, 1902.

"Hogen and Baker Sure of Success." *Plain Dealer*, November 6, 1911.

Holden, Matthew, Jr. "Ethnic Accommodation in a Historical Case." *Comparative Studies in Society and History* 8:2 (January 1966).

Holmgren, Daniel Martin. "Edward Webster Bemis and Municipal Reform." Ph.D. diss., Western Reserve University, 1964.

Hopwood, E. C. "Newton D. Baker's Administration as Mayor of Cleveland." *National Municipal Review* 2:3 (July 1913).

Howard, Nathaniel R. "I, Fred Kohler: Forty Years of Cleveland Politics." *Plain Dealer*, February 2–March 14, 1934.

Howe, Frederic C. "Cleveland's Education through Its Chamber of Commerce." *Outlook* 83 (July 28, 1906).

————. *Confessions of a Reformer.* New York: Scribner's, 1925.

Huff, Robert Arthur. "Frederic C. Howe, Progressive." Ph.D. diss., University of Rochester, 1966.

Johannesen, Eric. *Cleveland Architecture, 1876–1976.* Cleveland: Western Reserve Historical Society, 1979.

Johnson, Lewis J. "The Best Form of Preferential Vote." *Public* 16 (August 8, 1913).

Johnson, Tom. *My Story.* 1911. Reprint. Seattle: University of Washington Press, 1970.

————. Pamphlets. Freiberger Library, Case Western Reserve University, Special Collections. Cleveland.

Judis, John. "Decline and Fall: Cleveland Says No to Kucinich's Experiment in 'Urban Populism.'" *Progressive*, no. 44 (January 1980).

"Kill the Traction Proposal," editorial. *Plain Dealer*, October 20, 1915.

Kohler, Fred. "A Golden Rule Policy. Read before the Convention of the International Association of Chiefs of Police, at Detroit, Mich., June 2–6." *Public* 11 (June 12, 1908).

Kollar, Mary Ellen. "Cleveland City Government." In David D. Van Tassel and John J. Grabowski, eds., *The Encyclopedia of Cleveland History*. Bloomington: Indiana University Press, 1987.

Kusmer, Kenneth L. *A Ghetto Takes Shape: Black Cleveland, 1870–1920*. Urbana: University of Illinois Press, 1976.

Lorenz, Carl. *Tom L. Johnson: Mayor of Cleveland*. New York: A. S. Barnes, 1911.

Malin, W. C. "Government." In Wilfred Henry Alburn and Miriam Russell Alburn, *This Cleveland of Ours*. Chicago: S. J. Clarke, 1933.

Marschall, Dan, ed. *The Battle of Cleveland: Public Interest Challenges Corporate Power*. Washington, D.C.: Conference on Alternative State and Local Policies, 1979.

Maschke, Maurice. "Memoirs." *Plain Dealer*, August 1–September 15, 1934.

Maxey, Chester Collins. "An Analysis of Cleveland's New Charter." *National Municipal Review* 12:1 (January 1923).

———. "The Cleveland Election and the New Charter." *American Political Science Review* 16:1 (February 1922).

McCarthy, Michael P. "'Suburban Power': A Footnote on Cleveland in the Tom Johnson Years." *Northwest Ohio Quarterly* 45:1 (Winter 1972–73).

McGunagle, Fred. "Commissioner Jack Nicholl: Bargaining for the Public." *Cleveland Press*, July 28, 1978.

Miggins, Edward Michael. "Businessmen, Pedagogues, and Progressive Reform: The Cleveland Foundation's 1915 School Survey." Ph.D. diss., Case Western Reserve University, 1975.

Miggins, Edward Michael, and Mary Morgenthaler. "The Ethnic Mosaic: The Settlement of Cleveland by the New Immigrants and Migrants." In Thomas F. Campbell and Edward M. Miggins, eds., *The Birth of Modern Cleveland, 1865–1930*. Cleveland: Western Reserve Historical Society, 1988.

Miller, Carol Poh, and Robert Wheeler. *Cleveland: A Concise History, 1796–1990*. Bloomington: Indiana University Press, 1990.

Miller, William F. "Waxman Cultivates a Tough-Guy Stance." *Plain Dealer*, February 11, 1978.

Moulton, Eugene Russell. "An Evaluation of the Speaking Effectiveness of Newton D. Baker." Ph.D. diss., Western Reserve University, 1953.

Municipal Association/Civic League. Minutes. 1896–1915. Citizens League of Cleveland.

———. *[Municipal] Bulletin*. 1896–1914. Citizens League of Cleveland.

Murdock, Eugene C. "Cleveland's Johnson: The Burton Campaign." *American Journal of Economics and Sociology* 15:4 (July 1956).

———. "Cleveland's Johnson: The Cabinet." *Ohio Historical Quarterly* 66:4 (October 1957).

———. "Cleveland's Johnson: Elected Mayor." *Ohio Historical Quarterly* 65:1 (January 1956).

———. "Cleveland's Johnson: First Term." *Ohio Historical Quarterly* 67:1 (January 1958).

Norton, William J. "Chief Kohler of Cleveland and His Golden Rule Policy." *Outlook* 93 (November 6, 1909).

Otis, Charles Augustus. *Here I Am: A Rambling Account of the Exciting Times of Yesteryear*. Cleveland: Buhler, 1951.

Pangrace, Andrew. *The Citizens League of Cleveland*. Cleveland: Citizens League, 1946.

Porter, Philip W. *Cleveland: Confused City on a Seesaw*. Columbus: Ohio State University Press, 1976.

Randall, Prudence B. "The Meaning of Progressivism in Urban School Reform: Cleveland, 1901–1909." Ph.D. diss., Case Western Reserve University, 1971.

Raper, John W. *The Soviet Table, or the Rise of Civilization in Cleveland*. Cleveland: Public Affairs Committee, 1935.

Rarick, Holly M. *Progressive Vision: The Planning of Downtown Cleveland, 1903–1930*. Cleveland: Cleveland Museum of Art, 1986.

Rex, Frederick. "Municipal Dance Halls." *National Municipal Review* 4:3 (July 1915).

Richardson, James F. "Political Reform in Cleveland." In David D. Van Tassel and John J. Grabowski, eds., *Cleveland: A Tradition of Reform*. Kent, Ohio: Kent State University Press, 1986.

Rose, William Ganson. *Cleveland: The Making of a City*. Cleveland: World, 1950.

Saltzer, Robert. "Colorful Kohler Rebounds from Disgrace." *Cleveland Press*, October 11, 1941.

———. "The People's Choice." *Cleveland Press*, October 10, 1941.

Shaw, Archer H. *The Plain Dealer: One Hundred Years in Cleveland*. New York: Knopf, 1942.

Swanstrom, Todd. *The Crisis of Growth Politics: Cleveland, Kucinich, and the Challenge of Urban Populism*. Philadelphia: Temple University Press, 1985.

"Tom L. Johnson Memorial Number." *Public* 14 (July 21, 1911).

"Typewritten Manuscript of Johnson-Boyd Debates, 1905." Cleveland Public Library.

Van Tassel, David D., and John J. Grabowski, eds. *The Encyclopedia of Cleveland History*. Bloomington: Indiana University Press, 1987.

———. "Epilogue: The Reform Tradition Challenged, 1960–1980." In David D. Van Tassel and John J. Grabowski, eds., *Cleveland: A Tradition of Reform*. Kent, Ohio: Kent State University Press, 1986.

Wagner, Joseph L. "Barrett's Aim: Service to All. Mother's Slaying Pushed Him into Police Work." *Plain Dealer*, February 15, 1978.

———. "Corsi Acts the Bad Guy, Causes Aides to Tremble." *Plain Dealer*, February 9, 1978.

———. "Hey, Joe Tegreene: What's a Nice Guy Like You Doing with That Bunch?" *Plain Dealer*, June 25, 1978.

Waite, Florence T. *A Warm Friend for the Spirit: A History of the Family Service Association and Its Forbears*. Cleveland: Family Service Association of Cleveland, 1960.

Warner, Hoyt Landon. *Progressivism in Ohio, 1897–1917*. Columbus: Ohio State University Press, 1964.

Weiner, Ronald R., and Carol A. Beal. "The Sixth City: Cleveland in Three Stages of Urbanization." In Thomas F. Campbell and Edward M. Miggins, eds., *The*

Birth of Modern Cleveland, 1865–1930. Cleveland: Western Reserve Historical Society, 1988.

Whipple, James Beaumont. "Cleveland in Conflict: A Study in Urban Adolescence, 1876–1900." Ph.D. diss., Western Reserve University, 1951.

————. "Municipal Government in an Average City: Cleveland, 1876–1900." *Ohio State Archaeological and Historical Quarterly* 62:1 (January 1953).

Whitlock, Brand. *Forty Years of It.* 1914. Reprint. Cleveland: Press of Case Western Reserve University, 1970.

Wilcox, Delos F. "Municipal Government in Michigan and Ohio: A Study in the Relations of City and Commonwealth." *Columbia University Studies in History, Economics and Public Law* 5:3 (May 1896).

Witt, Peter. *Cleveland before St. Peter: A Handful of Hot Stuff.* Cleveland: Charles Lezius, 1899.

————. Papers. Western Reserve Historical Society. Cleveland.

"Witt Cuts Down Davis Lead." *Plain Dealer,* November 3, 1915.

Wittke, Carl. "Peter Witt, Tribune of the People." *Ohio State Archaeological and Historical Quarterly* 58:4 (October 1949).

"Witt Predicts End of Labor Battles." *Plain Dealer,* October 25, 1915.

Young, Dallas M. *Twentieth-Century Experience in Urban Transit: A Study of the Cleveland System and Its Development.* Cleveland: Press of Western Reserve University, 1960.

Chicago

Addams, Jane. *Twenty Years at Hull-House.* New York: Macmillan, 1910.

Allswang, John M. *A House for All Peoples.* Lexington: University Press of Kentucky, 1971.

Bach, Ira J. "A Reconsideration of the 1909 'Plan of Chicago.'" *Chicago History* 2:3 (Spring/Summer 1973).

Barker, Twiley W. "Political Mobilization of Black Chicago: Drafting a Candidate." *PS* 16:3 (Summer 1983).

Barnard, Harry. *Eagle Forgotten: The Life of John Peter Altgeld.* New York: Duell, Sloan and Pierce, 1938.

Barrett, Paul. *The Automobile and Urban Transit: The Formation of Public Policy in Chicago, 1900–1930.* Philadelphia: Temple University Press, 1983.

Becker, Richard Edward. "Edward Dunne, Reform Mayor of Chicago: 1905–1909." Ph.D. diss., University of Chicago, 1971.

Bennett, Larry. "Harold Washington and the Black Urban Regime." *Urban Affairs Quarterly* 28:3 (March 1993).

Bentley, Arthur F. "Municipal Ownership Interest Groups in Chicago: A Study of Referendum Votes, 1902–1907." Unpublished ms., 1908–1909(?). Newberry Library, Chicago.

Buenker, John D. "Dynamics of Chicago Ethnic Politics, 1900–1930." *Journal of the Illinois State Historical Society* 67:2 (April 1974).

————. "Edward F. Dunne: The Limits of Municipal Reform." In Paul M. Green and Melvin G. Holli, eds., *The Mayors: The Chicago Political Tradition.* Carbondale: Southern Illinois University Press, 1987.

————. "Edward F. Dunne: The Urban New Stock Democrat as Progressive." *Mid-America* 50:1 (January 1968).

Candeloro, Dominic. "The Chicago School Board Crisis of 1907." *Journal of the Illinois State Historical Society* 68:5 (November 1975).

Chicago Board of Education. *School Census Report.* 1908.

Chicago Bureau of Public Efficiency. "Administration of the Office of Coroner of Cook County, Illinois." December 1911.

————. "Administration of the Office of Recorder of Cook County, Illinois." September 1911.

————. "Administration of the Office of Sheriff of Cook County, Illinois." December 1911.

————. "Bureau of Streets, Civil Service Commission, and Special Assessment Accounting System of the City of Chicago." December 1911.

————. "Electrolysis of Water Pipes in the City of Chicago." July 1911.

————. "Methods of Preparing and Administering the Budget of Cook County." January 1911.

————. "The Municipal Court Acts: Two Related Propositions upon Which the Voters of Chicago Will Be Asked to Pass Judgment at the Elections of November 7: Vote No." October 1911.

————. "The Nineteen Local Governments in Chicago: A Multiplicity of Overlapping Taxing Bodies with Many Elective Officials: Chicago's Greatest Needs Are the Unification of Its Local Government and a Short Ballot." 2nd ed. March 1915.

————. "The Park Governments of Chicago—General Summary and Conclusion." December 1911.

————. "A Plea for Publicity in the Office of County Treasurer." October 1911.

————. "Preparing Asphalt Pavement: Work Done for the City of Chicago under Contract in 1911." October 1911.

————. "Proposed Purchase of Voting Machines by the Board of Election Commissioners of the City of Chicago." May 20, 1911.

————. "Street Pavement Laid in the City of Chicago: An Inquiry into Paving Materials, Methods and Results." July 1911.

————. "The Waterworks System of the City of Chicago." December 1911.

Chicago Charter Convention. *Proceedings.* October 1906–March 1907.

City Club [Chicago]. "The Work and Accomplishments of the Chicago Commission on City Expenditures." *City Club Bulletin* 4 (August 16, 1911).

"City Historian Given Real Work." *Chicago Tribune.* May 11, 1905.

Clavel, Pierre, and Wim Wiewel, eds. *Harold Washington and the Neighborhoods: Progressive City Government in Chicago, 1983–1987.* New Brunswick, N.J.: Rutgers University Press, 1991.

Collins, Lorin Cane, Jr. *Autobiography.* Chicago: Lincoln Publishing Co., 1934.

Cooling, W. F. *The Chicago Democracy.* Chicago: Platform Publishing, 1899.

Darrow, Clarence. *The Story of My Life.* 1932. Reprint. New York: Scribner's, 1960.

Diner, Steven J. *A City and Its Universities: Public Policy in Chicago, 1892–1919.* Chapel Hill: University of North Carolina Press, 1980.

Einhorn, Robin L. *Property Rules: Political Economy in Chicago, 1833–1872.* Chicago: University of Chicago Press, 1989.

Flanagan, Maureen A. *Charter Reform in Chicago*. Carbondale: Southern Illinois University Press, 1987.

———. "Fred A. Busse: A Silent Mayor in Turbulent Times." In Paul M. Green and Melvin G. Holli, eds., *The Mayors: The Chicago Political Tradition*. Carbondale: Southern Illinois University Press, 1987.

Gosnell, Harold F. *Machine Politics: Chicago Model*. 2nd ed. Chicago: University of Chicago Press, 1968.

———. *Negro Politicians: The Rise of Negro Politics in Chicago*. 1935. Reprint. Chicago: University of Chicago Press, 1967.

Gottfried, Alex. *Boss Cermak of Chicago: A Study of Political Leadership*. Seattle: University of Washington Press, 1962.

Gould, Alan B. "Walter L. Fisher: Profile of an Urban Reformer, 1880–1910." *Mid-America* 57:3 (July 1975).

Gove, Samuel K., and Louis H. Masotti, eds. *After Daley: Chicago Politics in Transition*. Urbana: University of Illinois Press, 1982.

Grant, Bruce. *Fight for a City: The Story of the Union League Club of Chicago and Its Times, 1880–1955*. Chicago: Rand McNally, 1955.

Green, Paul M. "The 1983 Chicago Democratic Mayoral Primary: Some New Players—Same Old Rules." In Melvin G. Holli and Paul M. Green, eds. *The Making of the Mayor: Chicago 1983*. Grand Rapids, Mich.: William B. Eerdmans, 1984.

———. "Anton Cermak: The Man and His Machine." In Paul M. Green and Melvin G. Holli, eds., *The Mayors: The Chicago Political Tradition*. Carbondale: Southern Illinois University Press, 1987.

———. "The Chicago Democratic Party, 1840–1920: From Factionalism to Political Organization." Ph.D. diss., University of Chicago, 1975.

———. "Irish Chicago: The Multiethnic Road to Machine Success." In Peter d'A. Jones and Melvin G. Holli, eds., *Ethnic Chicago*. Grand Rapids, Mich.: William B. Eerdmans, 1981.

Green, Paul M., and Melvin G. Holli, eds. *Restoration 1989: Chicago Elects a New Daley*. Chicago: Lyceum, 1991.

Grimshaw, William J. *Bitter Fruit: Black Politics and the Chicago Machine, 1931–1991*. Chicago: University of Chicago Press, 1992.

———. "The Daley Legacy: A Declining Politics of Party, Race, and Public Unions." In Samuel K. Gove and Louis H. Masotti, eds. *After Daley: Chicago Politics in Transition*. Urbana: University of Illinois Press, 1982.

———. "Is Chicago Ready for Reform? or, A New Agenda for Harold Washington." In Melvin G. Holli and Paul M. Green, eds. *The Making of the Mayor: Chicago 1983*. Grand Rapids, Mich.: William B. Eerdmans, 1984.

Grosser, Hugo S. "Chicago: A Review of Its Governmental History." In League of American Municipalities, *10th Annual Convention*. Chicago: League of American Municipalities, 1906.

Gunnell, John G. "Continuity and Innovation in the History of Political Science: The Case of Charles Merriam." *Journal of the History of the Behavioral Sciences* 28:2 (April 1992).

Harrison, Carter H. *Growing Up with Chicago*. Chicago: R. F. Seymour, 1944.

———. Papers. Newberry Library, Chicago.

———. *Stormy Years*. Indianapolis: Bobbs-Merrill, 1935.

Hatton, August Raymond. *Digest of City Charters*. Chicago: Chicago Charter Convention, 1906.

Hines, Thomas S. *Burnham of Chicago: Architect and Planner*. New York: Oxford University Press, 1974.

Hofmeister, Rudolf A. *The Germans of Chicago*. Champaign, Ill.: Stipes, 1976.

Holli, Melvin G., and Paul M. Green, eds. *The Making of the Mayor: Chicago 1983*. Grand Rapids, Mich.: William B. Eerdmans, 1984.

Hutchinson, William T. *Lowden of Illinois*. Chicago: University of Chicago Press, 1957.

Ickes, Harold L. *The Autobiography of a Curmudgeon*. New York: Reynal and Hitchcock, 1943.

Kantowicz, Edward R. "Carter H. Harrison II: The Politics of Balance." In Paul M. Green and Melvin G. Holli, eds., *The Mayors: The Chicago Political Tradition*. Carbondale: Southern Illinois University Press, 1987.

————. *Polish-American Politics in Chicago, 1888–1940*. Chicago: University of Chicago Press, 1975.

Karl, Barry D. *Charles E. Merriam and the Study of Politics*. Chicago: University of Chicago Press, 1974.

Kemp, Kathleen A., and Robert L. Lineberry. "The Last of the Great Urban Machines and the Last of the Great Urban Mayors? Chicago Politics, 1955–77." In Samuel K. Gove and Louis H. Masotti, eds. *After Daley: Chicago Politics in Transition*. Urbana: University of Illinois Press, 1982.

King, Hoyt. *Citizen Cole of Chicago*. Chicago: Horder's, 1931.

Kleppner, Paul. *Chicago Divided: The Making of a Black Mayor*. DeKalb: Northern Illinois University Press, 1985.

Komons, Nick Alexander. "Chicago, 1893–1907: The Politics of Reform." Ph.D. diss., George Washington University, 1961.

Lund, Eric R. "Swedish-American Politics and Press Response: The Chicago Mayoral Election of 1915." In Philip J. Anderson and Dag Blanck, eds., *Swedish-American Life in Chicago: Cultural and Urban Aspects of an Immigrant People, 1850–1930*. Urbana: University of Illinois Press, 1992.

Mayer, Harold M., and Richard C. Wade. *Chicago: Growth of a Metropolis*. Chicago: University of Chicago Press, 1969.

McCarthy, Michael Patrick. "Businessmen and Professionals in Municipal Reform: The Chicago Experience, 1877–1920." Ph.D. diss., Northwestern University, 1970.

————. "The New Metropolis: Chicago, the Annexation Movement, and Progressive Reform." In Michael H. Ebner and Eugene M. Tobin, eds., *The Age of Urban Reform: New Perspectives on the Progressive Era*. Port Washington, N.Y.: Kennikat, 1977.

————. "Prelude to Armageddon: Charles E. Merriam and the Chicago Mayoral Election of 1911." *Journal of the Illinois State Historical Society* 67:5 (November 1974).

McDonald, Forrest. *Insull*. Chicago: University of Chicago Press, 1962.

Merriam, Charles Edward. "The Chicago Charter Convention." *American Political Science Review* 2:1 (November 1907).

————. *Chicago: A More Intimate View of Urban Politics*. New York: Macmillan, 1929.

———. "Investigations as a Means of Securing Administrative Efficiency." *Efficiency in City Government. The Annals of the American Academy of Political and Social Science*, no. 41 (May 1912).

———. Papers. Joseph Regenstein Library, University of Chicago.

———. "Report of an Investigation of the Municipal Revenues of Chicago." 2nd ed. Chicago: City Club, 1906.

———. "The Work of the Chicago Bureau of Public Efficiency." *City Club Bulletin* [Philadelphia] 3 (November 2, 1910).

Miller, Joan. "The Politics of Municipal Reform in Chicago during the Progressive Era: The Municipal Voters' League as a Test Case, 1896–1920." M.A. thesis, Roosevelt University, 1966.

Morton, Richard Allen. "Edward F. Dunne: Illinois' Most Progressive Governor." *Illinois Historical Journal* 83:4 (Winter 1990).

Nelli, Humbert S. *Italians in Chicago, 1880–1930: A Study in Ethnic Mobility.* New York: Oxford University Press, 1970.

Peterson, Paul E. "Washington's Election in Chicago: The Other Half of the Story." *PS* 16:4 (Fall 1983).

Philpott, Thomas Lee. *The Slum and the Ghetto: Immigrants, Blacks, and Reformers in Chicago, 1880–1930.* Belmont, Calif.: Wadsworth, 1991.

Pierce, Bessie Louise. *A History of Chicago.* New York: Knopf, 1957.

Pinderhughes, Dianne M. *Race and Ethnicity in Chicago Politics: A Reexamination of Pluralist Theory.* Urbana: University of Illinois Press, 1987.

Preston, Michael B. "The Election of Harold Washington: Black Voting Patterns in the 1983 Chicago Mayoral Race." *PS* 16:3 (Summer 1983).

———. "The Resurgence of Black Voting in Chicago: 1955–1983." In Melvin G. Holli and Paul M. Green, eds. *The Making of the Mayor: Chicago 1983.* Grand Rapids, Mich.: William B. Eerdmans, 1984.

"The Proposed Charter for Chicago." *Real Estate News* 2 (August 1907).

Rakove, Milton. *Don't Make No Waves . . . Don't Back No Losers: An Insider's Analysis of the Daley Machine.* Bloomington: Indiana University Press, 1975.

———. "Jane Byrne and the New Chicago Politics." In Samuel K. Gove and Louis H. Masotti, eds. *After Daley: Chicago Politics in Transition.* Urbana: University of Illinois Press, 1982.

———. "Reflections on the Machine." In Melvin G. Holli and Paul M. Green, eds. *The Making of the Mayor: Chicago 1983.* Grand Rapids, Mich.: William B. Eerdmans, 1984.

Roberts, Sidney I. "Businessmen in Revolt: Chicago, 1874–1900." Ph.D. diss., Northwestern University, 1960.

Robins, Raymond. "An Analysis and Discussion of the Proposed New Charter." *Public Policy League Bulletin* 1:1 (September 1907).

Rose, Don. "How the 1983 Election Was Won." In Melvin G. Holli and Paul M. Green, eds. *The Making of the Mayor: Chicago 1983.* Grand Rapids, Mich.: William B. Eerdmans, 1984.

Schmidt, John R. *"The Mayor Who Cleaned Up Chicago": A Political Biography of William E. Dever.* DeKalb: Northern Illinois University Press, 1989.

Schottenhamel, George. "How Big Bill Thompson Won Control of Chicago." *Journal of the Illinois State Historical Society* 45:1 (Spring 1952).

Smith, Joan K. *Ella Flagg Young: Portrait of a Leader*. Ames: Educational Studies Press and the Iowa State University Research Foundation, 1979.

Stead, William T. *If Christ Came to Chicago*. 1894. Reprint. New York: Living Books, 1964.

Tarr, Joel Arthur. *A Study in Boss Politics: William Lorimer of Chicago*. Urbana: University of Illinois Press, 1970.

Taylor, Graham. *Pioneering on Social Frontiers*. Chicago: University of Chicago Press, 1930.

Tierney, Kevin. *Darrow: A Biography*. New York: Crowell, 1979.

Tingley, Ralph R. "From Carter Harrison II to Fred Busse: A Study of Chicago Political Parties and Personages from 1896 to 1907." Ph.D. diss., University of Chicago, 1950.

Tinzmann, Otto J. "The Education of Charles E. Merriam." M.A. thesis, DePaul University, 1969.

Tompkins, C. David. "John Peter Altgeld as a Candidate for Mayor of Chicago in 1899." *Journal of the Illinois State Historical Society* 56:4 (Winter 1963).

Wendt, Lloyd, and Herman Kogan. *Lords of the Levee: The Story of Bathhouse John and Hinky Dink*. Indianapolis: Bobbs-Merrill, 1943.

Werner, Morris R. *Julius Rosenwald: The Life of a Practical Humanitarian*. New York: Harper and Brothers, 1939.

"Why Municipal Reform Succeeds in Chicago and Fails in New York." *Independent* 56 (April 14, 1904).

Wilson, James Q. "Introduction." In Harold F. Gosnell, *Negro Politicians: The Rise of Negro Politics in Chicago*. Chicago: University of Chicago Press, 1967.

Zikmund, Joseph II. "Mayoral Voting and Ethnic Politics in the Daley-Bilandic-Byrne Era." In Samuel K. Gove and Louis H. Masotti, eds. *After Daley: Chicago Politics in Transition*. Urbana: University of Illinois Press, 1982.

Zoline, Elijah N. "Politics: Chicago." In Charles S. Bernheimer, ed., *The Russian Jew in the United States*. Philadelphia: John C. Winston Co., 1905.

Statistical Sources

Demographic data for New York, Cleveland, and Chicago were drawn from the 1900, 1910, and 1920 federal census. For each city, data have been conveniently broken down by ward or Assembly District, allowing use with electoral data aggregated on the same basis. New York electoral data can be found, in varying degrees of completeness, in the *Tribune Almanac* (until 1914) and the *World Almanac*, but the official and best sources are the election supplements to the *City Record*, usually published in December or January after each election. The *City Record* supplements are available at the New York Public Library or the New York County Board of Elections. Cleveland electoral data were collected from manuscript records at the Cuyahoga County Archives. Some Chicago electoral data were published in the *Chicago Daily News Almanac*; other results are on microfiche at the Chicago Municipal Reference Library in City Hall.

Index